TOBACCO:

ITS HISTORY AND ASSOCIATIONS.

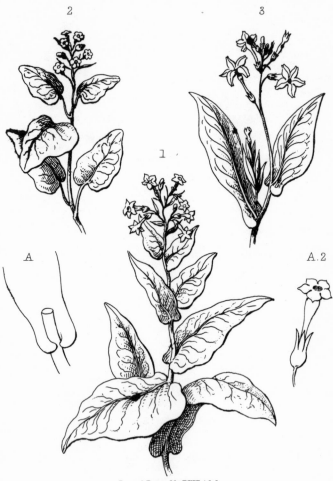

2   3

1

A   A.2

Drawn & Engraved by F.W. Fairholt.

TOBACCO PLANTS.

1 . Nicotiana Tabacum _ 2 . N. Rustica _ 3 . N. Persica

PUBLISHED BY CHAPMAN & HALL, PICCADILLY 1859

TOBACCO:

ITS HISTORY AND ASSOCIATIONS:

INCLUDING

AN ACCOUNT OF THE PLANT AND ITS MANUFACTURE; WITH ITS
MODES OF USE IN ALL AGES AND COUNTRIES.

By F. W. FAIRHOLT, F.S.A.,

Author of "Costume in England," &c. &c.;
Honorary Member of the Society of Antiquaries of Normandy, of Picardy,
and of Poitiers; and Corresponding Member of the
Society of Antiquaries of Scotland.

WITH 100 ILLUSTRATIONS BY THE AUTHOR.

" Sublime tobacco, which, from east to west,
Cheers the Tar's labour, and the Turkman's rest."
BYRON.

" The Old World was sure forlorn,
Wanting thee!"
C. LAMB.

LONDON:
CHAPMAN AND HALL, 193, PICCADILLY.
1859.

Now Reissued by
Singing Tree Press
1249 Washington Blvd., Detroit, Michigan 1968

Library of Congress Catalog Card
Number 68–21770

CHARLES ROACH SMITH, Esq.,

OF TEMPLE PLACE, STROOD, KENT.

My Dear Friend,

It was a custom with the old English authors to dedicate their works to persons for whom they felt esteem; and to make such dedications serve as familiar prefaces. I desire, in this instance, to revive the practice; and I inscribe your name on this page.

You, who know my early history, will feel no surprise at my choice of subject. Born in London, and never having been out of sight of St. Paul's until I had reached my twenty-second year, the tobacco-warehouse, where my father worked, became my play-ground; and my first remembrances are, of rolling in the tobacco-leaf, as country children would roll in a hay-field, and playing at "hide-and-seek" in the empty barrels. In after years, when I helped my father to manufacture many hundred pounds of tobacco-leaf, I little thought that my pen and pencil would be called into use over a book like this. I am willing to think, however, that the peculiarities of my early training have here been of use.

Disliking my father's trade, and, through many difficulties, happily emancipating myself, tobacco had not that charm for me that you and others find in it. But I hope these pages will show that I have no narrow notions on a pleasure in which I cannot participate; but rather a honest detestation of that want of Christian tolerance which has induced some persons to denounce a harmless indulgence as if it were a moral evil. I should be untrue to my father's memory— "an honest man and a good smoker"—if I did not contradict such gratuitous imputations. If I am proud of anything, it is of my father and his seventy-two years of industry and integrity.

That you are "a good smoker" also, I have had experience, at home and abroad, when I have examined in your society many of the finest relics of antiquity, the study of which has been the solace of our lives. In you I shall find a gentle critic: you will estimate, by your own experience, that which few who read consider, the time and trouble requisite to gather into one volume the results of reading many a score; and I have been embarrassed in my task of condensation by the abundance rather than the paucity of my materials.

I will not offer you any laudation here; friendship is too sacred a thing for public display. I only wish, that while one copy of this little book remains, it should exist to record the sincere esteem I feel for you.

F. W. FAIRHOLT.

11 MONTPELIER SQUARE,
　BROMPTON, LONDON,
　　　June 1, 1859.

CONTENTS.

—◆—

TOBACCO:

ITS HISTORY AND ASSOCIATIONS.

CHAPTER I.

THE TOBACCO PLANT.

TOBACCO is a hardy flowering perennial plant, growing freely in a rich moist soil, which is very necessary to its healthy development; but which it is said to exhaust in a remarkable degree. It varies in height according to species and locality; in some instances growing to the altitude of fifteen feet, in others not reaching more than three feet from the ground. There is also a dwarf kind discovered by Houston at Vera Cruz, the leaves of which grow in tufts near the ground, the flowers rising from a central stem to the height of eighteen inches. As many as forty varieties of the Tobacco plant have been noted by botanists, who class them all among the *Solanaceæ*, and narcotic poisons. The *Atropa Belladonna*, or deadly nightshade, is a member of this family; but it may be of use to the nervous to know that the common potato is in the same category; and that, though tobacco will produce

B

a virulent poison—*Nicotine*—by the chemical condensation of a large quantity,* in a similar manner the
Potato fruit and leaves give us *Solanine,* " an acrid
narcotic poison, two grains of which given to a rabbit,
produced paralysis of the posterior extremities, and
death in two hours. Traces of this are also found in
the healthy tubers." † It is therefore evident that in a
moderate manner, we may equally smoke our tobacco
or eat our potato as regardless of the horrors that
chemistry would seem at first to disclose, as when
enjoying the flavour of the bitter almond, which we
know to be owing to the presence of Prussic acid.
The three principal varieties of the plant most commonly grown are, the Virginian tobacco (*Nicotiana
tabacum*—Linnæus), which is that which was first
brought to Europe by Sir Francis Drake (fig. 1 of
Frontispiece) ; it sometimes reaches the height of seven
feet, and is of a strong coarse growth, the leaves,
sometimes two feet long, clasp the stem as shown at A,
and are covered with glandular hairs, which burst on
the smallest pressure, and impart a glutinous character
to the leaf, and an unpleasant odour to the hand. The
flowers grow in a bunch on the summit of the plant,
they are of a pink colour, the segments of the corolla

---

* Johnston, in his *Chemistry of Common Life,* tells us that Melseus
extracted three-quarters of a grain of nicotine from one hundred grains of
Virginian tobacco, so that the proportions are as 1 to 125. In 1851, the
Comte de Bocarmè was executed at Mons for poisoning a brother-in-law
by means of nicotine, in order to obtain the reversion of his property.

† Prescott (on the authority of Pereira), in his *Tobacco, and its
Adulterations.*

being pointed, as shown at A 2. *Shag, Returns,* and the ordinary cut tobaccos are prepared from this kind; of which there are many varieties, giving name to different qualities of tobacco, and chiefly adopted from the places of their growth. The Syrian Tobacco (*Nicotiana rustica*) differs from this in many essential particulars, as may be seen in our engraving (fig. 2), the principal being the branched stem, each offshoot bearing flowers; the leaves do not clasp the stem, but are attached by a long stalk, and they are not lanceolate, but ovate in form; the flowers are not pink, but green, and the segments of the corolla are rounded. It does not grow so high as the American plant by about two feet; it is milder than that in flavour, and is used for the more delicate cut tobaccos and cigars. The Latakia tobacco, and that known as Turkish and Syrian, are both manufactured from this plant. It is a native of America, but grows wild in other countries, and is a hardy annual in English gardens, flowering from Midsummer to Michaelmas, so that by some botanists it has been termed " common, or English tobacco." The Shiraz Tobacco (*Nicotiana persica*—Lindley) differs from both in the form of the leaves, and the colour of the flowers, which are white, and the segments of the corolla unequal. It is a native of Persia, and used for the manufacture of their most delicate kinds for smoking, but Lindley informs us that it is not fitted to form cigars, as it does not readily ignite. It is also never used medicinally as other tobaccos are, or have been.

The tobacco plant would grow freely in Great Britain, if government would allow its cultivation; it is now the policy to prohibit it, for the benefit of our colonies, whose trade with the mother country would be seriously damaged but for these restrictions. It was at one time extensively cultivated in the North-riding of Yorkshire; but in the early part of the reign of George III., penalties were inflicted on the growers, to the amount of £30,000, and the tobacco publicly burned. In Scotland it was also grown when our colonial trade was interrupted by the American war. About Kelso and Jedburgh a considerable tract of land was devoted to this purpose, the Act of Charles II. which made the growth illegal in England, of course not affecting Scotland; to meet which emergency the Act of the 19th of George III. was passed, which prohibits the cultivation of more than will occupy half a rod of ground; and which is to be used for medicinal purposes, or the destruction of insects.* In Ireland it was successfully grown, particularly in the county of Wexford, some years after the restrictive law just named was passed for England, and which, curiously enough, repealed the similar laws for Ireland. Tobacco could therefore be grown at home with us, as with other European nations; if it were our legal policy to permit it. Holland, which is in our latitude, but colder and damper in its soil, carries on

---

* It is frequently grown in the kitchen garden to destroy grubs and insects by its infusion in water, or to drive them from hothouses, by fumigation with dried leaves. In both ways it is most effective.

a large trade in its growth. France cultivates it also; but the larger quantity is grown in Germany: the time of harvesting the leaves is an interesting period for a stranger to visit the villages, which put on a new aspect as every house and barn is hung all over with the drying leaves. The European tobacco is less powerful in flavour than the American; and the native tobacco of Germany may be smoked to a continuous extent, which would be dangerous or disagreeable if the New World tobacco were used. Temperate climates, with a deep rich soil ranging from forty to fifty degrees of latitude, are said to be the most favourable for its free development. It is grown from seed; but frost is particularly injurious to young plants: the lower leaves are sometimes gathered as they ripen or begin to change colour, an operation performed at intervals till all are removed; or the growth of the plant is arrested by cutting off the top, to prevent the formation of flowers and seed, and enlarge the growth of leaves; or the plant is cut down entire, dried in the sun, and the leaves separated afterwards.

Mr. Prescott * thus enumerates the principal places from which tobacco finds its way into the English Market, and the peculiar uses to which each kind is devoted:—

"EUROPE.—*Germany, Holland,* and *Salonica* in European Turkey.

---

* Of the Inland Revenue department, in his valuable work on *Tobacco, and its Adulterations,* recently published by Van Voorst.

"ASIA.—*China, East Indies, Latakia,* and other parts of Asiatic Turkey; *Shiraz* in Persia; *Manilla* in Luzon, one of the Philippine Islands.

"NORTH AMERICA.—*Virginia, Kentucky, Maryland.*

"The Islands of *Cuba, Hayti,* and *Porto Rico.*

"SOUTH AMERICA.—*Varinas, Brazil, Columbia,* and *Cumana.*

"*Cuba, Havannah,* and Columbian leaf tobaccos: *Columbia, Varinas,* and *Cumana* are the most esteemed for Cigars. The leaves are marked with light yellow spots.

"The *Virginian, Kentucky,* and *Maryland* tobaccos are more frequently used for cut and spun tobaccos. *Turkey, Latakia,* or Syrian tobacco; and the *Persian* or *Shiraz* tobacco, are among the mildest and most delicately flavoured for the pipe.

"The Dutch tobaccos are mild and deficient in flavour. The darker kind is the strongest, and much esteemed for moist snuffs, the weaker kinds being employed in the commonest cigars and cheroots.

"Manilla tobacco is much esteemed for cheroots.

"Mixture of the leaves produced in different countries gives great variety in the flavour of manufactured tobaccos, requiring considerable skill and attention on the part of the manufacturer."

The same author also notes "among the adulterations which have from time to time been discovered in manufactured tobacco, the following substances may be named:—Leaves of Rhubarb, Dock, Burdock, Colts-foot, Beech, Plantain, Oak and Elm, Peat-earth,

Bran, Sawdust, Malt-rootlets, Barley-meal, Oatmeal, Bean-meal, Pea-meal, Potato-starch, and Chicory leaves steeped in tar-oil." To which may be added the leaves of the *cabbage* and *lettuce* in the manufacture of cheap cigars.*

A parliamentary return was made between the years 1852—4, of persons who had rendered themselves liable to prosecutions for infringement of the tobacco laws, from which it appeared that the cases of adulteration were numerous, and the materials used named therein add a few more to the above list: they consisted of sugar, alum, lime, flour of meal, rhubarb leaves, saltpetre, fuller's earth, starch, malt commings, chromate of lead, peat moss, treacle, common burdock leaves, common salt, endive leaves, lampblack, gum, red dye, and black dye, composed of vegetable red, iron, and liquorice.

It is not intended in this volume to renew the much vexed and always unsatisfied question—"Is tobacco injurious ? "

"Who shall decide when doctors disagree ?"

—has been asked in many similar cases : in this one

---

* A few years ago a cigar manufacturer resisted successfully an attempt at enforcing the legal penalty for the unlawful fabrication of cheap "Havannah Cigars," from tobacco which had paid no duty, as he was enabled to show in his own defence that he never made use of the tobacco leaf at all. Such cigars as are retailed at a penny, and leave a large profit for vendor and maker, must necessarily be constructed of less expensive material than tobacco leaves. They are sometimes steeped in infusion of strong tobacco water, to give them a little external flavour of a true kind.

doctors have disagreed to an unexampled extent; their opinions have been

"—far as the poles asunder,"

—and quite as unlikely to "join issue," as lawyers phrase it, and come to any satisfactory conclusion. Some opponents (and all "worshipful men," who write M.D. after their names, and are greatly in earnest) find every disease under the sun originating in tobacco-smoke. Others (equally good men, who also dignify their patronymics with a sprinkling of additional letters never given at christenings) declare as loudly in its favour, and quote quite as many instances of good resulting from the practice. Truth, as usual seems to lie between, undiscovered by the belligerents, but per-fectly well known to "the honest smoker" (as old Izaak Walton would style him) who wonders from amid his peaceful cloud what all the turmoil means. Can the smoking of "the pipe of peace;" the harmless sedative of an amiable man, raise all this storm? Can his quiet and consoling habit be the cause why so many "decent men" should grow quarrelsome and even vindictive about the matter? Alas! gentlemen-fighters, know you not that the herb first gained its reputation for its extremely sanatory uses? that it was styled "Sana sancta Indorum"—"Herbe propre à tous maux?"—and that doctors themselves first origi-nated the laudatory words of Captain Bobadil, and affirmed it to be "the most sovereign and precious

weed that ever the earth tendered to the use of man."
Look at the quarto volume *The Triall of Tobacco*,
by Dr. Edmund Gardiner, " practitioner of Physicke,"
(published in London 1610), or to that more portly
tome by Dr. John Neander of Bremen (published at
Leyden, 1622), who prescribes it for almost all the
diseases of life. Did not the " famous Physician"
Raphael Thorius smoke till he became inspired with
Latin poetry, and gave the world his *Hymnus Tabaci?*
The " common verse " which concludes his preface
may sum up the question,

> " Usus habet laudem, crimen abusus habet."

The disputes on tobacco remind one of that on
Rab Roryson's bonnet, as told by Tannahill :—

> "Some maintained it was black, some maintained it was blue,
> It had something of baith, as a body may trew."

There is a narrowness of spirit among the oppositionists which takes a persecuting feature, and induces
dislike and doubt of their tenets.

The same poet says elsewhere :—

> " I've heard some fouks descant sae freely
> On ither people's matters,
> As if themsel's war' real perfection,
> When had they stood a fair inspection,
> Th' abused war' far their betters."

In the words of a popular author the controversy
may be accepted as " An admirable illustration of the

effect which thought, constantly directed in a wrong channel, may have in warping the judgment." *

There is no doubt that tobacco, if much used by persons of lethargic temperament, is bad from the very nature of the herb, but "your hot and sanguine temper" may be much improved thereby. Instances in abundance occur where smoking really to excess, has not been accompanied by any injury to the smoker : not that for one moment we would here defend such practices. Men have lived to a good old age who have done so. The author's father died at the age of seventy-two : he had been twelve hours a day in a tobacco-manufactory for nearly fifty years; and he both smoked and chewed while busy in the labours of the workshop, sometimes amid a dense cloud of steam from drying the damp tobacco over the stoves; and his health and appetite were perfect to the day of his death ; he was a model of muscular and stomachic energy; in which his son, who neither smokes, snuffs, nor chews, by no means rivals him or does him credit. But we may best conclude with the following very sensible remarks, which appeared in the *Examiner* of January 17, 1852.

" Some physicians have been pleased to ascribe pernicious effects to the use of tobacco, upon about as good evidence as a gipsy tells fortunes by counting the furrows on the palm of a country girl's hand. A correspondent favours us with an extract from a paper read before the British Association at Southampton, in which a

* Inglis, *Rambles in the Footsteps of Don Quixote.*

truly horrid train of evils is traced to 'the continuous use of this poisonous substance.' The poison, it would seem, 'pervades the digestive and respiratory system,' 'the circulating system and the nervous system,' 'diminishing the moral and intellectual powers.' Instead of all this detail, and much more of the same sort, why did not the learned essayist say at once that the baneful drug pervaded 'soul and body?' With 'death in the pot' by one set of philosophers, and 'death in the pipe' by another, the wonder only is how we come to be alive at all; and the greater still, how we come to live longer than our ancestors of the reign of King Henry the Eighth, who never saw and never heard of a tobacco plant. Three hundred years ago a few American savages only consumed tobacco, and now it is consumed by all mankind, being the only commodity common to the consumption of all races and all social conditions. Are our lives shorter, our morals worse, or our intellects weaker, that for the better part of three centuries 'the poisonous drug,' according to this hypothesis, has been circulating through the veins of ourselves and our forefathers ?

"Men of every race and of every climate have been using stimulants of one sort or another from the days of Noah, and probably will continue to do so for the next four thousand years, in spite of chair or pulpit. The question to decide is which stimulant is most innocuous, and, after tea and coffee, we have no hesitation in ranking tobacco, for we are not to be frightened out of our wits by Dr. Laycock's awful array of terrors,

attested though they be 'by experiments demonstrating
the physiological action of the drug on animals,'—that
is, experiments to show that what may be injurious to
a dog that dies of old age at sixteen, and to a rabbit
which breeds seven times a year, and hardly lives five,
must be equally so to a creature that lives seventy or
eighty years, and whose ingenuity has altered the very
face of the planet he dwells on."

CHAPTER II.

TOBACCO IN AMERICA.

It was in the first week of November, 1492, that Europeans first noted the Indian custom of tobacco-smoking. The two sailors sent by Columbus to explore Cuba returned to the ships of their great commander, and told this among other things new and strange. They found the natives carried with them a lighted firebrand, and puffed smoke from their mouths and noses; this their European notions led them to conclude was some mode of perfuming themselves. A more intimate acquaintance with the natives, taught them that it was certain leaves of a herb rolled up in the dried leaves of the maize or Indian corn, that they thus burned, and inhaled the smoke. It was a novelty to the Spaniards, but it was an ancient and familiar custom with the natives: "the aborigines of Central America rolled up the tobacco-leaf, and dreamed away their lives in smoky reveries ages before Columbus was born, or the colonists of Sir Walter Raleigh brought it within the precincts of the Elizabethan court. The cocoa-leaf, now the comfort and strength of the Peruvian muletero, was chewed as he does it, in far remote

times, and among the same mountains, by the Indian
natives whose blood he inherits."* When the Spaniards
landed in Paraguay in 1503, the natives came forth to
oppose them, beating drums, throwing water, "chewing
herbs, and spurting the juice towards them ; " all very
rude and apparently absurd modes of defence against
invasion ; but the latter really formidable in close
combat, if the herb was tobacco, and the juice directed
to the eyes, as we find was done by natives in war.

Oviedo is the first author who gives a clear account
of smoking among the Indians of Hispaniola.† He
speaks of it among their " evil customs," as a thing
" very pernicious, used to produce insensibility. Their
mode of using it among the *caciques* and chief men, is
by inhalation through the nostrils by means of a
hollow forked cane, in one piece," of which he gives an

engraving: ‡ he describes it as " about a
span long; and when used the forked ends
are inserted in the nostrils, the other end
being applied to the burning leaves of the
herb. They thus inhale the smoke until
they become stupified. When forked canes
are not procurable, a straight reed or hollow
cane is used, and this implement is called *tabaco* by
the Indians; " and Oviedo is careful to observe

---

* *Chemistry of Common Life*, by Professor Johnston.

† *Historia General de las Indias*, 1526 ; enlarged 1535.

‡ The engraving does not occur in the earlier editions. The book was
very popular, and went through several. Our cut is copied from that published at Salamanca, 1547. It is remarkable as the first engraving ever
published of the primitive tobacco-pipe.

that that name is not given to the herb, or to the
stupor it produces, as some persons have erroneously
supposed. With similar inaccuracy the island of
Tobago is said to have given name to the plant;
but the author of " *Tobago* : or a Geographical
description, natural and civil history, together with
a full representation of the produce, and other
advantages arising from the fertility, excellent har-
bours, and happy situation of that famous Island,"
2 ed. p. 74, says :—" I do not recollect any author
who has given a clear account of this name, and as
many have expressed a doubt whether the island was
so called from the herb, or the herb from the island ;
I hope the curious and inquisitive reader will be well
pleased to see that matter set in its true light. For
the fact is that neither the island received its name
from the herb, nor the herb from the island. The
appellation is indeed Indian, and yet was bestowed by
the Spaniards. The thing happened thus : the Car-
ribees were extremely fond of tobacco, which in their
language they called *Kohiha*, and fancied when they
were drunk with the fumes of it, the dreams they had
were in some sort inspired. Now their method of
taking it was this ; they first made a fire of wood, and
when it was burnt out they scattered upon the living
embers the leaves of the plant, and received the smoke
of it by the help of an instrument that was hollow,
made exactly in the shape of the letter Y, putting the
larger tube into smoke, and thrusting the shorter tubes
up their nostrils. This instrument they called *Tobago*,

and when the Admiral Christopher Columbus passed
to the southward of this island, he judged the form of
it to resemble that instrument, and thence it received
its name."

In the narrative of the second voyage of Columbus
in 1494, we are informed by Roman Pane, the friar who
accompanied him, that this mode of inhaling by the
cane pipe was adopted in another way of taking tobacco.
The herb was reduced to a powder, which "they take
through a cane half a cubit long; one end of this they
place in the nose, and the other upon the
powder, and so draw it up, which purges
them very much." This is the earliest notice of snuff taking; and its effects upon the
Indians in both instances seem to have been
more violent and peculiar than upon Europeans since. He uses the name *cogiaba* for
the plant, which is its Hispaniolan name;
and is spelt by other travellers *cohiba*. It
was known as *petun* in Brazil, as *piecelt* in
Mexico, and at other places as *yoli*.

Lobel, in his *Novum Stirpia Adversaria*,
appended to his *History of Plants*, 1576,
gives an engraving of the tobacco rolled into
a tube, as first seen by Columbus in the
mouths of the natives of San Salvador, which is here
copied.* He describes it as a sort of small funnel

---

* It is traced in fac-simile. The reader must bear in mind that the
original artist has not attended to the comparative size of the tobacco tube
and the head of the smoker, the former being infinitely too large.

formed of the palm leaf, in which the dried leaves of
the tobacco are placed; fire is applied to it, and the
smoke inhaled. He speaks of this kind of smoking
being much used afterwards by Captains of ships
trading to the West Indies; and they attribute to it
the power of allaying hunger and thirst, exhilarating
the spirits, and renovating the animal powers.

We have thus the origin of snuff taking, and cigar
smoking clearly traced; and we can also discover the
use of the pipe among the chieftains of South America,
with scarcely any difference
in form to that universally
adopted in Europe. In the
engravings to Be Bry, *Historia Brasiliana,* 1590, is
one representing a native,
quietly enjoying a pipe,
which might be taken for
the clay pipe of a Dutchman
of the last century; a female
is bringing him a fresh sup-
ply of tobacco-leaves.* We can thus trace to South
America, at the period when the New World was first
discovered, every mode of using the tobacco-plant
which the Old World has indulged in ever since.

* Be Bry accompanies the print with this description : "This plant is
called *Petun* by the Brazilians ; *Tapaco,* by the Spaniards : the leaves of
which well dried they place in the open (wide-spread) part of a pipe, of
which (being burned) the smoke is inhaled into the mouth by the more
narrow part of the pipe, and so strongly that it flows out of the mouth and
nostrils, and by that means effectually drives out humours."

Francisco Lopez de Gomara, who was chaplain to
Cortez, when he made conquest of Mexico in 1519,
speaks of smoking as an established custom among the
people ; and Bernal Diaz relates that the king Monte-
zuma had his pipe brought with much ceremony by the
chief ladies of his court, after he had dined and
washed his mouth with scented water.   In the vicinity
of the city of Mexico large quantities of clay tobacco
pipes have been dug up of various fanciful forms,
which show that as great an amount of attention was
bestowed on their decoration by the old Mexicans, as
we have devoted to them in Europe.   Our engraving

 exhibits one of
very remark-
able form ; it
represents a
male figure with the characteristic features of the
Mexican type, at the back is the aperture for consuming the tobacco, which is smoked through the
straight leg; the bent one acting as a handle.*   The
ears of the figure are bored for the insertion of pendant
ornaments, which the natives devoted as willingly to
the heads of their pipes, as to their own.

In the History of the New World, by Giralamo
Benzoni of Milan, narrating his travels in America
from 1541 to 1556 (and which has been translated
from the Venetian edition of 1573 by Rear-Admiral

---

* In our chapter on Pipes is engraved a clay pipe of English make, precisely on the same principle, and is a curious example of undesigned coin-
cidence, or of the unchanging essential modes of tobacco smoking.

Smyth for the Hakluyt Society, 1857), speaking of the Island of Hispaniola, he says :—

" In this island, as also in other provinces of these new countries, there are some bushes, not very large, like reeds, that produce a leaf in shape like that of the walnut, though rather larger, which (where it is used) is held in great esteem by the natives, and very much prized by the slaves whom the Spaniards have brought from Ethiopia.

" When these leaves are in season, they pick them, tie them up in bundles, and suspend them near their fireplace till they are very dry; and when they wish to use them, they take a leaf of their grain (maize), and putting one of the others into it, they roll them round tight together; then they set fire to one end, and putting the other end into the mouth, they draw their breath up through it, wherefore the smoke goes into the mouth, the throat, the head, and they retain it as long as they can, for they find a pleasure in it ; and so much do they fill themselves with this cruel smoke, that they lose their reason. And there are some who take so much of it, that they fall down as if they were dead, and remain the greater part of the day or night stupified. Some men are found who are content with imbibing only enough of this smoke to make them giddy, and no more. See what a wicked and pestiferous poison from the devil this must be. It has happened to me several times that, going through the provinces of Guatemala and Nicaragua, I have entered the house of an Indian who had taken this herb, which in the Mexican language is called *tabacco*, and immediately perceiving the sharp fetid smell of this truly diabolical and stinking smoke, I was obliged to go away in haste, and seek some other place.*

"In La Española and the other islands, when their doctors wanted to cure a sick man, they went to the place where they were to administer the smoke, and when he was thoroughly intoxicated by it, the cure was mostly effected. On returning to his senses, he told a thousand stories of his having been at the council of the gods, and other high visions." Benzoni gives a woodcut of the ceremony of tobacco-taking by means of inhalation at the mouth from a pipe ; a second figure has dropped the pipe, and lies on his back in a state of insensibility, while a third is tended by a physician in his *hamoc*, the origin of those used by our sailors.

In North America the custom was even more general.† Not one tribe was found to be unacquainted with the habit when they were first discovered by European travellers; and it is generally supposed the custom had its origin among them. The old Indian tradition favours this belief, which is thus related by

* This is strong language ! Benzoni was evidently not the man to introduce smoking to Venice ! Admiral Smyth remarks on this passage: "Surely the royal author of the famous Counterblast must have seen this graphic and early description of a cigar !"

† The Indians were so constant in their devotions to the pipe, that they used them as Europeans use a watch, and in reckoning the time anything occupied would say, "I was one pipe (of time) about it."

Franklin, in the course of a narrative he gives of a Swedish minister who took occasion to inform the chiefs of the Susquehannah Indians, in a kind of sermon, of the principal historical facts on which the Christian religion is founded; and particularly the fall of our first parents. When the sermon was over, an old Indian orator replied: " What you have told us is very good; we thank you for coming so far to tell us those things you have heard from your mothers; in return we will tell you what we have heard from ours.

" In the beginning we had only flesh of animals to eat; and if they failed, we starved. Two of our hunters having killed a deer, and broiled a part of it, saw a young woman descend from the clouds, and seat herself on a hill hard by. Said one to the other : ' It is a spirit, perhaps, that has smelt our venison ; let us offer some of it to her.' They accordingly gave her the tongue ; she was pleased with its flavour, and said : ' Your kindness shall be rewarded ; come here thirteen moons hence, and you shall find it.' They did so ; and found, where her right hand had touched the ground, maize growing; where her left hand had been, kidney-beans ; and where she had sat, they found tobacco."

Hariot, who joined the expedition of 1584, under the auspices of Sir Walter Raleigh, which resulted in the discovery of Virginia, states, that the natives considered tobacco as a gift from the Great Spirit for their special enjoyment,—one that the Great Spirit also indulged in. The pipe was therefore sacred, and smoking partook of the character of a moral, if not a religious act. We quote as much as relates to the herb (the first detailed English narrative) published by him in 1588 in *A Briefe and True Report of the New Found Land of Virginia*, the truth of which is attested by Rafe Lane, the governor.

He thus writes :—" There is an herbe which is sowed apart by itselfe, and is called by the inhabitants *uppówoc*. In the West Indies it hath divers names, according to the severall places and countries where it groweth and is used : the Spaniards generally call it *Tobacco*. The leaves thereof being dried and brought into powder, they use to take the fume or smoke thereof by sucking it through pipes made of clay into their stomacke and heade, from whence it purgeth superfluous fleame and other grosse humors ; openeth all the pores and passages of the body ; by which means the use thereof not only preserveth the body from obstructions, but also if any be so that they have not beene of too long continuance, in short time breaketh them ; whereby their bodies are notably pre- served in health, and know not many grievous diseases wherewithall we in England are oftentimes affected.

" This *uppówoc* is of so precious estimation amongest them that they thinke their gods are marvellously delighted therewith ; whereupon sometime they make halowed fires, and cast some of the powder therein for a sacrifice. Being in a storme uppon the waters, to pacifie their gods, they cast some up into the aire and into the water : so a weare for fish being newly set up, they cast some therein and into the aire ; also after an escape of danger they cast some into the aire likewise ; but all done with strange gestures, stamping, sometime dauncing, clapping of hands, holding up of hands, and staring up into the heavens, uttering therewithal and chattering strange wordes, and noises.

" We ourselves during the time we were there used to suck it after their manner, as also since our returne, and have found many rare and wonderful experiments of the vertues thereof; of which the relation would require a volume by itselfe ; the use of it by so manie of late, men and women, of great calling as else, and some learned phisitions also, is sufficient witnes."

We may here conveniently quote some other early notices of the plant by English voyagers :—

In the voyage of Sir Francis Drake * it is noted that the natives of North America " brought a little basket made of rushes, and filled with an herbe which they called *Tobah;*" and he afterwards notes, they " came now the second time to us, bringing with them as before had been done, feathers and bags of *Tobah* for presents, or rather indeed for sacrifices, upon this persuasion that we were gods."

In *The Historie of Travaile into Virginia Britannica,* published by the Hakluyt Society from the original MS. of William Strachey, first secretary to

* *The World Encompassed.* Lond. 1628. The voyage commenced 1572, and ended August, 1573.

the colony, and supposed to have been written between 1610 and 1612, he says: "Here is great store of tobacco, which the salvages call *apooke*: howbeit it is not of the best kynd, it is but poor and weake, and of a byting taste; it grows not fully a yard above ground, bearing a little yellow flower like to henbane; the leaves are short and thick, somewhat round at the upper end; whereas the best tobacco of Trynidado and the Oronoque, is large, sharpe, and growing two or three yardes from the ground, bearing a flower of the breadth of our bellflowers in England; the salvages here dry the leaves of this *apooke* over the fier, and sometymes in the sun, and crumble yt into poudre, stalks, leaves, and all, taking the same in pipes of earth, which very ingeniously they can make."

In the old Indian grave mounds, many of which are of the remotest antiquity, pipes of ingenious fabrication have been found. Some are cut into the form of heads ; and it is remarkable that the features are singularly truthful and expressive, bearing a striking similarity to the Mongolian type, and so far favouring the theory of some ethnologists who suppose America to have been peopled by migrations from the eastern part of Asia. The great antiquity of these mounds is attested by the fact of colossal trees growing upon them, which are several centuries old, as an examination of the sectional rings of the stem can prove. Squier and Davis in their *Ancient Monuments of the Mississippi Valley,*[*]

---

[*] Published in 4to by the Smithsonian Institution, Washington, 1848.

say : " The mound-builders were inveterate smokers, if the great number of pipes discovered in the mounds, be admitted as evidence of the fact. These constitute not only a numerous, but a singularly interesting class of remains. In their construction the skill of the makers seems to have been exhausted. Their general form, which may be regarded as the *primitive* form of the implement, is well exhibited in the accompanying sketch. They are always carved from a single piece, and consist of a flat curved base, of variable length  and width, with the bowl rising from the centre of the convex side. From one of the ends, and communicating with the hollow of the bowl, is drilled a small hole, which answers the purpose of a tube; the corresponding opposite division being left for the manifest purpose of holding the implement to the mouth. The specimen above represented is finely carved from a beautiful variety of brown porphyry, granulated with various-coloured materials, the whole much changed by the action of fire, and somewhat resembling porcelain. It is intensely hard, and successfully resists the edge of the finest-tempered knife. The length of the base is five inches, breadth of the same one inch and a quarter ; the bowl is one inch and a quarter high, slightly tapering upwards, but flaring near the top. The hollow of the bowl is six-tenths of an inch

diameter. The perforation answering to the tube is
one-sixth of an inch diameter, which is about the usual
size. This circumstance places it beyond doubt that
the mouth was applied directly to the implement,
without the intervention of a tube of wood or metal.
It will be observed that it is ornamented with cup-
shaped holes an eighth of an inch broad, and about the
same depth. Seven of these are placed in a circle
upon each side of the bowl, which has a line of them
extending spirally round it."

Such is the general form of these implements. The
larger proportion of those found in the mounds, however, are of much more elaborate workmanship. They
are sculptured with figures of beasts, birds, and reptiles,
all executed with a strict fidelity to nature; the atti-
tudes are characteristic, and the very habit of the
creatures occasionally given. Some represent animals
peculiar to the lower latitudes, and illustrate important
questions on the migrations of the race. Most are
worked in porphyry, and all exhibit a truthfulness,
delicacy, and finish we should scarcely expect to find in
the works of the aborigines of America. The otter is
shown in a characteristic attitude, holding a fish in his
mouth; the heron also holds a fish; and the hawk
grasps a small bird in its talons, which it tears with its
beak. The panther, the bear, the wolf, the beaver,
the otter, the squirrel, the racoon; the hawk, the
heron, the crow, swallow, buzzard, paroquet, toucan,
and other indigenous and southern birds; the turtle,
the frog, toad, rattlesnake, &c., are recognised at a

glance. But the most interesting and valuable in the
list are a number of sculptured human heads, no
doubt faithfully representing the predominant physical
features of the ancient people by whom they were
made. We here engrave two of the best examples:
Fig. 1. was obtained from the famous ancient works
known as " Mound City," on the Sciato River, in Ross
County, Ohio. It represents the head, apparently of

Fig. 1.   Fig .2.

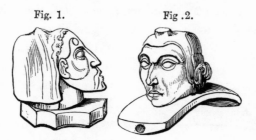

a chief, decorated with a raised head-dress, the forehead having a border of pearls inserted in the black
stone of which the pipe is composed; the face is
tattooed or decorated with incised lines deeply cut.
Fig. 2. is considered by Mr. Squier as the "most
beautiful head of the series, and is evidently that of
a female. It is carved from a compact stone, smooth
and well polished. The muscles of the face are well
exhibited, and the forehead finely moulded. The eyes
are prominent and open, and the lips full and rounded.
Whether the head is encased in a sort of hood, or
whether the hair is platted across the forehead and
down the sides of the face, is not easy to say, as the
action of fire used in the service of the dead has

impaired the contour in some degree. The knots observable at the top of the forehead and behind the ears, may represent the way in which the hair was wound." The workmanship of this head is unsurpassed by any specimen of ancient American art which had fallen under the notice of Messrs. Squier and Davis in their researches, "not excepting the best productions of Mexico and Peru."

The Lamantin, Manitus, or Sea-cow, from the peculiarity of its form, was well adapted to the shape of the

old Indian pipe. The fact of this creature being thus represented, as it is peculiar to tropical America, at a distance of a thousand miles from the home of the mound-builders, is a proof of a system of intercourse, most probably by barter, kept up by the Indians throughout the continent; and thus, so apparently insignificant a relic as an old Indian pipe-stem affords us an important trait in their past history, which the ethnologist will know how to value.

The beaver is given with characteristic fidelity in another pipe; and the reader will observe that all

these decorations are made to face the smoker, and increase his pleasure as he indulges in the weed; and not for the ostentatious display of a showy pipe as among "civilized" moderns.

The wild cat in our next engraving, is equally good; the ferocity and watchfulness which combine in the features of the species, are well displayed.

Birds are also represented with equal truthfulness. We engrave one pipe decorated with the figure of a toucan, which is represented receiving its food from a human hand (the latter indicated by incised lines in the base of the pipe). This bird is only found in the tropical countries of North America. Pozzo, a distinguished naturalist, speaks of taming

them very easily. Other travellers inform us that they are very highly prized by the Indians of Guiana and Brazil, principally on account of their brilliant plumage; they pluck off the skin from the breast, containing the most beautiful feathers, and glue it upon their cheeks by way of ornament. In these districts the toucan was almost the only bird the aborigines attempted to domesticate.

It will be noticed that all these ancient pipes are constructed of the hardest materials—granite, porphyry, and basaltic stone. The time and labour expended in perfecting these elaborate works, must have given them a high value when finished. They appear to have been first rudely fashioned by tools of copper

or obsidian (as used by the Peruvians and Mexicans),
and then carefully finished by rubbing or grinding on
stones possessing a sharp grit.

" From the appearance of these relics it is fairly
inferable that, among the mound-builders, as among
the tribes of North American Indians, the practice of
smoking was very general if not universal. The con-
jecture that it was also more or less interwoven with
their civil and religious observances, is not without its
support. The use of tobacco was known to nearly all
the American nations, and the pipe was their grand
diplomatist. In making war and in concluding peace
it performed an important part. Their deliberations,
domestic as well as public, were conducted under its
influences; and no treaty was ever made unsignalised
by the passage of the calumet. The transfer of the
pipe from the lips of one individual to those of another
was the token of amity and friendship, a gage of honour
with the chivalry of the forest which was seldom
violated. In their religious ceremonies it was also
introduced, with various degrees of solemnity. A sub-
stitute for tobacco was sometimes furnished in the
tender bark of the young willow; other substitutes were
found among the Northern tribes in the leaves and
roots of various pungent herbs. The custom extended
to Mexico, where however it does not seem to have
been invested with any of those singular convention-
alities observed in the higher latitudes. It prevailed
in South America and in the Caribbean islands. The
form of the Indian pipe in North America is extremely

variable, and very much the subject of individual taste. Some are excessively rude, but most are formed with great labour from the finest materials within reach. Along the Mississippi and among the tribes to the westward of that river, the material most valued for the purpose was, and still is, the red pipe-stone of the *Côteau des Prairies*, a beautiful mineral resembling steatite, easily worked, and capable of a high finish. The spot whence it is obtained, and which is certainly one of the most interesting mineral localities of the whole country, is regarded with superstitious veneration by the Indians. It is esteemed to be under the special protection of the Great Spirit, and is connected with many of their most singular traditions. Until very recently it was the common resort of the tribes, where animosities and rivalries were forgotten, and where the most embittered foes met each other on terms of amity. In carving pipes from this material they expended their utmost skill, and we may regard them as the *chefs d'œuvre* of modern Indian art. The following

engraving, from originals, will exhibit their predominant form, which, it will be observed, is radically different from that of the mound pipes. The larger of the two was once the favourite pipe of the eloquent Keokuk, chief of the Sacs and Foxes, whose name occupies a conspicuous place in the Indian history of the North-west. These pipes were smoked with long tubes of wood, from twenty inches to three feet in length, fantastically ornamented with feathers and beads." (*Squier and Davis.*)

The sculpture of these articles, which is sometimes attempted in imitation of the human figure and of various animals, is often tasteful. But they never display the nice observation, and true, artistic appreciation and skill exhibited by those of the mounds, notwithstanding their makers have all the advantages resulting from steel implements for carving, and from the *suggestions* afforded by European art. The only fair test of the relative degrees of skill possessed by the two races would be in a comparison of the remains of the mounds with the productions of the Indians before the commencement of European intercourse. A comparison with the works of the latter however, at any period, would not fail to exhibit in a striking light the greatly superior skill of the ancient people.

There are also pipes of clay found in Virginia, but they are generally of rude workmanship ; one of these

with a singular head-dress, closely resembling some of those observed on the idols and sculptures of Mexico, is here copied from Squier and Davis, from whence we also copy the plain pipe-head from a mound in Florida.

Most of the ancient clay-pipes that have been discovered have this form, which is not widely different from that adopted by the later Indians. "The Virginians we observed to have pipes of clay before even the English came there; and from those barbarians we Europeans have borrowed our mode and fashion of smoking." *

Pipe-stems seem to be a much later addition to the Indian pipe. I engrave an example of one from the collection of the late T. Crofton Croker; it is of black stone, and is all cut from one piece; it bears traces of European influence, if indeed the figure be not intended for an European. It came from Upper Canada.

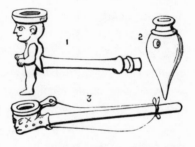

A second from the same place, also formed of black stone, seems constructed to condense the oil of tobacco at the pointed termination of the bowl, a thin reed being inserted in the small hole above, when the pipe is smoked. Fig. 3, from the New York Government collection, has a wooden tube inserted in the head of dark green obsidian, which is sculptured with a loop to allow of its being tied by a string to the stem.

* *Natural History of Tobacco* in the Harleian Miscellany, vol. i. p. 535.

Dr. Wilson, of Toronto, U.S., * in his clever Ethnographical sketch of *Pipes and Tobacco,* has been at
some pains to describe the varieties of pipes in use by
the North American Indians, of which I avail myself
briefly. He is inclined to think that the pipe-stem
"is one of the characteristics of modern race, if not
distinctive of the Northern tribes of Indians," who
used the bowl very small, as we see it in the earliest
English pipes. " Specimens of another class of clay
pipes," he tells us, " of a larger size, and with a tube
of such length as obviously to be designed for use
without the addition of a pipe-stem," he thinks,
peculiar to the Canadian frontier. " Most of the
ancient clay pipes that have been discovered are stated
to have the same form ; and this, it may be noted,
bears so near a resemblance to that of the red clay
pipe used in modern Turkey, with the cherry-tree
pipe-stem, that it might be supposed to have furnished
the model. The bowls of this class of ancient clay
pipes are not of the miniature proportions which
induce a comparison between those of Canada and the
early examples found in Britain; neither do the stone
pipe-heads of the mound-builders suggest by the size
of the bowl either the self-denying economy of the
ancient smoker, or his practice of the modern Indian
mode of exhaling the fumes of the tobacco, by which

* Once Curator of the Royal Society of Antiquaries of Scotland, and
author of *Prehistoric Annals of Scotland, Memorials of Edinburgh,* &c. ;
now Professor of History and English Literature in University College,
Toronto.

so small a quantity suffices to produce the full narcotic effects of the favourite weed. They would rather seem to confirm the indications derived from other sources, of an essential difference between the ancient smoking usages of Central America and of the mound-builders, and those which are still maintained in their primeval integrity among the Indians of the North West.

"Great variety of form and material distinguishes the pipes of the modern Indians : arising in part from the local facilities they possess for a suitable material from which to construct them.; and in part also from the special style of art and decoration which has become the traditional usage of the tribe. The favourite red pipe-stone of the *Côteau des Prairies*, has been generally sought after, both from its easiness of working and the beauty of its appearance.* * *A pipe of this favourite and beautiful material, found on the shores of Lake Simcoe, and now in my possession, measures five inches and three-quarters in length, and nearly four inches in greatest breadth, yet the capacity of the bowl hollowed in it for the reception of tobacco is even less than in the smallest of the ' Elfin Pipes.' In contrast to this, a modern Winnebago pipe recently acquired by me, made of the same red pipe stone, inlaid with lead, and executed with ingenious skill, has a bowl of large dimensions illustrative of Indian smoking usages modified by the influence of the white man. From the red pipe-stone, as well as from lime-stone and other harder rocks, the Chippeways, the Winnebagos, and the Siouxs, frequently make a

peculiar class of pipes, inlaid with lead. * * * The
Chinook and Puget Sound Indians, who evince little
taste in comparison with the tribes surrounding them,
in ornamenting their persons or their warlike and domestic implements, commonly use wooden pipes. Sometimes these are elaborately carved, but most frequently
they are rudely and hastily made for immediate use;
and even among these remote tribes of the flat head
Indians, the common clay pipe of the fur trader begins
to supersede such native arts.

"Among the Assinaboin Indians a material is used
in pipe manufacture altogether peculiar to them. It
is a fine marble, much too hard to admit of minute
carving, but taking a high polish. This is cut into
pipes of graceful form, and made so extremely thin,
as to be nearly transparent, so that when lighted the
glowing tobacco shines through, and presents a singular appearance when in use at night or in a dark
lodge. Another favourite material employed by the
Assinaboin Indians is a coarse species of jasper also
too hard to admit of elaborate ornamentation. This
also is cut into various simple but tasteful designs,
executed chiefly by the slow and laborious process of
rubbing it down with other stones. The choice of the
material for fashioning the favourite pipe, is by no
means invariably guided by the facilities which the
location of the tribe affords. A suitable stone for such
a purpose will be picked up and carried hundreds of
miles. Mr. Kane informs me that, in coming down
the Athabaska River, when drawing near its source in

the Rocky Mountains, he observed his Assinaboin guides select the favourite bluish jasper from among the water-worn stones in the bed of the river, to carry home for the purpose of pipe manufacture, although they were then fully five hundred miles from their lodges. Such a traditional adherence to a choice of material peculiar to a remote source, may frequently prove of considerable value as a clue to former migrations of the tribes.

"Both the Cree and the Winnebago Indians carve pipes in stone, of a form now more frequently met with in the Indian curiosity stores of Canada and the States than any other specimens of native carving. The tube, cut at a sharp right angle with the cylindrical bowl of the pipe, is ornamented with a thin vandyked ridge, generally perforated with a row of holes, and standing up somewhat like the dorsal fin of a fish. The Winnebagos also manufacture pipes of the same form, but of a smaller size, in lead, with considerable skill.

"Among the Cree Indians a double pipe is occasionally in use, consisting of a bowl carved out of stone without much attempt at ornament, but with perforations on two sides, so that two smokers can insert their pipe-stems at once, and enjoy the same supply of tobacco. It does not appear, however, that any special significance is attached to this singular fancy. The Saultaux Indians, a branch of the great Algonquin nation, also carve their pipes out of a black stone, found in their country, and evince considerable skill in the execution of their elaborate details. * * * But the

most remarkable of all the specimens of pipe sculpture
executed by the Indians of the north-west, are those
carved by the Babeen, or Big-lip Indians, so called
from the singular deformity they produce by inserting
a piece of wood into a slit made in the lower lip. The
Babeen Indians are found along the Pacific Coast,
about latitude 54° 40′, and extend from the borders
of the Russian dominions east-ward nearly to Frazer
River. The pipes of the Babeen, and also of the
Clalam Indians occupying the neighbouring Vancou-
ver's Island, are carved with the utmost elaborateness,
and in the most singular and grotesque devices, from a
soft blue claystone or slate. Their form is in part determined by the material, which is only procurable in thin
slabs ; so that the sculptures, wrought on both sides,
present a sort of double bas-relief. From this, singular
and grotesque groups are carved, without any apparent
reference to the final destination of the whole as a pipe.
The lower side is generally a straight line, and in the
specimens I have examined they measure from two or
three to fifteen inches long ; so that in these the pipe-
stem is included. A small hollow is carved out of
some protruding ornament to serve as the bowl of the
pipe, and from the further end a perforation is drilled
to connect with this. The only addition made to it
when in use is the insertion of a quill or straw as a
mouth-piece." Of this latter kind we present an engraving ; they are among the most remarkable productions of the northern Indians, partaking of most
grotesque features, and generally representing men

swallowed by serpents and monsters; an extraordinary jumble of human and animal form; occasionally an

European appears among them in his round hat and tail coat, which never looks more ridiculous than when it is exhibited by the "native artists" of the Northern Pacific. Large and unwieldy as these pipes appear, they have but a very small aperture for tobacco, as may be seen in the upper portion of the woodcut given above.*

Catlin says, in his *Letters on the North American Indians*, 1841, they are all excessive smokers, and many of them would seem to be smoking one-half of their lives.† He thus describes their pipe-making :—

"The Indians shape out the bowls of their pipes from the solid stone, which is not quite as hard as

* A savage in want of his pipe has been known to dig a small hole in the ground, light his tobacco in it, and draw the smoke through a reed.

† When they can get no tobacco, they smoke weeds or leaves, and bark of trees which are narcotics; these they sometimes dry or pulverise and carry in pouches, smoking it to great excess : this is called *Knick k'neck.* A peculiar expedient resorted to by them, when they undertake a long journey, and are like to be destitute of provisions, is to mix the juice of tobacco with powdered shells, in the form of little balls, which they keep in their mouths, and the gradual solution serves to counteract the uneasy craving of the stomach.

marble, with nothing but a knife. The Indian makes the hole in the bowl of the pipe by drilling into it a hard stick shaped to the desired size, with a quantity of sharp sand and water, kept constantly in the hole, subjecting him therefore to very great labour, and the necessity of much patience." The smoking stems " are uniformly made of the stalk of the young ash, which generally grows straight, and has a small pith through the centre, which is easily burned out with a hot wire or a piece of hard wood."

With a brief notice of the War Pipe and the Peace Pipe we will conclude this section of our labour. The

first, a true tomahawk, is smoked through the reed handle, the tobacco being placed in the small receptacle above the hatchet; the smoke is drawn through the handle, which is perforated in its entire length, making it the pipe-stem. The Calumet, or peace-pipe, is the cherished heir-loom of the tribe, and is decorated with all the splendour of savage taste by the women, who vie with each other in rendering it as showy as possible with birds' feathers of the brightest colour, beads of various hues, and bows of ribbon. Each Indian knows to what tribe the pipe belongs at a glance, and it is only used on great political or religious celebrations to ratify good feeling by solemnly smoking it among the assembled tribes. The bowl is made of the sacred red pipe-stone from

the *Côteau des Prairies* in the Sioux country already
noted, and is affixed to a stem 4 or 5 feet in length.
The earliest travellers in North America noted this
custom : the Knight Montmagny, Governor of Canada
in 1645, used it to confirm the treaty of peace with
Algonquins, Montagnez, Hurons, and Cherokees ; one
of the latest travellers, the American artist Catlin,
has also described it, and accompanied his description
with the sketch we now copy.

" The calumet, or pipe of peace, ornamented with
the war-eagle's quills, is a sacred pipe, and never

allowed to be used on any other occasion than that of
peace-making, when the chief brings it into treaty,
and unfolding the many bandages which are carefully
kept around it, has it ready to be mutually smoked by
the chiefs, after the terms of the treaty are agreed
upon, as the means of solemnising it ; which is done
by passing the sacred stem to each chief, who draws
one breath of smoke only through it, thereby passing

the most inviolable pledge they can possibly give for
keeping the peace. This sacred pipe is then carefully
folded up and stowed away in the chief's lodge until a
similar occasion calls it out to be used in a similar
manner.

" There is no custom more uniformly in constant
use amongst the poor Indians than that of smoking,
nor any more highly valued. His pipe is his constant
companion through life—his messenger of peace ; he
pledges his friends through its stem and its bowl, and
when its care-drowning fumes cease to flow, it takes a
place with him in his solitary grave with his tomahawk
and war-club, companions to his long-fancied ' mild
and beautiful hunting-grounds. ' "

Such were " the modes to savage nations dear " of
smoking tobacco. In our next chapter we will con·
sider its European styles.

CHAPTER III.

TOBACCO IN EUROPE.

(AND ITS LITERARY ASSOCIATIONS.)

THE history of the origin of popular customs is generally involved in obscurity, it is the natural result of that very popularity which seems to render the office of historian unnecessary. Tradition thus occupies the place of the written chronicle, and when the latter has to be compiled, many facts have been lost or distorted. It is thus that the European use of Tobacco has been descanted on by various writers, some of whom, not content with doubting the persons who are popularly thought to have introduced it in the sixteenth century, have asserted its use in the East as an historic fact some centuries before the discovery of America. It is certain that the fumes of plants were used in medicine from a very early period; but the wild assertions deduced therefrom as to the early custom of tobacco smoking in the Old World, can only be classed among "the curiosities of literature," * inasmuch as no one

---

* We must dispose of some few of these in a note. The "tradition" of the Greek Church that Noah was intoxicated by tobacco would seem to be the production of some holy humourist. The grave assertion of Dr. Yates that he saw a representation of a smoking party in an ancient tomb in

of these writers has attempted to explain the extraordinary fact of the total silence of all persons as to the custom in Europe, either in ancient or modern times. It is in fact not till long after its European advent, in comparatively modern times, that we meet with these assertions and conjectures, which presuppose the monstrous improbability that the world had smoked on unwittingly for some three thousand years, and then accepted the " weed " from the aborigines of America as a new gift!

The proper name of the herb is also a subject of discussion, but the weight of evidence is certainly not in favour of the present one so extensively adopted in Europe. The name *tabaco* certainly appears, from the testimony of the oldest authors, to be that applied to the tube used by the Indians to inhale the smoke; and that the plant itself bore the name of *yoli, petun,*

Egypt may pass uncontradicted, as the author of this work has seen in the collection of drawings formed by a late distinguished antiquary to illustrate Norfolk, one representing a carved panel, of the age of Edward the Third, and from the mouth of one figure a pipe comfortably depends. The Egyptian pipe may have been added to an old figure in a similar manner by some idler—or, what is more probable, the picture may have represented glass-blowers at work, as engraved in *Wilkinson's Egypt,* vol. iii. p. 89, which on a cursory glance looks exactly like a smoking party. Irish antiquaries have also seen native instances as old or apparently older, but no notice has been taken of the "ingenious artists" who have added "the little tube of magic power" to these really extraordinary "ancient monuments." China, that very safe country, where all investigators repose when their labours in every other are refuted, is now the "happy home" whence the use of tobacco is declared to have emanated for the benefit of "outer barbarians." The determination to find what is sought for in all these theories is the most amusing part of them ; and the manner in which facts are ignored, for the stultification of fancies, would make a curious chapter on the idiosyncracies of authors.

piecelt, or *cohiba,* according to the varied language of
the different tribes who inhabited the great continent. *

"About 1560" is the date generally awarded to the
introduction of Tobacco to Europe, and a Spanish
physician, Franceso Hernandez, is believed to have
brought some plants to Spain for the inspection of his
"Most Catholic" Majesty Philip the Second, who had
commissioned him to visit Mexico and note its natural
productions. Almost at the same period France and
Italy were made acquainted therewith, chiefly by
the aid of members of the church. Jean Nicot, Lord
of Villemain, and master of the Requests of the
French King's household, was sent as ambassador to
the Portuguese Court in 1559, and purchased while at
Lisbon some tobacco seed from a Flemish merchant
who had obtained it in Florida. † He sent it to the
Grand Prior of France, and the herb was originally
known as *Herbe du Grand Prieur.* When Nicot
returned to France in 1561 he presented the Queen,
Catharine de Medicis, with some of the plants, and its
name was then altered in compliment to her to *Herbe
de la Reine,* and *Herbe Medicée.* The native name of
petun was, however, occasionally used; but all were
allowed to fall into disuse for one constructed in honour of the original importer; thus *Nicotiana* became its
recognised name, a term still preserved to us in *Nico-*

---

* These, and other native terms noted by early voyagers to America,
will be found in the previous chapter.

† In the castle of Belem is still preserved a letter in which he tells of
his first acquaintance with this "herb of a peculiarly pleasant taste, good
medicinally in fevers and other diseases."

tine, the scientific name for the essential oil the
tobacco-plant contains. * Italy received the gift direct
from the hands of Cardinal Prosper Santa Croce, who
also obtained it in Portugal, and in honour of him it
was christened *Erba Santa Croce.* An envoy from
France, who had probably obtained some of the plants
that Nicot introduced, brought them to another part of
Italy where it was called *Tornabona* from his name.
But the Spanish name, *tabaco,* given to it by Hernandez ultimately triumphed over all, and became
(with slight variations) that universally recognised over
the world.†

It was to the supposed sanitary effects of tobacco
that its honorable introduction to Europe was due.
Queens and Cardinals bowed to the dictum of physicians, who seemed to look upon the plant as a divine
remedy for most diseases, and so speedily propounded
cures for all that "flesh is heir to" from various
applications of it, that it also was christened *Herba
Panacea* and *Herba Santa*; and the "tabaco of Trinidado" is termed *Sana sancta Indorum* in Gerard's

---

* The author of the *Flora Domestica* (1823, p. 365) says :—"The
French have many names for it ; as, le tabac, nicotiane, petum, herbe du
Grand Prieur, herbe à la Reine, Medicée (from the Queen's family name),
buglosse antarctique, panacée antarctique (southern all-heal), herbe sainte,
herbe sacrée (holy herb), herbe propre à tous maux (herb fit for all
diseases), jusquiame de Perou (Peruvian henbane), herbe de Tourbanon,
herbe de St. Croix, herbe de l'ambassadeur."

† The Spaniards still use the name in its old purity of spelling ; the
Portuguese and Italians add an additional letter and term it *tabacco ;* we
alter the first vowel improperly and call it *tobacco*; the Poles term it
tabaka ; the Danes and Swedes shorten it to *tobak* ; the Germans, Dutch,
and Russians spell it *tabak,* a close approach to the French *tabac.*

Herball, 1597.* It was grown in small quantities as a medical herb for a long period in France, the English having long preceded that nation in the indulgence of smoking.

The curative virtues of the tobacco-plant are noted by two of our old poets. First Spenser in his *Fairy Queen* makes his Belphœbe include it with other medicinal herbs gathered to heal Timais :—

> "Into the woods thence-forth in haste she went,
> To seeke for herbes that mote him remedy ;
> For she of hearbes had great intendiment,
> Taught of the Nymph which from her infancy
> Her nursed had in true nobility :
> There whether it *divine Tobacco* were,
> Or Panachæa, or Polygony,
> She found and brought it to her patient deare,
> Who all this while lay bleeding out his heart-blood neare."

This was written soon after the introduction of the plant to England. Next William Lilly, the Euphuist and court-poet to Elizabeth, in his play *The Woman in the Moone,* 1597, makes Pandora after wounding a lover with a spear, send her servant for herbs to cure it :—

> "Gather me balme and cooling violets,
> And of our holy herb *nicotian,*
> And bring withall pure honey from the hive,
> To heale the wound of my unhappy hand." †

Henry Buttes, in his curious little volume entitled

* Some of the German writers describe it under the name of the *Holy Healing Herb* (Heilig wundkraut).

† This poet, from the testimony of his friend Nash, appears to have been a "great tobacco-smoker."

Dyets Dry Dinner (12mo, 1599), treats of the virtues of
Tobacco as a digestive power:—

> " Fruit, herbs, flesh, fish, whitemeats, spice, sauce, all
> Concoct are by Tobacco's cordiall."

He says he names his book a dry dinner, not only
Caminum Prandium, without wine, but *Accipritinum*
without all drink except tobacco, which also is but dry
drink. That it was " translated out of India in the seede
or roote; native or sative in our own fruitfullest soils.
It cureth any griefe, dolour, imposture, or obstruction
proceeding of colde or winde, especially in the head or
breast. The fume taken in a pipe is good against
Rumes, Catarrhs, hoarseness, ache in the head,
stomacke, lungs, breast: also in want of meate, drinke,
sleepe, or rest."
" The name in India is *piecelt*, surnamed *Tabacco*
by the Spaniards of the Ile *Tabaco*. By their meanes
it spred farre and neare : but yet wee are not beholden
to their tradition. Our English Ulisses, renowned Syr
Walter Rawleigh, a man admirably excellent in Navi-
gation, of Natures privy counsell, and infinitely read
in the wide booke of the worlde, hath both farre fetcht
it, and deare bought it ; the estimate of the treasure I
leave to other ; yet this all know, since it came in
request there hath bene *Magnus fumi questus*, and
Fumi-vendulus is the best Epithite for an Apothecary."
We shall meet with other instances of Tobacco sold

as a sanatory by Apothecaries;* and we may here most conveniently note some of the old medical recipes for its use. Edmund Gardiner, in his *Triall of Tobacco*, 1610,† gives this recipe for persons with asthma, or consumptive tendency :—

> Foliorum sana sancta Indorum.
> Styracis,
> Sandarachæ.
> Terebenthiæ,
> Mastichis, ana partes equales. ‡

Our author says "a medicine in the plague thus prepared I should judge to be verie effectual," if taken warm, and perspiration be induced :—

> Pulveris radicis Angelica Hortensis, vel sylvestris, ℨj.
> Theriacæ optima, 31, Ə℥.
> Aqua stillatitia, sana sancta Indorum, ℥iiij.
> Aceti optimi, ℥℥. Misce.

One more instance of the many given by our author,

---

* In Middleton's *Roaring Girl* one asks an apothecary : "Have you any good pudding tobacco, sir ?" (See also the extract from Dekker, p. 56.)

† The title is worth giving in full for its prolix detail of the contents of the book :—"*The Triall of Tobacco*, wherein his worth is most worthily expressed : as, in the name, nature, and qualitie of the same hearb ; his special use in all Physicke, with the right and 'true use of taking it, as well for the seasons and times, as also the complexions, dispositions, and constitutions of such bodies and persons as are fittest ; and to whom it is most profitable to take it." The author was an old man when he compiled the book ; but he did it, he tells us, to supply the want of a proper knowledge of a plant "so much in use amongst Englishmen."

‡ The Doctor notes the success attendant on a patient of his own, who could scarcely breathe, and was given over by his physicians, but "was at length counselled to take tobacco in fume : which he daily did, and only by this way, by little and little, he recovered his former health and strength of bodie." He also says : "a sirup made of the decoction of this herbe, with sufficient sugar, and so taken in a very small quantitie, dischargeth the breast from phlegmatic matter."

E

and we have done. It is "an unguent to take away all
pains of the gout," made by baking the ingredients for
five hours in a glass vessel :—

> Succi foliorum san. sanct. Indorum, ℥viij.
> Axung. porci masculi.
> Axung. caponis, ana unc. ii. Misce.

"What is a more noble medicine, or more readie at
hand, than Tobacco?" asks this author; and his view
of its virtues was taken afterward in a more ambitious
volume, by Dr. John Neander of Bremen, whose quarto
volume entitled *Tabacologia* was published at Leyden
in 1622, and who prescribes its use in a multitude of
recipes after the fashion of those just given for almost
all the diseases of life; it should be noted, however,
that it is never used without admixture with other
good and powerful medicaments.*

Sir Walter Raleigh is the popular hero English
tradition has chosen as the originator of smoking
among ourselves. He certainly made it fashionable,
sanctioned it by his custom, and gave it "a good
standing in society;" but it seems to have been introduced by Mr. Ralph Lane, who was sent out by
Raleigh as governor of Virginia, returning to England
in 1586. The historian of the voyage, Mr. Thomas
Harriot, and the learned Camden, who both lived at
the period, unhesitatingly affirm that Lane has the
honour of being the original English smoker.† The

* Dr. Everard had published at Antwerp in 1587 a similar work.
† Pennant, in *Tour in Wales* 1810 (vol. ii. p. 151), speaking of Captain

tobacco-plant seems, however, to have been known in England earlier. Stow in his *Annals*, declares, that "tobacco came into England about the twentieth year of Queen Elizabeth" (1577), but Taylor the Water-poet assigns an earlier date, he says "Tobacco was first brought into England in 1565, by Sir John Hawkins."* Lobelius, in his *Novum Stirpium Adversaria* (Antwerp 1576), declares that "within these few years" the West Indian tobacco had become "an inmate of England." Raleigh was certainly the first devoted adherent of smoking in England, and in spite of his courtiership when a queen ruled, ostentatiously enjoyed his pipe. Aubrey has noted, "He was the first that brought tobacco into England, and into fashion. In our part of North Wilts—*e.g.* Malmsbury Hundred—it came first into fashion by Sir Walter Long. They had first silver pipes. The ordinary sort made use of a walnut shell and a strawe. I have heard my grandfather Lyte say, that one pipe was handed from man to man round the table. Sir W. R.

Myddelton, who fought at Azores in 1591 :—"It is sayed that he, with Captain Thomas Price of Plasyollin, and one Captain Koet, were the first who smoked, or (as they called it) drank tobacco publickly in London, and that the Londoners flocked from all parts to see them. Pipes were not then invented, so they used the twisted leaves or *segars*." He gives this on the authority of the Sebright MS., and adds, "The invention is usually ascribed to Sir Walter Raleigh. It may be so, but he was too good a courtier to smoke in public, especially in the reign of James."

* Postscript to *The Old, Old, Very Old Man, or Life of Thomas Parr*. 1635. The translator of Everard's *Panacea*, in 1659, says :—" Captain Richard Grenfield and Sir Francis Drake were the first planters of it here, and not Sir Walter Raleigh, which is the common error ; so difficult is it to fix popular discoveries."

standing in a stand at Sir Ro. Poyntz parke at Acton
tooke a pipe of tobacco, which made the ladies quitte
it till he had donne;" this was after the accident
recorded as happening to him when " he took a private
pipe," and occasioned his servant to cast the ale over
him as the smoke induced him to fear his master
was on fire. If there be little credit attached to his
memory for thus " disgusting the ladies," there is still
less for having indulged in a pipe as he sat to see his
friend Essex perish on the scaffold.*

It is curious to note this well-known anecdote of
Raleigh, reported of other persons (a fact not hitherto
noted by historians of the herb). The famous jester
Dick Tarlton who died in 1588, is one of them, and in
his *Jests* (1611) the tale is thus told ; " How Tarlton
took tobacco at the first coming up of it :—Tarlton as
other gentlemen used, at the first coming up of
tobacco, did take it more for fashions sake than otherwise, and being in a roome, sat betweene two men
overcome with wine, and they never seeing the like,
wondered at it, and seeing the vapour come out of
Tarlton's nose, cryed out *fire, fire !* and threw a cup of
wine in Tarlton's face. ' Make no more stirre,' quoth
Tarlton, ' the fire is quenched : if the sheriffs come, it
will turne a fine as the custom is.' And drinking that
againe, ' fie,' says the other, ' what a stinke it makes, I

* He was "faithful to the end " in his love of tobacco, for Aubrey
relates, that he smoked a short time before his own execution, and thus
defends the action :—" He tooke a pipe of tobacco a little before he went
to the scaffolde, which some female persons were scandalised at ; but I
think 'twas well and properly donne to settle his spirits."

am almost poysoned.' 'If it offend,' quoth Tarlton, 'let's every one take a little of the smell, and so the savor will quickly go:' but tobacco whiffes made them leave him to pay all." Rich, in his *Irish Hubbub* (1619), gives another version of the story—"I remember a pretty jest of tobacco which was this. A certain Welchman coming newly to London, and beholding one to take tobacco, never seeing the like before, and not knowing the manner of it, but perceiving him vent smoke so fast, and supposing his inward parts to be on fire; cried out, 'O Jhesu, Jhesu man, for the passion of Cod hold, for by Cod's splud ty snowt's on fire,' and having a bowle of beere in his hand, threw it at the other's face, to quench his smoking nose."

Steadily and quietly the art of smoking made its way in England, until about ten years after its introduction the satirists began to complain of the prevalence of this habit; but it was too firmly fixed then for their invectives to have any effect; and to take tobacco "with a grace" was looked upon as the necessary qualification of a gentleman. Ben Jonson, in his *Every Man out of his Humour*, introduces such a character in Sogliardo, who is described as "an essential clown, yet so enamoured of the name of a gentleman, that he will have it though he buys it. He comes up every term to learn to take tobacco." The hangers-on of society, the needy cavaliers, the tavern-sharpers, and captains of the Bobadil sort, made a profession of the art of smoking. In the play just quoted "rare Ben" gives the form of a placard hung

in St. Paul's, at that time the fashionable promenade
of the gallants of the day, and offering instruction in
these words :—" If this City, or the suburbs of the
same, do afford any young gentleman of the first,
second, or third head,* more or less, whose friends are
but lately deceased, and whose lands are but new come
into his hands, that, to be as exactly qualified as the
best of our ordinary gallants are, is affected to enter-
tain the most gentlemanlike use of Tobacco; as first
to give it the most exquisite perfume, then to know all
the delicate sweet forms for the assumption of it, as
also the rare corollary and practice of the Cuban
ebolition, Euripus † and Whiffe, which he shall receive
or take in here at London, and evaporate at Uxbridge,
or farther, if it please him. If there be any such
generous spirit, that is truly enamoured of these good
faculties; may it please him but by a note of his hand,
to specify the place or ordinary where he uses to eat
and lie, and most sweet attendance with Tobacco and
pipes of the best sort shall be ministered. *Stet, quæso,
candide lector.*" The highflown style and ridiculous
asseverations of the virtues of "the most divine herb,"

---

* Terms used in hunting to denote the ages of *bucks*.

† Euripus, a term for a particular mode of smoking; in what its
peculiarity consisted it is not easy now to determine; the name appears to
be derived from the narrow and rapid strait between the island of Euboea
and the continent, proverbial for its flux and reflux; hence it may perhaps
mean a rapid inhaling and emitting of the smoke. The Germans still
practise many quaint modes of emitting tobacco-smoke; one accomplish-
ment of this kind consists in breathing it gently forth till it forms a ring,
and before it loses that form, sending another ring at right angles through
it. (See quotation from Dekker, p. 56.) The *Studenten* of the Universities
devote some time to acquiring the power of such feats.

indulged in by these needy professors, who dogged the steps of every silly young country gentleman, are well depicted in the same author's Captain Bobadil.

Lodge, in his *Wit's Miserie, and the World's Madnesse* (1596), speaking of "another devil of this age *Adulation*" and his subserviency, says, " This Damocles amongst the retinue carries alwaies the tabacco-pipe," and is the toady to silly young gallants.

In *Every Man out of his Humour* (1599), the author notes one gallant who takes lessons in smoking in a hired chamber at an ordinary, " private to practise in." " There we might see Sogliardo sit in a chair holding his snout like a sow under an apple-tree, while the other open'd his nostrils with a poking-stick, to give the smoke a more free delivery."

Samuel Rowlands, in his *Paire of Spy-knaves* (circa 1610), has a tale how a countryman was cheated in a London tavern, by a knave who pretended to teach him smoking.

> ——— "I'll teach thee (do observe mee heere)
> To take tobacco like a cavalier ;
> Thus draw the vapour through your nose, and say,
> *Puffe, it is gone*, fuming the smoke away."

Dekker, in that very curious picture of manners, *The Gull's Horn-book* (1602), thus narrates the approved fashion among smokers in his day:—"Before the meat come smoking to the board, our gallant must draw out his tobacco-box, the ladle for the cold snuff into the nostril, the tongs, and priming-iron ; all which artillery

may be of gold or silver, if he can reach the price of
it; it will be a reasonable useful pawn at all times,
when the amount of his money falls out to run low.
And here you must observe to know in what tobacco is
in town, better than the merchants, and to discourse of
the apothecaries where it is to be sold; then let him
show his several tricks in taking it, as the whiff, the
ring, &c., for these are compliments that gain gentlemen no mean respect."

What we now call *smoking* was at this period generally termed *drinking* tobacco. The author of " *Vox
Civitatis*, or London's complaint against her children
in the country " (1636); speaking of the dissolute and
debauched who loiter about taverns and public places
says, "Men will not stand upon it to *drink* either wine,
or *tobacco* with them who are more fit for Bride-
well." *

The term, no doubt, originated in the custom of inhaling the smoke, and allowing it to escape through the
nose;† a fashion in which it was originally enjoyed by
the Indians. The Duke of Newcastle, in his Comedy
of *The Triumphant Widow* (Act 3, Sc. 1), speaks of a

* Two more illustrations of the use of the term are here given:—
"We'll stay here to drink tobacco."—*Miseries of Inforced Marriage*,
1607. (Dodsley's Old Plays.) " The smoke of tobacco (the which Dodo-
neus called rightly Henbane of Peru) *drunke* and *drawen* by a pipe, filleth
the membranes of the braine, and astonisheth and filleth many persons
with such joy and pleasure, and sweet losse of senses, that they can by no
means be without it."—*The Perfuming of Tobacco, and the great abuse
committed in it*, 1611.

† Marston in his *Mountebank's Masque* says, humorously, "The
divell cannot take tobacco through his nose, for St. Dunstan hath seared
that up with his tongs."

joker making a party laugh, so that " the *tihie* took a
reverend old gentlewoman when she was a drinking,
and she did squirt the beer out of her nose, as an Indian
does tobacco." The term was constantly used until the
middle of the seventeenth century; for the catalogue
of Rubens' effects, sent over by Sir Balthazar Gerbier
to Charles I. in 1640, calls a Dutch picture of smokers
" the Tobacco-*drinkers*." The fashionable mode of
thus inhaling tobacco-smoke, and expelling it by the
nose, is curiously shown in the accompanying cut,

copied from a rare little volume in 12mo, printed at
Rotterdam in 1623, and entitled, *Een Korte beschry-
vinge van het wonderlycke kruyt Tobacco.** The
engraving is valuable for the clear way in which it

---

* This work is dedicated to an Englishman, " The worthy nobleman,
M. Humphry King, Knight, and Chief Sovereign of the Order of Glorious
Tobacco." The Dutch were always enthusiasts for the herb.

depicts the whole paraphernalia of a smoker, with
the roll of Tobacco on the table before him, and the
knife and trencher with which he cuts it up for use.
This was termed carotte and " Pudding-cane tobacco,"
by which latter name it is described in Chapman's
Comedy, *All Fooles*, 1605. In the same play, Dariotto
says :—" My boy once lighted a pipe of cane Tobacco
with a peece of a vile ballad, and I'll sweare I had a
singing in my head a whole week after."

In Field's *Amends for Ladies* (1618) is a scene with
London swaggerers at a wineshop in Turnbull-street
where one jestingly asks a silly nobleman, " Will your
lordship take any tobacco ? " and another sneeringly
remarks " 'Sheart! he cannot put it through his
nose !" A severe comment on the incapacity of a
" fast man " of the days of James I.

Paul Hentzner, who visited England in 1598, notes
the constant custom of smoking at all public places :
He visited the Bear Garden in Southwark, and says :—
" At these spectacles, and everywhere else, the English
are constantly smoking tobacco, and in this manner :
They have pipes on purpose, made of clay, into the
farther end of which they put the herb, so dry that
it may be rubbed into powder, and putting fire to it,
they draw the smoak into their mouths, which they
puff out again, through their nostrils, like funnels,
along with it plenty of phlegm and defluxion from the
head." This was in fact one of the chief " medical
virtues " for which the herb was professedly taken.

The prevalence of tobacco-smoking on the stage,

where gallants were accommodated with stools to sit during the play at an increased charge, is alluded to by Cokes in Ben Jonson's admirable play, *Bartholomew Fair*. He has gone into a booth to see a puppet-play, and asks of the master, "Ha' you none of your pretty impudent boys, now; to bring stooles, fill Tobacco, fetch ale, and beg money as they have at other houses?" The inconvenience occasionally felt by the female part of the audience is demonstrated by the Grocer's wife in Beaumont and Fletcher's *Knight of the Burning Pestle*, who taking her seat on the stage, exclaims, "Fie! this stinking tobacco kils men; would there were none in England: now I pray, gentlemen, what good does this stinking tobacco?—doe you nothing?—I warrant you make chimnies of your faces!" * Collier, in his *Annals of the Stage*, notes † that one of the boy-actors in the induction to *Cynthia's Revels*, imitating a gallant supposed to be sitting on the stage, speaks of having his "three sorts of tobacco in his pocket, and his light by him." Dekker in 1609 tells his gallant to " get his match lighted;" and in the *Scornful Lady* (1616) Captains of gally-foists are ridiculed, who only "wear swords to reach fire at a play," for the purpose of lighting their pipes. Hutton, in his

* This idea seems to have been taken from a tirade against tobacco smoking, entitled *Worke for Chimney Sweepers*, which Gardiner, in his *Triall of Tobacco*, says the author was " commanded or compelled to write" (probably by James the First, who afterwards took pen in hand himself); it was answered in 1602 by *A Defence of Tobacco*, in which the author shows that his opponent has injured his own cause, by his desire to prove too much—a not uncommon case!

† Vol. iii. p. 416.

Follies Anatomie (1611), speaks of the custom of taking
tobacco at theatres (instancing the Globe—Shakespeare's theatre):—

> "—— the crowded stage
> Must needs be graced with you and your page,
> Sweare for a place with each controlling foole,
> And send your hackney servant for a stoole."

Tobacco was even sold at the play-house, and in
Bartholomew Fair, Ben Jonson talks of those "who
accomodate gentlemen with tobacco at our theatres." *

Ben Jonson thus further alludes to the general
prevalence of smoking :—

> "—— Carmen
> Are got into the yellow starch, and chimney sweepers
> To their tobacco, and strong waters, Hum,
> Meath and Obarni."
>
> *The Devil is an Ass*, Act i. Sc. i.

The same author makes his *Volpone*, when disguised
as a Mountebank, declare if his nostrums had been
well known—

> "No Indian drug had e'er been famed—
> *Tobacco*, sassafras, not named."

The affected phrases used by tobacco-smokers, and
the pretences they made to carry the choicest tobacco
about them, much as the modern "swells" do expensive cigars, is very excellently ridiculed, in the old
Comedy known as *Greene's Tu Quoque*, 1614. The
scene is a fashionable London ordinary, where some
"fast men" of the day meet, and one asks of another,

---

* See also the *Actor's Remonstrance.* 1645.

who is smoking—" Please you to impart your smoke?"
To which he replies, "very willingly, Sir." The other,
after a whiff or two, exclaims, " In good faith, a pipe of
excellent vapour!" which the donor confirms by
declaring it "the best the house yields." To which the
other rejoins in some surprise, " Had you it in the
house? I thought it had been your own : 'tis not so
good now as I took it for!" The custom of passing
the pipe from one to another is noted in Barnaby
Rich's *Irish Hubbub* (1622), " One pipe of tobacco will
suffice three or four men at once," and he adds, that
the custom was indulged in by men of all grades.

Lodge, in his *Wit's Miserie, and the World's Madnesse* (1596), speaks of a foolish fellow, " Who will hug
you in his armes, kisse you on the cheeke, and rapping
out an horrible oath, crie ' Gods soule, Tom, I love
you. You know my poore heart, come to my chamber
for a pipe of tobacco ; there lives not a man in this
world that I more honour.' "

Samuel Rowlands, a prolific writer of ephemera in
the reign of Elizabeth and James ; and whose works,
now exceedingly rare, are chiefly valuable for the
pictures they afford of popular manners ; has the
following poem on tobacco, which contains four lines
still popularly quoted as a vindication of smoking,
without knowledge of their antiquity. It occurs in
his *Knave of Clubbs*, 1611. We have marked them
with inverted commas :—

" Who durst dispraise tobacco whilst the smoke is in my nose,
  Or say, but fah ! my pipe doth smell ? I would I knew but those

Durst offer such indignity to that which I prefer,
For all the brood of blackamoors will swear I do not err.
In taking this same worthy whif with valiant cavalier,
But that will make his nostrils smoke, at cupps of wine or beer.
When as my purse can not afford my stomach flesh or fish,
I sup with smoke, and feed as well and fat as one can wish.
Come into any company, though not a cross you have,*
Yet offer them tobacco, and their liquor you shall have.
They say old hospitalitie kept chimnies smoking still ;
Now what your chimnies want of that, our smoking noses will.
' Much victuals serves for gluttony, to fatten men like swine,
' But he's a frugal man indeed that with a leaf can dine,
' And needs no napkins for his hands his finger's ends to wipe,
' But keeps his kitchen in a box, and roast meat in a pipe.'
This is the way to help down years, a meal a day's enough ;
Take out tobacco for the rest by pipe, or else by snuff,
And you shall find it physical ; a corpulent, fat man,
Within a year shall shrink so small that one his guts shall span.
It's full of physic rare effects, it worketh sundry ways,
The leaf green, dried, steept, burnt to dust, have each their several
    praise.
It makes some sober that are drunk, some drunk of sober sense,
And all the moisture hurts the brain it fetches smoking thence.
All the four elements unite when you tobacco take,
For earth and water, air and fire, do a conjunction make.
The pipe is earth, the fire's therein, the air the breathing smoke ;
Good liquor must be present too, for fear I chance to choke.
Here, gentlemen, a health to all, 'tis passing good and strong.
I would speak more, but for the pipe I cannot stay so long.

The four lines alluded to are appended to a well executed engraving (copied on the opposite page) of the time of Charles I; which afterwards was made to do duty against smokers by being printed in a most pious broadside against spendthrifts published in 1641, and entitled *The Sucklington Faction, or (Suckling's) Roaring boys;* an evident blow levelled by the puritanic party at the cavalier-poet Sir John Suckling.

---

* Equivalent in meaning to *penniless,* from the cross then so constantly impressed on the reverse of the current coin.

The commencement of the seventeenth century was the golden age of tobacco. It was favoured by all, and

valued for imputed virtues more than it possessed. It received a large amount of literary notice, larger than ever after fell to its share. Poets were inspired with a desire to sing its praises, and exert their fancy in its honour. *The Metamorphosis of Tobacco* is one of these effusions, an ambitious addition to those narrated by Ovid. It is dedicated by its unknown author to Michael Drayton, one of England's worthiest poets, and was printed in 1602 ; on the title is a cut of the tobacco-plant growing in the cleft of "the bi-forked hill," with the motto round it *Digna Parnasso et Apolline.* The author takes a dignified view of his subject as he exclaims :—

> "Me let the sound of great Tobaccoes praise
> A pitch above those love-sick poets raise.

> Let me adore with my thrice happie pen,
> The sweete and sole delight of mortal men ;
> The Cornucopia of all earthly pleasure,
> Where Bankrupt nature hath consum'd her treasure.
> A worthy plant springing from Flora's hand,
> The blessed offspring of an uncouth land."

Our author then proceeds to tell us—

> " On what occasion and by whom it stood,
> That the blest world received so great a good."

He imagines a " sudden parliament " called of the Elements to hear Prometheus complain that his work is not perfected, and ask their help.   The Earth proposes that—

> " A plant shall from my wrinkled forehead spring,
> Which once inflam'd with the stolne heavenly fire,
> Shall breath into this lifeless corse inspire."

The Elements now combine to form " the herb composed in despite of fate—" the tobacco-plant.

> " And had not Tellus temper'd too much mud,
> Too much terrene corruption in the bud,
> The man that tasted it should never die,
> But stand in record of eternitie."

Jupiter becomes enraged at this ; and banishes the plant to a world unknown to Europe.   Here it is long hidden until the Graces travel to the New World, and are much delighted when—

> " They in the palace of great Montezume,
> Are entertained with this celestial fume,"

that they remain there eternally smoking ; and our only chance of " studying the graces," according to our

author, is to do the same. He furnishes another
legend of its origin by imagining a fair nymph of Virginia whom Jove visits in the garb of a shepherd,
and Juno changes into the herb. Esculapius

> " Descried this herbe to our new golden age,
> And did devise a pipe, which should asswage
> The wounds which sorrow in our hearts did fix ; "

and he further declares, that had the Romans known it,
instead of a Saturnalia,

> " A new *Tabacconalia* had been made.
> All goods, all pleasures in it it doth linke—
> 'Tis phisicke, clothing, music, meat and drink."

In Ben Jonson's *Every Man out of his Humour*
(1599), one of the characters, Fastidious Brisk, an
impersonation of the "swell" of his day, takes tobacco,
attended by a boy to trim the pipe ; and makes love to
his mistress, between the whiffs he puffs forth in
smoking. In Heywood's *Fair Maid of the Exchange*
(1607), one of the characters is advised to court a girl
by " asking her if she'll take a pipe of tobacco." In
Edward Sharpham's comedy, *The Fleire* (1615), one
"Signior Petoune, a traveller and a great tobacconist,"*
is one of the characters introduced as a type of the
fashionable smoker of the day. He says, "I take it
now and then, fasting, for the purification of my wit,"
and he tells the ladies, "If you use but a' mornings

---

* *Smokers*, it must be remembered, were then termed *tobacconists*, a
name now exclusively applied to vendors of the herb.

when you rise, the divine smoke of this celestiall
herbe," it will do their complexions most good of any
thing known. His friends jestingly allow its good
qualities toward himself, by assuring him that before
he took it he "was an arrant ass." He assents, "indeed
I was," and adds, "Faith, these gentlemen have not
long used my company, yet you see how tobacco hath
already refined their spirits." He very gallantly offers
to share his pleasure, "Dear Lady, please you take a
pipe of tobacco," but he becomes ultimately so trouble-
some, that he is "sworne on his owne tobacco-pipe,"
not to trouble them more; "you shall never come
with your squibs, and smoke squirts, amongst ladies
and gentlewomen, flinging out fume at your nostrils,
as a whale doth salt water, unlesse you be entreated
by them."

Rossaline in Marston's first part of *Antonio and
Mellinda* (1602), speaks of a courtier as

> " A great tobacco-taker too, that's flat ;
> For his eyes look as if they had been hung
> In the smoake of his nose."

The same lady is asked, in another part of the play,
"Faith, mad niece, I wonder when thou wilt marry,"
to which she replies, "Faith, kind uncle, when men
abandon jealousy, forsake taking of tobacco, and cease
to wear their beards so rudely long. Oh, to have a
husband with a mouth continually smoking, with a
bush of furs on the ridge of his chin, readie still
to flop into his foaming chaps, 'tis more than most

intolerable." The Duke is represented in the same author's play, *What you Will* (1607), smoking among the ladies, and lighting his pipe with a petition sent to him.

In 1602, when Dekker printed his *Satiromastix*, ladies smoked. Asinius Babo, offering his pipe, observes:—"'Tis at your service gallants, and the tobacco too: 'tis right pudding, I can tell you; a lady or two took a pipe full or two at my hands, and praised it, fore the heavens." *

Prynne, the famous-Puritanic inveigher against stage-plays, tells us that in his time, ladies at the theatre were sometimes " offered the tobacco-pipe " as a refreshment instead of apples,† which appear to have been " the staple commodity." Mary King, better known as " Moll Cutpurse," that

"Bold Virago stout and tall,"

as described by Butler in his *Hudibras*, is depicted on the title-page of Middleton's comedy, *The Roaring Girle*, of which she is the heroine, in the costume of a man smoking tobacco (the upper part of the cut is here

---

* Dekker, in his *Gull's Horn-book*, thus apostrophises tobacco :— "Make me thine adopted heir, that, inheriting the virtues of thy whiffes, I may distribute them amongst all nations, and make the fantastic Englishman, above the rest, more cunning in the distinction of thy roll Trinidado, leaf, and pudding, than the whitest-toothed black-a-moor in all Asia." Dr. Nott, in a note, thinks these the three kinds of tobacco mentioned by Ben Jonson in *Cynthia's Revels* :—Dekker also speaks of gallants "able to discourse whether your cane or your pudding be sweetest, and which pipe has the best bore, and which burns black, which breaks in the burning."

† *Histriomastix*, 1633, marginal note to page 363.

given in fac-simile). She was a notorious courtesan, who generally dressed in man's apparel, and varied her profession occasionally as a fortune-teller, pick-pocket, thief, receiver of stolen goods, or forger, as " accident

suited." Her most notable exploit was robbing the parliamentary general, Fairfax, on Hounslow Heath, for which she narrowly escaped hanging. She lived till 1659, when, according to Granger, "she died of the dropsy in the seventy-fifth year of her age ; but would probably have died sooner, if she had not smoked tobacco, in the frequent use of which she had long indulged herself."

But tobacco smoking was not restricted to ladies " fair and free," for as many young ladies of Spain and South America, still " indulge in the weed," without offence ; and many old ones do yet in England ; so when tobacco was first introduced among us, did some few of our own fair dames. Appended is a copy of a curious

female portrait, painted about 1650, in the possession
of W. H. Rolfe, Esq., of Sandwich. The fair lady has
in her hand a tobacco-box, and is indulging in the
solace of her pipe; which she wields in a very graceful

and "lady-like" manner. Miss Pardoe, in her *History
of the Court of Louis XIV.*, has shown that the
daughters of the *Grande Monarque* did not disdain to
do the same, although he had a great dislike to tobacco.
When the ladies became wearied by the " gravity and
etiquette of the court circle, they were accustomed to
celebrate a species of orgie in their own apartments,
after supper; and on one occasion, when the Dauphin
had at a late hour quitted the card-table, and hearing
a noise in their quarter of the palace, entered to
ascertain its cause; he found them engaged in smoking,
and discovered that they had borrowed their pipes from
the Officers of the Swiss guard! "

Tobacco was necessarily an expensive habit, and one of the earliest objections made to the custom of smoking, was its ruinous cost. Among the papers at Penshurst, is a note of expenses of Sir Henry Sidney, Lord Deputy of Ireland, among which occurs "three shillings for an ounce of tobacco." This was within about three years of its first introduction to England, and would be equivalent to about eighteen shillings of our present money. Between 1606 and 1638, the accounts of Francis fourth Earl of Cumberland, show the great consumption of money to be in wines, journeys, clothes, presents, and tobacco. Whittaker, in his *History of Craven*, p. 275, says, "The last heavy article of expence, was tabacco, of which the finest sort cost eighteen shillings per pound, and an inferior kind ten shillings. A single bill for this article amounted to £36 7s. 8d." By multiplying this by four, we shall be able to judge of the price, as compared with that of our own day, and so understand the heavy expense of an indulgence in tobacco at this period. Aubrey narrates that in his early days:—"It was sold then for its wayte in silver. I have heard some of our old yeomen neighbours say, that when they went to Malmesbury or Chippenham Market, they culled out their biggest shillings to lay in the scales against the tobacco; now (1680) the customes of it are the greatest his majestie hath."

Drayton, in the sixteenth song of his *Poly-olbion*, (1613), complains that—

> "Our gold goes out so fast, for foolish foraine things,
> Which upstart gentry still into our country brings;

Who their insatiate pride seek chiefly to maintaine
By that which only serves to uses vile and vaine:
Which our plaine fathers earste would have accounted sinne,
Before the costly coach, and silken stock came in ;
Before that Indian weed so strongly was imbrac't ;
Wherein such mighty summes we prodigally waste."

The popularity of smoking, naturally and speedily led to adulterations ; and one of them is noted in Ben Jonson's *Bartholomew Faire*, where Ursula, the vendor of roast pig, a lady who " can but hold life and soule together" with drink "and a whiff of tobacco," orders her tapster to look to her interests; "Look too't, sirrah, you were best! three pence a pipe full, I will ha' made of all my whole halfe pound of tabacco, and a quarter of a pound of coltsfoot, mixt with it too, to eke it out."

Dr. Barclay, of Edinburgh, in his *Nepenthes* (1614), notes that " avarice and greedines of gaine have moved the marchants to apparell some European plants with Indian coats, and to enstal them in shops as righteous and legitimate tabacco. Some others have tabacco from Florida indeede, but because either it is exhausted of spiritualitie, or the radicall humour is spent, and wasted, or it hath gotten moysture by the way, or it hath bene dried for expedition in the sunne, or carried too negligently ; they sophisticate and farde the same in sundrie sortes, with black spice, galanga, aqua vitæ, Spanish wine, anise seedes, oyle of Spicke, and such like." Armin, in his *Nest of Ninnies* (1608), speaks of tobacco "sophisticated to taste strong." *

* Stephens, in his *Essays and Characters*, 1615, speaks of one who "deceives with his commodity worse than a tobacco-man."

Ben Jonson, in his *Alchemist* (1610), speaking in praise of the tobacconist, Abel Drugger, notes the adulteration then practised, and the luxuries used in smoking:—

> He lets me have good tobacco ; and he does not
> Sophisticate it with sack—lees or oil,
> Nor washes it in muscadel and grains,
> Nor buries it in gravel, under ground,
> Wrapp'd up in greasy leather, or piss'd clouts ;
> But keeps it in fine lilly pots, that, open'd
> Smell like a conserve of roses, or French beans.
> He has his maple block, his silver tongs,
> Winchester pipes, and fire of juniper."

Rowlands, in his *Knave of Harts* (1613), says of a prodigall knave :

> " In a tobacco-shop (resembling Hell,
> Fire, stink, and smoke must be where devils dwell),
> He sits, you cannot see his face for vapour,
> Offering to Pluto with a tallow taper."

The spendthrift Folly-wit, in Middleton's play, *A Mad World, my Masters* (1608), speaks of the tavern and tobacco-shop as consequences, " to sink down dead in a tavern, and rise in a tobacco-shop," is his mode of action. In Heywood's *Fortune by Land and Sea* is a scene at a tavern, where the gallants indulge in sack and tobacco. Ardelio, the cashier'd servingman in Marmion's play, *Holland's Leaguer* (1632), says:—

> " The best thing I am fit for is a Tapster,
> Or else to get a wench of mine own, and sell
> Bottell Ale and Tobacco."

Among the Roxburgh ballads in the British Museum, is a wood-cut of this period, which we here copy in fac-simile (on a reduced scale), it is an excellent tavern scene. The table is supplied with a huge " pottle-pot " of drink, and pipes for smoking.

The swaggering gallant who is indulging in his pipe, is a sketch from nature, worthy of Dekker. The trio might be fitly employed in chanting the following praises of Ale and Tobacco : *—

> Tobacco fumes away all nastie rheumes,
> But health away it never lightly frets,
> And nappy Ale makes mirth (as Aprill raine doth Earth)
> Spring like the pleasant spring, where're it soaking wets.
>
> CHORUS.
> But in that spring of mirth,
>   Such madnes nye doth growe,
> As fills a foole by birth
>   With crotchets, with Ale and Tobacco.

---

* From Ravenscroft's *Briefe Discourse of Music*, to which is prefixed songs " Concerning the pleasure of five usuall recreations, Hunting, Hawking, Dauncing, Drinking, and Enamouring." 1614.

One cleares the braine, the other glads the hart,
Which they retaine, by nature and by Art ;
The first by nature cleares, by Arte makes giddy will,
The last by nature cheares, by Art makes heady still.

CHORUS.

So we, whose braynes else lowe,
Swell hye with crotchet rules,
Feed on these two, as fat,
As headdy giddy fooles.

Another song, of an earlier date, may here be given as a popular sample of the Nicotian Muse.*

Come sirrah Jacke hoe,
Fill some Tobacco,
Bring a wire
And some fire,
Hast, hast away,
Quicke I say,
Do not stay,
Shun delay,
For I dranke none good to-day ;
I sweare that this Tobacco,
It's perfect Trinidado,
By the very very mas,
Never, never, never was
Better gere then is here,
By the roode, for the bloud.
It is very, very good.

Fill the pipe once more,
My braines daunce *trenchmore,* †
It is headdy,
I am geeddy,
My head and braines,
Back and raines,
Jointes and vaines,
From all paines,

---

* It occurs in John Weelkes' *Ayeres or Phantasticke Spirites,* 1608.
† A popular dance tune. See Chappell's *Popular Music of the Olden Time.*

It doth well purge and make cleane.
Then those that doe condemne it,
Or such as not commend it,
Never were so wise to learne,
Good Tobacco to discerne,
    Let them go plucke a crow,
    And not know as I do,
    The sweet of Trinidado.

Edmund Gardiner, the author of *The Triall of Tobacco* (1610), complains that, "The patrimony of many noble young gentlemen, have been quite exhausted, and have vanished cleane away with this smoky vapour, and hath most shamefully and beastly flyen out at the master's nose;" and that, "othersome there be that spend whole daies, moneths, times, and yeares (for the most part) in tabacco taking, not sparing to take it even in their bed," a custom now chiefly indulged in by the Germans. "Thus," he continues, "you see that tobacco is a fantasticall attracter, and glutton-feeder of the appetite, rather taken of many for wantonnesse, when they have nothing else to do than of any absolute or necessarie use."

A most curious account of the increase of the tobacco trade in London, is furnished in the following words by Barnaby Rich, in his *Honestie of this Age* (1614):—"There is not so base a groome that comes into an ale-house to call for his pott, but he must have his pipe of tobacco; for it is a commodity that is nowe as vendible in every taverne, wine, and ale-house, as eyther wine, ale, or beare; and for apothecaries' shops, grocers' shops, chandlers' shops, they are (almost) never without company, that from morning till night are still taking of tobacco. What a number are there besides, that doe keepe houses, set open shoppes, that have no other trade to live by, but by the selling of tobacco.

"I have heard it told, that now very lately there hath been a catalogue of all those new erected houses that have sett up that trade of selling tobacco in London, and neare about London ; and if a man may believe what is confidently reported, there are found to be upward of seven thousand houses that doth live by that trade. I cannot say whether they number apothecaries' shops, grocers' shops, and chandlers' shops, in the computation, but let it bee that these were thrust in to make up the number : let us now look a little into the *vidimus* of the matter, and let us cast upp but a sleight account what the expense might be that is consumed in smoakie vapour.

" If it be true that there be seven thousand shops in and about London, that doth vent tobacco, as it is credibly reported that there be over and above that number, it may well be supposed to be but an ill-customed shop, that taketh not five shillings a day, one day with another, throughout the whole year ; or, if one doth take lesse, two other may take more : but let us make our account, but after two shillings sixpence a day, for he that taketh lesse than that would be ill able to pay his rent, or to keepe open his shop-windows ; neither would tobacco houses make such a muster as they do, and that almost in every lane, and in every by-corner round about London.

"Let us then reckon thus, seven thousand halfe-crownes a day, amounteth just to three hundred nineteen thousand, three hundred seventie-five pounds a yeare, *summa totalis,* all spent in smoake." *

It must not be imagined that the lovers of the herb were allowed their enjoyment unmolested. It was soon denounced in unmeasured terms by those who did not partake of it; and the rancour of the attack was characterised by that total want of charity which has ever marked those who—

> "Compound for sins they are inclined to
> By damning those they have no mind to."

"Modern lovers of the pipe" (observes a writer in the *New York Literary World,* of Feb. 1848,) "seldom think of the worthies to whom they are indebted for its free enjoyment; and of those who delight in nasal aliment, how few ever call to mind the Diocletian persecutions their predecessors passed through in adhering to their faith in, and transmitting to their descendants, the virtues of tobacco. Europe frowned, and Asia threatened; Pagan, Manommedan, and Christian monarchs combined to crush them. The world was roused like a famishing lion from its lair, and gloated on them. James I. of England, foaming with rage, sent forth his *Counterblast;* the half savage ruler of

---

* "The 3 companies," he also tells us, that are "now more gainefull than all the seven sciences, and have gotten all the trade into their own hands; the first is to keepe an ale-house, the second a tobacco-house, and the third to keep a brothell-house."

the Muscovites followed suit; the King of Persia,
Amurath IV. of Turkey, the Emperor Jehan-Geer, and
others, all joined the crusade.* Arming themselves
with scourges, halters, knives, and bearing gibbets on
their banners, they denounced death to all found
inhaling fumes of the plant through a tube, or caught
with a pellet of it under their tongues. Such as used
it as a sternutative only were dealt with more gently—
they were merely to be deprived of their organs of
smelling—of nostrils and nose. To perfect the
miseries of the pitiable delinquents, Urban VIII. went
in awful pomp to the Vatican, where, tremulous with
holy anger, he shook his garments to intimate that the
blood of the offenders would be on their own heads,
and then thundered excommunication on every soul
who took the accursed thing, in any shape, into a
church! †

Was ever destruction of body and spirit threatened
so unjustly? Mutilation for taking a pinch! Loss of
life for lighting a pipe! Exclusion from heaven for
perhaps harmlessly reviving attention to a wearisome
sermon in chapel or church! Merciful heavens! what
comminations these to emanate from Christian kings

---

* In Russia it was punished with amputation of the nose ; and in the
Swiss canton of Berne it ranked in the table of offences next to adultery ;
even so late as the middle of the last century, a particular court was held
there for trying delinquents. But persecution only increased the practice.

† Urban VIII. in 1624 published a decree of excommunication against
such as used tobacco in churches, and Innocent XII., A.D. 1690, solemnly
excommunicated all those who should "take snuff or tobacco in St. Peter's
at Rome."

and Christ's successor! Present and eternal death,
tortures here, and endless torments hereafter, for a
whiff or quid of tobacco! Our sympathies are naturally excited for the sufferers. One wonders how they
managed to preserve their integrity, or pass through
the fires unscathed, or even escape annihilation. Yet
most of them did escape, and they did more—they
converted the Nebuchadnezzars who sought to consume them. Conscious of their innocence and of their
rights, they mildly persisted in maintaining them. Of
retiring habits, they avoided agitation and debate,
declaring that the properties of the proscribed herb
made such efforts uncongenial, while it strengthened
them in passive resistance, composed their spirits, and
rendered them, in a great measure, indifferent to
abuse, and often insensible to pain. Hence they
smoked, and chewed, and sneezed at home until their
hottest enemies became their warmest friends, and
greater sinners than themselves had ever been."

This is no overcharged picture of the great tobacco
persecution, of the early part of the seventeenth
century. Sandys notes in his travels, having seen an
unfortunate Turk conducted about the streets of
Constantinople in 1610, mounted backward on an ass
with a tobacco-pipe driven through the cartilage of his
nose, for the crime of smoking. Now we cannot
dissever a Turk from his tobacco, in our idea of him,
so little ultimate real effect had this insane crusade.
Our King James I. had fortunately not the power to
torture his subjects' bodies like Amurath; or d—n

their souls like Pope Urban (whose name certainly belied his actions), but he did all that laid in his power to damage the cause of tobacco, and the character of smokers. He has been happily described by Barham,* as—

> "A gentleman called King James,
> In quilted doublet and great trunk breeches,
> Who held in abhorrence tobacco and witches."

Sir John Harrington, in his *Nugæ Antiquæ*, relates a conversation he had with the king in the first year of his accession to the throne, when he strongly denounced it. Ben Jonson, in his Masque, *The Gipsies Metamorphosed*, three times played before James I., politely wished his Majesty's sense of smelling protected

> "From tobacco, with the type
> Of the devil's glyster-pipe."

On his visiting Oxford in 1605, the University gratified the king, by debating on the salutary character of the herb, and of course deciding against it; though to the honour of some of the number be it said,† that after the monarch had confirmed the verdict in very strong language, Dr. Cheynell holding a tobacco-pipe in his hand, extolled the virtues of the herb in the highest terms, placing it in advance of every other remedial agent. The king had written his famous *Counterblaste to Tobacco*, in which all his

* *Ingoldsby Legends—The Witches' Frolic.*
† See Wake's *Rex Platonicus.* 1627.

pent-up dislike burst forth in 1603, so that the boldness
of the Doctor was all the more creditable to his con-
science. James had often declared his unmitigated
dislike to tobacco, and when he wrote against it made
no compromise. His Majesty treats the argument (if
it can be called one) in a right royal style, after the
fashion of a condemned sentence from the bench to
convicted criminals.

This is a specimen of the arrogant tone of argument
adopted in this renowned treatise :—" Surely smoke
becomes a kitchen farre better than a dining chamber ;
and yet it makes a kitchen oftentimes in the inward
parts of men, soyling and infecting with an unctuous
and oyly kind of soote as hath been found in some
great tobacco takers, that after death were opened.
A custom loathsome to the eye, harmfull to the braine,
dangerous to the lungs, and in the black stinking
fume thereof, nearest resembling the horrible Stygian
smoke of the pit that is bottomless." Elsewhere his
dislike to Raleigh peeps forth covertly in the following
passage :—

" Now the corrupted baseness of the first use of this
tobacco doeth very well agree with the foolish and
groundless first entry thereof into this kingdome. It
is not so long since the first entry of this abuse
amongst us here, as this present age can very well
remember both *the first* author and the form of the
first introduction of it amongst us. It was neither
brought in by King, great conqueror, nor learned
Doctor of Physic. With the report of a *great dis-*

G

covery for a conquest, some two or three savage men
were brought in together with this savage custom.
But the pity is the poor wild barbarous men died, but
that vile barbarous custom is yet alive, yea, in fresh
vigour, so as it seems a miracle to me how a custom
springing from so vile a ground, and brought in by a
father so generally hated should be welcomed on so
slender a warrent." *

The general opinion of James, forcibly expressed and
powerfully condensed, is given in *A Collection of Witty.
Apophthegms* by him, as follows:—

"That *tobacco was the lively image and pattern of
hell;* for that it had, by allusion, in it all the parts and
vices of the world whereby hell may be gained; to
wit; First, *It was a smoke;* so are the vanities of this
world. Secondly, *It delighteth them who take it;* so
do the pleasures of the world delight the men of the
world. Thirdly, *It maketh men drunken, and light in
the head;* so do the vanities of the world, men are
drunken therewith. Fourthly, *He that taketh tobacco
saith he cannot leave it, it doth bewitch him:* even so

---

* This passage appears clearly to allude to Raleigh, as James's dislike
to him was sufficient to induce him to apply such spiteful terms to the
man he judicially murdered. The *report* of discovery also agrees with
Raleigh's discovery and attempted colonisation of Virginia by his expedition. The notice of the savage men brought in with the custom appears
to settle the question that has been raised, whether tobacco was brought
to England first by the expedition that discovered Virginia, or by the
colonists brought back by Drake, 1586. Captains Amidas and Barlow,
of Raleigh's first expedition (27th April, 1584), who discovered Virginia,
had the pipe of peace presented to them, and brought away two Indians.
They are alluded to as one of the "London Sights" by Trinculo, in
Shakspere's *Tempest.*

the pleasures of the world make men loath to leave
them, they are for the most part so inchanted with
them : and further, besides all this, *It is like hell in
the very substance of it, for it is a stinking loathsome
thing;* and so is hell. And further, his majesty pro-
fessed that, *were he to invite the devil to dinner,* he
should have three dishes ; 1. *A pig*; 2. *A pole of ling
and mustard;* and 3. *A pipe of tobacco* for digesture."

King James had the power not only to write viciously
but to act strongly ; and he it was who first imposed a
heavy tax on tobacco. "However absurd his reason-
ing may appear, it unfortunately happened that he
possessed the power to reduce his aversion to practice,
and he may be considered as the author of that
unwarrantable persecution of the tobacco plant, which,
under varying circumstances, has been injudiciously
continued to the present time."* The importation
duty was originally twopence per pound. James at
once raised it to the monstrous sum of *six shillings
and ten pence.* The *animus* which affected his weak
mind bursts forth in the preamble of his Act, against
what he is pleased to term an "evil vanitie;" by which,
he adds "the health of a great number of people is
impayred, and their bodies weakened, and made unfit
for labour, and the estates of many mean persons so
decayed and consumed, as they are thereby driven to
unthriftie shiftes only to maintain their gluttonous
exercise thereof." †

* Brodigan's *Treatise on the Tobacco Plant,* 1830.
† He gives one instance of the luxurious use of the herb by those "not

When Kings make unnecessary and unjust laws, subjects naturally study how to evade them : it is a mere system of self-defence ; and as James nearly suppressed the importation of tobacco, the English farmers began to grow it on their own land. But the Scottish Solomon,* who was on the alert, added another law restraining its cultivation " to misuse and misemploy the soil of this fruitfull Kingdom." † As this enforced the trade with the English colony of Virginia alone, it was soon found that Spanish and Portuguese tobacco might be brought into port on the payment of the old duty of twopence a pound ; thus a large trade was carried on with their planters to the injury of the British colonists. Its use increased in spite of all legislative measures, and James ended by prohibiting any person from dealing in the article, who did not hold his letters patent. By this means the trade was monopolised, the consumer oppressed, importation diminished, and the London Company of Virginian traders ultimately ruined. Those who are fond of excusing the evil acts of one of the worst of English Kings, pretend to see James's care for his subjects' health and wealth in these restrictions ; totally regardless of the fact that

caring at what price they buy the drug, but rather devising how to add to it *other mixtures*, thereby to make it the more delightful to the taste."

* This term, so very composedly taken as a compliment to James, was really intended for the reverse. It was applied to him by Henry the Fourth of France, in allusion to his mother's intimacy with *David* Rizzio, —Solomon being "the son of David."

† The tyrannic selfishness of James peeps forth in the first phrase of his Act :—" Whereas *We*, out of the dislike *we have* to tobacco," a strange reason for crushing the pleasure and trade of his subjects !

James cared for neither when the monopoly brought large sums into his own pocket.

Joshua Sylvester, the translater of *Du Bartas*, and a favourite poet of James I., gratified that royal hater of the herb by tuning his harp to a poem, bearing the strange title of *Tobacco battered, and the pipes shattered (about their eares that idely Idolize so base and barbarous a weed ; or at leastwise overlove so loathsome a vanitie) by a volley of holy shot, thundered from Mount Helicon.* The verbosity of the title page is carried out in the poem, which is intolerably dull, and only strong when abusive. The author, in a dedication to the favourite, George, Duke of Buckingham, ventures :

" To call your aide against the proud oppression
Of th' Infidel, usurping Faith's possession,
    That Indian tyrant, England's only shame.
Thousands of ours he here hath captive taken,
    Of all degrees, kept under slavish yoak,
Their God, their good, king, country, friends, forsaken,
    To follow Follie, and to feed on smoake."

In this spirit the whole is written, and one small sample more may suffice :

" Two smokie engines in this latter age
(Sathan's short circuit ; the more sharp his rage)
Have been invented by too-vaunted wit,
Or rather vented from the infernal pit, *
Guns and *tobacco pipes*, with fire and smoak,
At least a third part of mankind to choak ;

---

* Taylor, the water poet, had an equal enmity to tobacco and coaches, and he says, " It is a doubtful question whether the devil brought tobacco into England in a coach, for both appeared about the same time."

> (Which happely* th' Apocalyps foretold)
> Yet of the two we may (think I) be bolde,
> In some respects to think the last the worst,
> However both in their effects accurst."

In this spirit of piety and intolerance, he condemns
at last, all smokers to Tophet :—

> " For hell hath smoke
> Impenitent Tobacconists to choake,
> Though never dead ; there shall they have their fill.
> In heaven is none, but light and glory still."

In a very different spirit, Dr. William Barclay
dedicated his little work, *Nepenthes, or the Vertues of
Tobacco* (published at Edinburgh, 1614),—" to my Lord
Bishop of Murray," in these lines :—

> " The statelie, rich, late conquer'd Indian plaines,
>   Foster a plant, the princess of all plants,
> Which Portugall, after perill and paines,
>   To Europe brought, as it most justly vaunts ;
> This plant at home the people and priests assure,
>   Of his goodwill, whom they as God adore ;
> Both here and there it worketh wondrous cure,
>   And hath much heavenlie vertue hid in store.
> A stranger plant shipwracked on our coast,
>   Is come to helpe this colde phlegmatic soyle,
> Yet cannot live for calumnie and boast,
>   In danger daylie of some greater broyle.
>   My Lord, this sacred herbe which never offendit,
>   Is forced to crave your favour to defend it."

In his treatise the author defends not only the herb,
but speaks as rapturously of the land of its growth,
" the country which God hath honoured and blessed
with this happie and holy herbe." He compares

* The Author here refers to *Revelations*, ix. 17.

himself to Hercules, whose only arms were a bag and
a club when he went to war; he says, " I have armed
myself with a boxe for his bagge, and a pipe for his
club : a box to conserve my tobacco, and a pipe to use
it; by these two, God willing, to overcome many
maladies." He narrates many that may be so cured,
and imagines that physicians might be done without
in all cases of defluxion and catarrh "if they knew
the vertue of tobacco;" concluding by decrying the
imputations against it, as—

> " Forged by scurvie, leud, unlearned leiches,
>   As time hath taught and practise thatt all tryis.
> Tobacco neither altereth health nor hew,
>   Ten thousand thousands know that it is true."

One of the most curious and rare books which
the taste for " the Indian novelty " generated, is
Richard Brathwait's little volume, bearing the following title :—*The Smoaking Age, or, the Man in the
Mist: with the Life and Death of Tobacco. Dedicated to
those three renowned and imparallel'd heroes, Captain
Whiffe, Captain Pipe, and Captain Snuffe; to whom
the Author wisheth as much content as this smoaking
age can afford them. At the signe of Teare-nose*, 1617.
The following is an analysis of its contents :

An exceedingly well executed frontispiece by Mar-
shall, representing a tobacconist's shop, faces the title,
which we here engrave. The shop is open to the
street, in accordance with ancient usage ; and has a
pent-house of boards, from which hangs a double hoop,
used to hold pipes; "strong water," glasses, and

A TOBACCONIST'S SHOP, TEMP. JAMES I.

From Brathwait's *Smoaking Age.*

measures, are behind, on shelves; the counter is covered with a "faire linen cloth," upon which pipes are laid ; upon it stands a carved figure of a negro smoking, showing the antiquity of using such a figure as a sign for a tobacconist's shop. A curtain drawn aside discloses the private room, where three smokers are indulging at a table formed of a board laid upon tobacco barrels. In the original, they are named Captain Whiffe, Captain Pipe, and Captain Snuffe. From the mouth of the first a label issues, with the words " Qui color albus erat;" from that of the second, " Quantum mutatis ab illo;" and from the third, ",Anglus in Æthiopium." From each pipe other labels proceed, with these words on them "Itum est in viscera terra," "Fistula dulce canit," and "Mea messis in herba est." The book, the title-page tells us, is divided into three lectures :—1. The Birth of Tobacco ; 2. Pluto's blessing to Tobacco; and 3. Time's complaint against Tobacco. The epigram "Upon Tobacco " in the title-page, shows the unfavourable view its author took of his theme :

> " This some affirme, yet yeeld I not to that,
> 'Twill make a fat man leane, a leane man fat ;
> But this I'm sure (hows'ere it be thy meane)
> That many whiffes will make a fat man leane."

The author in his Introduction, "to whomsoever, whensoever, or wheresoever," affirms that he was entreated by a friend "that I would address my pen to treat of that subject ; being, as he verie truly affirmed, a principal help to discourse, especially to our young

English gallants, whose first salutation to their acquaintance is, *Will you take a pipe of Tobacco ?* " A
custom which he reprobates in this long preface.

The book is a fanciful tale; the scene first laid
in Tartary, "not farre from the Bermudoes," where
dwelt a rich Islander, named Nepenthes, and his wife
Usquebaughin. One day, upon the sea-coast, they met
with an Apothecary, who had been cast on shore, after
having been rifled by pirates, and swallowed by a
Polypus, who was compelled to disgorge him by the
medicine he carried about him. He is carried home
by the islanders, and by his art, the wife, before
childless, has a son. About the same time, a high
feast is held in Pluto's court, whither comes Bacchus,
who, making the god drunk, makes love to Proserpine;
a child is born, and delightedly acknowledged by
Pluto, until he is undeceived by Mercury, and goes
with a complaint to Jupiter. Meanwhile, the child, to
elude suspicion, is changed for that borne by Usquebaughin, but having obtained the former before she can
send her own in its place, Pluto returns, meets the
messenger, Iris, with it, and announces Jove's decree,
that to root out his disgrace, it shall be changed to a
plant—"which, to expresse his father, shall still reserve
the name of his progenitor Bacchus ; and therefore,
have we in his memory, called him (as one commended
to the care, protection, and tuition of his father)
Tobacco." He then pronounces a farewell speech to
him, in which he tells him he will be favourably received everywhere, and aid him in bringing souls to

destruction, particularly in England : " Thou wilt be
the onely enlarger of my kingdom, the enricher of my
state, and the stablisher of my state eternally ; " and
that all, rich and poor, will reverence him : "Not a
complete Gallant that hath not his utensils to conduct
thee to his nose," or waterman or tankard carrier that
will not accost him joyfully. Then follows "Especiall
advertisements given by Pluto to Tobacco," in these
words :—

" The first caution I propound is, that in everie place
where thou commest, thou take the best booth in the
faire. Plant thyself in the eye of the Citie ; set mee
the picture of some sallow-faced Blackamoore, or a
Virginia-man, for that will rather draw custome, upon
the Frontespice of thy doore : A Zeuxes, or Apelles,
would doe well in these cases to enforce passengers by
the picture, to draw nere the substance : make a
partition in thy shop; it may bee the hot Venetian
comes to bathe with thee, rather than to drink tobacco
with thee." He then particularly desires him to court
the Scholar, the Lawyer, and the Poet : " The Scholler
will bee thine, if thou talke in his element ; sooth him
in his arguments, and call him most profound, dogma-
ticall, and literate Trismegistus." The Lawyer is to be
won by being compared with the Romans for oratory.
" For the Poet, I cannot tell what to say to it, he is so
oft out of his wits, as he verily imagines himselfe the
Man in the Moone : There's quick-silver in his braine;
and if he were not now and then encountered by
Sergeants, and kept under locke and key, hee would

verily turne Bedlame. Yet because phrensie must be
purged, and thou (my Wag-halter) hast vertue and
operation to love such, becken to the thred-bare con-
temned Urchin, give him a pipe on my score, hee'll pay
it at the next new play he makes, if the Doore-keepers
will bee true to him: and if not, hee'll make thee up
some scurvy end of a ballad deserves a pipe of smoak."
He concludes by saying: "But now (my Rogue in graine)
if thou couldst set up a private Refectorie, for the
young effeminate sort (for they would, like Adamants,
draw continuall recourse) I would hug thee eternally.
Sell me Potato-roots, Eringoes, all Electuaries, Con-
fections, Receipts, Conceipts, Deceipts, Pomatum,
Cerusse, with a large recitall of thy brave commodities;
and a little smooth-faced Ganymede standing at the
doore, who, like another parret or mag-pie, may cry ever
in one tune: What doe you lacke? Pomatum of the
best, Cerusse of the finest?" He also enjoins him to
obtain the custom of ladies, so that assignations would
appear to have been thus carried on at tobacconists',
who combined in some degree the perfumer's trade.

The plant being shipped to the world "in Charon's
vessel," is very successful in entrapping men. Time is
described "with a scythe in his hand, and blubber'd
face, standing in the publique street of Troynovant, for
there this plant took first planting," uttering his "complaint upon tobacco, and the miserie of man's securitie,
losing that treasure by Time's expense, which can never
be repurchased, or redeemed, but by bitter and inces-
sant repentance;" adding, "none to me so profest

enemies as these smoakers of our age; they whiffe me
out in fume, and spend my best of houres in candle-
light; their wits goe and come by pipe and pipe; thus
am I taken in snuffe by every pesant. * * * Believe
Time's words! it is not the swarty-chopt tobacco-drugge,
that will yeeld you content in the expense of your time:
you may smoake it long ere you better your owne discourse, or make your accounts even, which Time expects
at your hands. A whole ounce of tobacco will hardly
purchase one dram of wit; repentance is the best fruit
you shall reape out of such an unsavoury herbe." He
ends with invectives against the three captains named
in the title; a short historical account of tobacco
succeeds;* and then comes the following:—

TIME'S SONNET.

Sweet youth, smoake not thy time,
    Too precious to abuse;
    Th'ast fitter feats to choose:
What may redeeme that prime,
    Thy smoaking age doth loose?

Good Oldman, eye thy glasse,
    See, how those sands doe fall!
    None can a graine recall:
Old houres doe quickly passe,
    Shall smoake consume them all?

---

* Two other works on tobacco are incidentally mentioned: 1. *A pleasant
poeticall paradox in the praise of the plant, wherein is learnedly proved,
and by impregnable reasons convinced, that Tobacco is the only sovereign
experimentall cure, not only for the Neapolitan itch, but generally for all
maladies incident to man's body.* 2. *A little Tract, entitled Tobacco,
published by especiall direction of the author upon his death-bed, dedicated
to Humphry King, one well-experienced in the use, benefit, and practise of
that herbe, and printed for Will Barlow (with Tobacco armes) then keeping
shop in Gracious streete.*

Love's Lady, whom sunne, weather,
  Yea, the least airy touch,
  (Complexion it is such)
May taint ; cinge not your feather,
  Tobacco may doe much.

Shunne smoake, East, West, North, South,
Love's Lady, Oldman, Youth.

This is followed by a poem in seventeen stanzas entitled *Chaucer's Incensed Ghost*, in which he complains of having his name affixed to a poem in praise of tobacco, deprecates its use, and concludes with :—

"Yee then, whose measures merit well the name,
And litle yee retaine,—Poets I meane,
Bedew'd with influence from Hippocrene,
As yee professants seeme, so be the same
And with your owne pennes eternize yonr fame ;
  Shun these pipe-pageants; for there seldome come
  Tobacco-factors to Elysium."

In a totally different spirit did Sir Robert Aytoun (born 1570, died 1638) write the following sonnet on tobacco :—

"Forsaken of all comforts but these two,
  My faggot and my pipe, I sit to muse
  On all my crosses, and almost excuse
The Heavens for dealing with me as they do.
When Hope steps in, and with a smiling brow,
  Such cheerful expectations doth infuse
  As makes me think ere long I cannot choose
But be some grandee, whatsoe'er I'm now.
  But having spent my pipe, I then perceive
  That hopes and dreams are cousins—both deceive.
Then mark I this conclusion in my mind,
  It's all one thing—both tend into one scope—
  To live upon Tobacco and on Hope,
The one's but smoke, the other is but wind."

In a MS. volume of poetry in the possession of Mr.
J. Payne Collier, is a poem on tobacco, which seems to
be an amplification of Mr. Butler's *Busse against
Tobacco** (Gough's *Norfolk MS.*, 43 Bodl. Lib.), and
begins thus :

> " Tobacco's an outlandish weed,
>   Doth in the land strange wonders breed ;
>   It taints the breath, the blood it dries,
>   It burns the head, it blinds the eyes ;
>   It dries the lungs, scourgeth the lights,
>   It 'numbs the soul, it dulls the sprites ;
>   It brings a man into a maze,
>   And makes him sit for other's gaze ;
>   It makes a man, it mars a purse,
>   A lean one fat, a fat one worse ;
>   A sound man sick, a sick man sound,
>   A bound man loose, a loose man bound ;
>   A white man black, a black man white,
>   A night a day, a day a night ;
>   The wise a fool, the foolish wise,
>   A sober man in drunkard's guise ;
>   A drunkard, with a draught or twain,
>   A sober man it makes again ;
>   A full man empty, and an empty full,
>   A gentleman a foolish gull ;
>   It turns the brain like cat in pan,
>   And makes a Jack a gentleman."

In Brewer's "pleasant comedy" entitled *Lingua ;
or the Combat of the Tongue and the Five Senses for
superiority*, 1617, tobacco is impersonated as one of
the suite of *Olfactus*, or the sense of smelling, and his
appearance is thus described : " Tobacco apparelled in

---

* This appears to have been written jestingly, as Lamb wrote his verses
against smoking. Butler was an eminent physician and humorist. See
a recipe of his, p. 98, note. He was a lover of tobacco.

a taffata mantle, his armes brown and naked; buskins
made of the pilling of osiers; his neck bare, hung with
Indian leaves; his face brown, painted with blew
stripes; in his nose swines' teeth; on his head a painted
wicker crown, with tobacco-pipes set in it; plumes of
tobacco-leaves; led by two Indian boyes, naked, with
tapers in their hands, tobacco-boxes, and pipes lighted."
On his appearance, *Phantastes* exclaims :

"*Ph.* Foh, foh, what a smell is here ! Is this one of your delightfull
objects ?

Olfactus. It is your only scent in request, Sir.

Communis Sensus. What fiery fellow is that which smokes so much in
the mouth ?

Ol. It is the great and puissant god of Tobacco.

*Tobacco. In doch guevarroh pufuer shelvaro baggon,
        Olfia di quanon, Indi cortilo vraggon.**

Ph. Ha, ha, ha, ha, this in my opinion is the tongue of the Antipodes.

Memoria. No, I remember it very well; it was the language the Arca-
dians spake, that lived long before the Moon.

Co. Sen. What signifies it, Olfactus ?

Ol. This is the mighty Emperor, Tobacco, King of Trinidado, that in
being conquered, conquered all Europe, in making them pay tribute for
their smoke.

*Tobacco. Erfronge inglues conde hisingo,
        Develin floscoth ma pu cocthingo.*

Ol. Expeller of catarrhs, banisher of all agues, your guts' only salve for
the green wounds of a *non-plus.*

*Tobacco. Al Vulcam vercu, I parda pora si de gratam ka famala,
        Mara, che Baccho respartera, quirara!*

Ol. Sonne to the god Vulcan, and Tellus, kin to the father of Mirth,
called Bacchus !

*Tobacco. Viscardonok, pillostuphe, parcano, tinaromagas,
        Pagi dagen stollisinfe, carocibato scribus.*

Ol. Genius of all swaggerers, grossest enemy to physitians, sweet

---

* This speech, like the rest in which Tobacco is supposed to describe his
own virtues, is in an imaginary language, to represent Indian, which
Olfactus translates in the ensuing speeches.

ointment for sowre teeth,* first knot of good fellowship,† adamant of company, swift wind to spread the wings of time, hated of none but those who know him not, and of so great deserts that whoso is acquainted with him can hardly forsake him."

The latter words seem to bear out the remark made by Sir Kenelm Digby, in his *Observations upon Religio Medici :* "Who was ever delighted with tobacco, the first time he took it? And who could willingly be without it, after he was a while habituated to the use of it ? "

The writers of this era abound with allusions to the use of the "divine weed." The poets and dramatists celebrate its sway.‡ It is recorded that James I. sat out very uneasily the performance of Dr. Barton Holiday's *Technogamia*, or marriage of the Arts (played at Woodstock, August 26, 1621), in which the following song is sung :—

> Tobacco's a Musician,
> And in a pipe delighteth ;
> It descends in a close,
> Through the organs of the nose,
> With a relish that inviteth.

---

* This will be best understood from the following passage in Ashmole's *Diary*, bearing date January 24, 1685 : "I was much troubled with my teeth, in my upper jaw, on my left side, which, by fits, continued for a week; and then I held pills in my mouth, made of burned allom, pepper, and *tobacco*, which drew much rheum from me, and so I was eased."

† So Stephens in his *Essayes*, 1615, declares "good fellows take tobacco for company sake."

‡ In the *Epigrams* by Marlowe and Sir John Davis, appended to Dyce's edition of *Marlowe* (vol. iii. p. 249), may be read a poem on the *peculiar* curative virtues once attributed to the herb.

This makes me sing so ho, so ho, boyes,
  Ho boyes sound I loudly,
    Earth ne'er did breed
    Such a jovial weed,
  Whereof to boast so proudly.

Tobacco is a Lawyer,
  His pipes do love long cases,
    When our braines it enters,
    Our feete do make indentures ;
  While we seale with stamping paces,
This makes me sing, &c.

Tobacco's a Physician,
  Good both for sound and sickly ;
    Tis a hot perfume,
    That expells cold rheume,*
  And makes it flow downe quickly.
This makes me sing, &c.

Tobacco is a Traveller,
  Come from the Indies hether ;
    It passed sea and land,
    Ere it came to my hand,
  And scaped the wind and weather.
This makes me sing, &c.

---

* In the MS. *Common-place Book of Thomas Brampton, of Kinton, Suffolk* [Gough's Norfolk MS., Bodleian Lib. (No. 46)], is the following dog-Latin recipe, entitled " Mr. Butler's true medycine for the Rewme " :

      Saccio cum sugarro,
      Nobilis ala cum gingero
      Et nutmeggo et tosta bruno
      Bona phisica curare morbum de rheumo,
          Et ego indico,
      Melior est quam tobacco.

Fuller, in his *Worthies*, styles Dr. Butler the "Esculapius of the age ;" he was born at Ipswich, 1535, and died at Cambridge, 1617. He was especially consulted in the last illness of Prince Henry, son of James I. His curious treatment of a confirmed smoker is given in a note to our next chapter. Sir John Hawkins, in his edition of *The Angler*, 1784, says, "he invented a medicated drink called Dr. Butler's Ale, which, if not now, was a few years ago sold at certain houses in London, that had his head for a sign."

Tobacco is a Critticke,
That still old paper turneth,
Whose labour and care,
Is as smoke in the aire,
That ascends from a rag when it burneth.
This makes me sing, &c.

Tobacco's an ignis fatuus
A fat and fyrie vapour,
That leads men about
Till the fire be out,
Consuming like a taper.
This makes me sing, &c.

Tobacco is a Whyffler,
And cries 'huff snuff' with furie,
His pipes, his club, and linke,
He's the wiser that does drinke ;
Thus armed I fear not a furie.
This makes me sing so ho, so ho, boyes,
Ho boyes sound I loudly ;
Earth ne're did breed
Such a jovial weed,
Whereof to boast so proudly.

In *Wit's Recreations* (1640), is the following jovial-
ity, entitled, " *The tryumph of Tobacco over Sack and
Ale.*"

Nay, soft by your leaves,
Tobacco bereaves
    You both of the garland : forbeare it :
You are two to one,
Yet tobacco alone
    Is like both to win it, and weare it.
Though many men crack,
Some of ale, some of sack,
    And think they have reason to do it ;
Tobacco hath more
That will never give or'e
    The honour they do unto it.
Tobacco engages
Both sexes, all ages,

The poor as well as the wealthy,
From the court to the cottage,
From childhood to dotage,
    Both those that are sick and the healthy.
It plainly appears
That in a few years
    Tobacco more custom hath gained,
Then sack, or then ale,
Though they double the tale,
    Of the times, wherein they have reigned.
And worthily too,
For what they undoe
    Tobacco doth help to regaine,
On fairer conditions,
Than many physitians,
    Puts an end to much griefe and paine ;
It helpeth digestion,
Of that there's no question,
    The gout and the tooth ache it easeth :
Be it early, or late,
'Tis never out of date,
    He may safely take it that pleaseth.
Tobacco prevents
Infection by scents,
    That hurt the brain, and are heady.
An antidote is,
Before you're amisse,
    As well as an after remedy.
The cold it doth heate,
Cools them that do sweat,
    And them that are fat maketh lean :
The hungry doth feed,
And, if there be need,
    Spent spirits restoreth again.
The poets of old,
Many fables have told,
    Of the gods and their symposia :
But tobacco alone,
Had they known it, had gone
    For their nectar and ambrosia.*

---

* This idea occurs in an Epigram on Tobacco in the same work, which
savours of hyperbole :
    " Nature's idea, Physicke's rare perfection,
    Cold rheumes expeller, and the wit's direction ;

It is not the smack
Of ale or of sack,
    That can with tobacco compare :
For taste and for smell,
It bears away the bell
    From them both, wherever they are :
For all their bravado,
It is Trinidado,
    That both their noses will wipe
Of the praises they desire,
Unless they conspire
    To sing to the tune of his pipe.

The verse that has been written in the praise and dispraise of tobacco, would, of itself, fill a volume; but, among the quantity, no piece has been more enduringly popular than the song of *Tobacco is an Indian weed*. It has undergone a variety of changes (deteriorating rather than improving it), and through these it may be traced, from the reign of James I., down to the present day.

The earliest copy I have seen (says Mr. Chappell, in his *Popular Music of the Olden Time*) is in a manuscript volume of poetry transcribed during James's reign, and which was most kindly lent to me by Mr. Payne Collier. It there bears the initials of G[eorge] W[ither], a very likely person to have written such a song. A courtier poet would not have sung the praises of smoking—so obnoxious to the King as to induce him to write a *Counterblaste to Tobacco*—but Wither despised the servility which would have tended to his advancement at court. " He could not refrain," says

---

O had the gods known thy immortal smack,
The heavens 'ere this time had been *colored black*."

Wood, "from showing himself a Presbyterian satirist."
It was the publication of his *Abuses stript and whipt*
which caused his committal to the Marshalsea prison.
The following is Wither's song :—

> " Why should we so much despise
> So good and wholesome an exercise
> As, early and late, to meditate ?
>   Thus think, and drink tobacco.

> " The earthen pipe, so lily white,
> Shows that thou art a mortal wight ;
> Even such—and gone with a small touch :
>   Thus think, and drink tobacco.

> " And when the smoke ascends on high,
> Think on the worldly vanity
> Of worldly stuff—'tis gone with a puff :
>   Thus think, and drink tobacco.

> " And when the pipe is foul within,
> Think how the soul's defiled with sin—
> To purge with fire it doth require :
>   Thus think, and drink tobacco.

> " Lastly, the ashes left behind
> May daily shew, to move the mind,
> That to ashes and dust return we must :
>   Thus think, and drink tobacco."

About 1670, we find several copies of Wither's song,
but the first stanza changed in all, besides other minor
variations. In *Merry Drollery Complete* (1670), it
commences, "Tobacco, that is withered quite." On
broadsides, bearing date the same year, and having the
tune at the top, the first line is, " The Indian weed
withered quite." In 1669 it appeared in its present
form, in the first volume of *Pills to purge Melancholy.*

and so remained until 1719, when D'Urfey became editor of that collection, and transferred it, with others, to the third. The following is the song printed on the broadsides, and in the *Pills* :—

> " Tobacco's but an Indian weed,
>   Grows green at morn, cut down at eve,
>   It shows our decay, we are but clay :
>   Think of this when you smoke tobacco.
>
> " The pipe, that is so lily white,
>   Wherein so many take delight,
>   Is broke with a touch—man's life is such :
>   Think of this when you smoke tobacco.
>
> " The pipe, that is so foul within,
>   Shews how man's soul is stain'd with sin,
>   And then the fire it doth require :
>   Think of this when you smoke tobacco.
>
> " The ashes that are left behind
>   Do serve to put us all in mind
>   That unto dust return we must :
>   Think of this when you smoke tobacco.
>
> " The smoke, that does so high ascend,
>   Shews us man's life must have have an end,
>   The vapour's gone—man's life is done :
>   Think of this when you smoke tobacco." *

Bishop Earle in his *Micro-cosmography* (1628), has this character of a tobacco-seller : " He is the only man

---

* After the *Pills*, it was printed with alterations, and the addition of a very inferior second part, by the Rev. Ralph Erskine, a minister of the Scotch Church, in his *Gospel Sonnets*. This is the "Smoking Spiritualized," which is still in print among the ballad-vendors of Seven-Dials, and a copy of which is contained in *Songs and Ballads of the Peasantry of England*, by J. H. Dixon, or the new edition by Robert Bell.

In the Rev. James Plumptre's *Collection of Songs* (8vo, 1805), *Tobacco is an Indian weed* was adapted to a more modern tune by Dr. Hague ; and about 1830, the late Samuel Wesley again re-set the words, to music of his own composition.—*Chappell.*

that finds good in it which others brag of, but do not;
for it is meat, drink, and clothes to him. No man
opens his ware with greater seriousness, or challenges
your judgment more in the approbation. His shop is
the rendezvous of spitting, where men dialogue with
their noses, and their communication is smoak.* It
is the only place where Spain is commended and
preferred before England itself. He should be well
experienced in the world, for he has daily trial of men's
nostrils, and none is better acquainted with humours.
He is the piecing commonly of some other trade,
which is bawd to his tobacco, and that to his wife,
which is the flame that follows this smoak." In
another part of his work our author says of a Tavern,
" it is the torrid zone, that scorches the face, and
tobacco the gun-powder that blows it up."

Scattered in the diaries of this era we occasionally
meet with a few notices of the prices of tobacco.
Thus in the MS. notes made by Sir Henry Oglander
of Nunwell in the Isle of Wight, in the year 1626
he records among other expenses, "for eight ounces
of tobacco, five shillings : " he frequently puts down
other sums for the same luxury, and in one of his
letters to his son in London mentions his disappoint-
ment at not getting tobacco with other things ordered
to come from the Capital. In the Journal of the
Reverend Giles Moore, published by the Sussex Archæological Society (Vol. I. *Transactions*), he notes the

---

* Minshew calls a tobacconist *fumi-vendulus,* a *smoak-seller*.

payment in 1656 for " two ounces of tobacco, one shilling."

The expense of the custom was one fertile source of objection to the "fragrant weed." We have heard the satirists declare it ruined the smaller gentry, and grave elders occasionally "put out the pipes " of fast young heirs by testamentary legislation. Thus the will of Peter Campbell, a Derbyshire gentleman in 1616, bequeathed all his household goods to his eldest son Roger; but if at any time his brothers or sisters "fynd him takeing of tobacco," he shall forfeit all, " or their full valew." Now, as he had five brothers and three sisters, he must have been well watched.*

The " rigidly righteous " were in those days as bitterly tyrannical on tobacco, as they still continue to be on any other practice that does not accord with their particular idiosyncracies. They prophesied as we have seen in the course of our researches, all sorts of evil and ruin to those who used tobacco. But there were not wanting some few who saw the ruin of England in the habit. In the Parliament of 1620 the member for Pontefract, Sir Edwin Sandys, summed up the evil thus :—

" There was wont to come out of Spain a great mass of money, to the value of £100,000 per annum, for our cloths and other merchandises; and now we have from thence for all our cloths and merchandises, nothing but tobacco : nay that will not pay for all the

* *Gent's Mag.*, April, 1769.

tobacco we have from thence, but they have more from us in money every year, £20,000 ; so there goes out of this kingdom as good as £120,000 for tobacco every year."*

Certainly the sapient James I. had done his best by pen and penalty to stop the pipes of his southern subjects. He left no small tyranny untried by which he might hinder others of an enjoyment he could not share. The petty meddlings of this wretched sovereign with the minor liberties of the subjects he unfortunately ruled, increased to a tyranny which, bequeathed as a heir-loom to his son, brought him to the scaffold. James was "little" in everything. He could take no enlarged view of life, or that political economy which regulates and balances for the good of all, even the follies or extravagancies of the few. Hence he deprived the country of a large revenue, crushed and repressed the fair trade, and indulged himself in fines, and others in monopolies of the plant, making restrictions which led to evasion and dishonesty, and granting power of selling only to those who could pay exorbitant fines. Garrard in *the Stafford Letters*, vol 1. notes in 1633 the Life-leases for selling tobacco; as being £15 fine, and as much rent by the year. "Some towns have yielded 20 marks, £10, £5, and £6 fine and rent, none goes under ; and three or four allowed in great market-towns and thoroughfares. I hear Plymouth hath yielded £100, and as much

* *Parl. Hist.* vol. i. p. 1195.

yearly rent." Under 1634 is noted, " The tobacco-
licencers go on apace ; they yield a good fine, and a
constant yearly rent."

History proves that persecution never triumphs in its
attempted eradications. Tobacco was so generally liked
that no legislative measures could prevent its use. Nor
was it confined to " the fast men " of the age. " There
are also some," says Dr. Venner of Bath in his *treatise
concerning the taking the fume of tobacco* (1637), " who
are grave and seemingly wise and judicious, that take
it moderately, and most commonly at fixed times ; but
with its proper adjunct, which (as they doe suppose) is
a cup of sack, and this they think to bee no bad
physick." The clergy occasionally indulged in "a quiet
pipe." Archbishop Harsnett, in his Ordinances for
the regulation of his schools at Chigwell in Essex,
ordains that the Latin schoolmaster be " of a sound
religion, neither papist nor puritan, of a grave be-
haviour, of a sober and honest conversation, no tippler
nor haunter of ale-houses," and, as a climax, " no
puffer of tobacco ! " Aubrey, writing in 1680, says,
" within these thirty-five years it was considered scandalous for a divine to take tobacco ; " but Lilly, the
Astrologer, in his *Memoirs*, under the year 1633,
tells a different tale. He says :—

" In this year also William Bredon, parson or vicar
of Thornton in Buckinghamshire, was living, a profound divine, but absolutely the most polite person
for nativities in that age, strictly adhering to Ptolomy,
which he well understood ; he had a hand in com-

posing Sir Christopher Heydon's defence of judicial
astrology, being that time his chaplain; he was so
given over to tobacco and drink, that when he had no
tobacco, he would cut the bell-ropes and smoke
them."

Prefixed to Rand's edition of Skelton's *Elinour
Rumming*, 1624, are some verses by a rhymer of the
day, curiously descriptive of the general habit of
tobacco smoking, supposed to be uttered by Skelton's
Ghost,* who says of his own era :—

> " Nor did that time know
> To puffe and to blow
> In a peece of white clay,
> As you doe at this day,
> With fier and coale,
> And a leafe in a hole ;
> As my ghost hath late seene,
> As I walked betweene
> Westminster Hall
> And the church of Saint Paul,
> And so thorow the citie,
> Where I saw and did pitty
> My countrymen's cases,
> With fiery-smoke faces,
> Sucking and drinking
> A filthie weede stinking,
> Was ne're knowne before
> Till the devil and the More
> In th' Indies did meete,
> And each other there greete
> With a health they desire
> Of stinke, smoke, and fier.

---

* It may be worth while here to note, as a sample of the sort of arguments people *will* adduce for the antiquity of smoking, that this poem has
been quoted as a proof that the custom was usual when Skelton lived, in the
reign of Henry the Eighth ! The argument is not more unsound than fifty
others used pertinaciously by determined discoverers of mare's nests.

But who e're doth abhorre it,
The citie smoakes for it ;
Now full of fier shops
And fowle spitting chops,
So neesing and coughing,
That my ghost fell to scoffing,
And to myself said,
Here's filthie fumes made ;
Good phisicke of force
To cure a sicke horse."

In the curious Pamphlet published about 1626, comprising a dialogue between the Proctor and Parator,
or informer to the Ecclesiastical Courts; the latter
notes his gains from closing the tobacco shops on
stated days, having " gotten good booty from transgres-
sors against holy dayes, of Chandlers, Ale-Houses,
Tavernes, Tobacco-shops, Butchers, Comfit-makers,
Gunsmiths, Bakers, Brokers, Cookes, Weavers, and
divers other malefactors against our terrible Canons
and Jurisdiction : for had I but given them a severe
looke, I could by that meanes have made them draw
their purses, or else they knew whither they were to
be fetcht up with a *Coram Nomine.* I have put 80
of these fearfull Birds into one net, and I alwaies held
correspondency with the Clarks of Parishes, so that I
could stand by a pillar in the Church, and heare them
all excommunicated at once, by the poore Curate, who
durst not disobey for fear of the mighty command of
the Judges of the Courts, whose awfull injunctions
were as formidable to such ten pound a year fellowes,
as Canon shot to young Sea-men."

D'Avenant, writing in 1634, speaks of the custom of

smoking as " so much in fashion, that methinks your children begin to play with broken pipes instead of corals, to make way for their teeth."

During the reign of Charles I., no alteration was made in the restrictive laws against tobacco. He also continued its sale only as a royal monopoly, and prohibited it from being dealt in by any but such as he had appointed to the trade, who paid him a heavy sum for the privilege ; a measure that proved most injurious to the planters. Charles seized all the profits of their industry, and disregarded their remonstrances. It is recorded that when, in his days of misfortune, he sat in the guard-chamber at Westminster, the soldiers of Cromwell blew their tobacco smoke in his face, knowing that he had almost as strong a dislike to it as his father had.

In the Ashmolean MSS. at Oxford (No. 38, art. 439) is the following tirade " against tobacco : "—

" Of all the plants that Tellus' bosome yields
In groves, glades, gardens, marshes, mountaines, fieldes,
None so pernitious to man's life is knowne
As is tobacco, saving hemp alone ;
Betwixt which two there seemes great sympathy
To ruinate poore Adam's progeny.
For in them both a strangling virtue note ;
And both of them doe worke upon the throate.
The one within it, and without the other,
And th' one prepareth worke unto the t'other.
For there doth meete, I meane at jaile and gallowes,
More of these beastly, base tobacco fellowes,
Than hence to any prophane haunt doe use,
Excepting still the playhouse and the stewes,
Seeth to there comon lot so double choaked,
Just bacon like to be hanged up and smoaked ;

A destiny as proper to befall
To mortal swine, as to swine naturall.
Upon this point we may this riddle bring—
This subject hath more subjects than the king.
Variety and surfit doth feed the spittle,
And fill the grave ; Nature's content with little.

Cromwell believed with King James I., that growing tobacco in England was "thereby to misuse and
misemploy the soill of this kingdom;" and he sent
his troopers to trample down the growing crops where-
ever they found them.* It is recorded that the soldiers
smoked at the Protector's magnificent funeral, as if to
publicly triumph over their recovered liberty. Evelyn,
in his *Diary*, on the 22nd of October, 1658, notes, that
the Protector's funeral " was the joyfullest funeral I
ever saw ; for there were none that cried but dogs,
which the soldiers hooted away with a barbarous noise,
drinking and taking tobacco in the streets as they
went."

The Puritans, from the earliest days of their " plantation " among us, abhorred the fume of the pipe. Ben
Jonson notes it, and the puritanical *Justice Overdoo*
rails against it in *Bartholomew Faire*. A citizen's

* It had been extensively grown in Gloucestershire, as appears from the
following passage : In " *Harry Hangman's Honour ; or the Gloucestershire Hangman's Request to the Smoakers or Tobacconists in London :* a
quarto pamphlet in the king's collection (marked in ink, June 11, 1655),
he says : "the very planting of tobacco hath proved the decay of my
trade, for since it hath beene planted in Gloucestershire, especially at
Winchcourt, my trade hath proved nothing worth." He adds, "Then
'twas a merry world with me ! for indeed before tobacco was there planted
there being no kind of trade to employ men, and very small tillage, necessity compelled poor men to stand my friends, by stealing of sheep and
other cattel, breaking of hedges, robbing of orchards, and what not."

wife, in Marston's comedy, *The Dutch Courtezan*, 1605, preparing for the entertainment of her friends, says to her servants, " Perfume this parlor, it does so smell of prophane tobacco. I could never endure this ungodly tobacco, since one of our elders assured me upon his knowledge, tobacco was not used in the congregation of the family of Love " (a religious sect then notorious). Hutton, in his *Follies Anatomie*, 1611, speaks of a puritan who—

> " Abhorres a sattin suit, a velvet cloak,
> And sayes tobacco is the devill's smoke."

Penn, the Quaker, disliked tobacco. Clarkson, in his *Life* of him, records this, and says, that while in America he was often annoyed by it, but here submitted in good humour. Once, on his way to Pensburg, he stopped at Burlington to see old friends, who happened to be smoking; knowing his dislike, they concealed their pipes. Perceiving, from the smell when he entered the room, that they had been smoking, and discovering that the pipes had been hid, he said pleasantly, " Well, friends, I am glad that you are at last ashamed of your old practice." " Not entirely so," replied Samuel Jennings, one of the company; " but we preferred laying down our pipes to the danger of offending a weak brother."

The old colonists who planted tobacco were equally severe against Quakers. Thus, in what are termed the "Blue Laws" of old Virginia, 1663, we find it enacted : " Every master of a ship or vessel, that shall bring in any quakers to reside here after the 1st of July next, shall be fined 5000 pounds of tobacco." This is followed by another:—" Any person inhabiting this country, and entertaining any Quaker in or near his house, to preach or teach, shall, for every time of such entertainment, be fined 5000 pounds of tobacco." It was the custom in the colony at this period to pay invariably all fines for crimes in pounds of tobacco.*

It must not, however, be too hastily inferred from this that the "religious world" did not smoke. Some sectarians prided themselves on it; and when they stabled their horses in our cathedrals, fumigated them also with tobacco. In the *Conference between a Puritan Preacher and a Family of his Flock*, printed in the (spurious) posthumous works of Butler, 1732, the preacher exclaims before dinner—

> '"——— I must crave thy leave to light
> One pipe to whet my appetite ;"

and in the *Rump Songs* mention is made of one of " the Saints " who was a lover of the pipe :—

> " Salloway, with tobacco
> Inspired, turned State Quack O !"

The translator of Everard's treatise† says of its

---

* In the early colonisation, the charge made to settlers as the price of a young woman "imported there" was 120 lbs. of tobacco.

† *Panacea, or the Universal Medicine ; being a Discovery of the Wonderfull Virtues of Tobacco taken in a Pipe; with its Use and Operation both in Physick and Chyrurgery.* By Dr. Everard. 1659. Translated by J. R., and dedicated to the Merchants and Planters of Tobacco.

I

increased consumption in England:—"It is like Elias'
cloud, which was no bigger than a man's hand, that
hath suddenly covered the face of the earth; the low
countries, Germany, Poland, Arabia, Persia, Turkey,
almost all countries, drive a trade of it; and there is
no commodity that hath advanced so many from small
fortunes to gain great estates in the world.

"Seamen will be supplied with it for their long
voyages. Soldiers cannot (but) want it when they keep
guard all night, or upon other hard duties in cold and
tempestuous weather. Farmers, ploughmen, porters,
and almost all labouring men plead for it, saying they
find great refreshment by it, and very many would as
soon part with their necessary food as they would be
totally deprived of the use of tobacco."

"Scholars use it much, and many grave and great
men take tobacco to make them more serviceable in
their callings. Tobacco is grown to be not only the
physick, but even the meat and drink of many men,
women, and children. In a word, it hath prevailed so
far, that there is no living without it.

"If we reflect upon our forefathers, and that within
the time of less than one hundred years, before the
use of tobacco came to be known amongst us, we
cannot but wonder how they did to subsist without
it; for were the planting or traffick of tobacco now
hindered, millions of this nation in all probability
must perish for the want of food, their whole livelihood almost depending upon it. So many druggists,
grocers, tobacco-shops, taverns, inns, alehouses, vic-

tuallers, carriers, cutters and dryers of tobacco, pipe-makers, and the like, that deal in it, will prove no less."

The popularity of tobacco-smoking at the time of the Restoration of Charles II., may be gathered from the following curious narrative from *The Life and Times of Lilly the Astrologer*, who was seized as a suspected person in January, 1661,—" one Everard, a Justice of Peace in Westminster, ere I was stirring, sent a Serjeant and thirty four musqueteers for me to White-Hall : he had twice that night seized about sixty persons, supposed fanaticks, very despicable persons, many whereof were aged, some were water-bearers, and had been Parliament-soldiers ; others, of ordinary callings : all these were guarded unto White-Hall, into a large room, until day-light, and then committed to the Gate-House : I was had into the guard-room, which I thought to be hell ; some therein were sleeping, others swearing, others smoking tobacco. In the chimney of the room I believe there was two bushels of broken tobacco pipes, almost half one load of ashes."

Charles II., on his Restoration, confirmed the old laws for the suppression of its culture, and extended the restriction to Ireland, under a penalty of confiscation and fine of forty shillings for every rood so planted, except " in any physick-garden of either University, or in any other private garden for physick or chirurgery," but then only half a pole of land to be so planted. Three years afterwards the penalty was

raised to a fine of 10*l.* per rood. It is recorded
that Charles sent a letter to the University of Cambridge, forbidding the members to wear perriwigs,
smoke tobacco, and read the sermons they delivered.*
Tobacco did not become popular at court; but smoking
it was a practice very constantly indulged as "the
contemplative man's recreation" (to use Walton's term
for fishing), particularly in the provinces. Thus, in
Shadwell's comedy, the *Virtuoso*, 1676, an old country
gentleman orders "a pipe and a match" in the garden;
another exclaims, "here's old Snarl, he has called for
his tobacco too; he smoaks all day like a kitchen
chimney." A French traveller, Monsieur Jorevin de
Rochefort,† thus relates his experiences of an evening
spent with a friend at Worcester :—

"The supper being finished, they set on the table
half a dozen pipes and a pacquet of tobacco for
smoking, which is a general custom, as well among the
women as men, who think that without tobacco, one
cannot live in England, because they say it dissipates
the evil humours of the brain."

"Whilst we were walking about the town, he asked
me if it was the custom in France, as in England, that
when the children went to school, they carried in their
satchel, with their books, a pipe of tobacco, which
their mother took care to fill early in the morning, it
serving them instead of a breakfast; and that at the

* *Hone's Every Day Book*, vol. i., col. 1264.

† His travels were printed at Paris in 1672, and have been translated in
the *Antiquarian Repertory*, vol. ii., p. 99.

accustomed hour, every one laid aside his book to light his pipe, the master smoking with them, and teaching them how to hold their pipes and draw in the tobacco ; thus accustoming them to it from their youths, believing it absolutely necessary for a man's health. This put me in mind of a Spaniard, who being accustomed to take tobacco, I found him at a seaport of Calabria in Italy, where we were detained by bad weather on our return from Malta; here, he not being able to procure tobacco, cut off a piece of the cable, with which he filled his pipe, to draw and suck down the smoke thereof, instead of tobacco. I have also seen an Irishman, twenty-four years old, who during his whole life had smoked tobacco ; he, having fallen sick, was forbid the use of that plant, as being too great a dryer of the body ; this he submitted to for some time, but he became so low, and so melancholy, that he could at length take nothing but a little tobacco, which was at last permitted him, and he in a short time recovered his perfect health. I have known several who not content with smoking in the day, went to bed with their pipes in their mouths, others who have risen in the night to light their pipes, to take tobacco with as much pleasure as they would have received in drinking either Alicant or Greek wine."

M. Rochefort's mention of the prevalence of smoking among females, calls to mind Tom Brown's " exhortatory letter to an old lady that smoked tobacco," written about the same period, which runs as follows :—
" Though the ill-natured world censures you for

smoking, yet I would advise you, Madam, not to part
with so innocent a diversion. In the first place it is
healthful ; and as Galen rightly observes is a sovereign
remedy for the toothache, the constant persecutor of
old ladies. Secondly, tobacco, though it be an heathen-
ish word, it is a great help to Christian meditations ;
which is the reason I suppose, that recommends it to
your *parsons*, the generality of whom can no more
write a sermon without a pipe in their mouths, than a
concordance in their hands ; besides, every pipe you
break, may serve to put you in mind upon what
slender accidents man's life depends. I knew a dis-
senting minister who on fast-days used to mortify upon
a rump of beef, because it put him, as he said, in mind
that all flesh was grass ; but I am sure much more is
to be learnt from tobacco. It may instruct you that
riches, beauty, and all the glories of the world, vanish
like a vapour. Thirdly, it is a pretty plaything.
Fourthly, and lastly, it is fashionable, at least 'tis in a
fair way of becoming so."

Walton and Cotton at this period enjoyed " a quiet
pipe " on the banks of the Dove, in the lovely county
of Derbyshire. Both have recorded it in their immortal *Angler*. There is a strong sense of enjoyment after their " light supper," when Piscator (Cotton
himself) says to his attendants, " Come, take away, and
bring us some pipes and a bottle of ale." And then
addressing his guest Viator, asks, " Are you for this
diet, sir ? " to which he replies, " Yes, sir, I am for one
pipe of tobacco ; and I perceive yours is very good by

the smell." Piscator answers, "the best I can get in London, I assure you;" no small recommendation, in an age when much difficulty and expense was attendant on communication with the capital; but it has been well observed "if a man does smoke, let him smoke good tobacco, that no extra and unnecessary offence be given to the 'weaker brethren.'"

In the middle of the seventeenth century, tobacco formed the subject of a curious ballet at Lisbon, which may be thus briefly described. The scene was laid in the Island of Tobago, the supposed native place of tobacco, and a troop of its inhabitants were introduced chanting in celebration of the good fortune of people to whom the gods had granted a plant so precious. Four priests, taking tobacco in powder from golden boxes pendant from their girdles, cast it in the air to appease tempests. The rest then marched in solemn procession round their idols, with long pipes in their mouths, fumigating them as with incense. A second scene exhibited manufacturers at work, tying up the leaves of the plant, cutting it for the smoker, and pounding it for the snuff-takers. The third and last scene introduced the consumers of the herb, and a general dance, in which all mixed together, and offered pinches from each other's snuff-boxes. The smokers of all nations, in appropriate costume, joined the dance, to indicate the reunion of all peoples and creeds under the powerful influence of tobacco ; the natives leaping among them all till the curtain fell.

During the prevalence of the Great Plague of

London (1665), tobacco was recommended and generally taken, as a preventive of infection. The physicians and those who attended the sick, took it very freely; those who went round with the dead-carts, had their pipes continually lighted. It was popularly reported, and as generally believed, that no tobacconists or their households were afflicted by the pestilence. This gave tobacco a new popularity, and it again took the high medical position assumed for it by the earlier physicians of the French Court.

In a broadside poem published about 1670, entitled "*Nicotianæ Encomium;* or the Golden Leaf Tabacco display'd in its sovereignty and singular vertues," its efficacy against the plague is particularly dwelt upon:—

> " If the Grand Bugbear Toad, the Plague, ye fear;
> Lo ! under God your antidote is here."

All diseases are declared to be quelled by it:—

> " Ye hot, ye cold, ye Rheumatick draw nigh ;
> In this rich leafe a sovereign dose doth lie.
> We'll cure ye all : Physick ye need not want,
> Here 'tis, i' th' gummy entralls of a Plant."

At the feasts of the Mayor and citizens of London, pipes and tobacco were served; and in the Lord Mayor's Show of 1672, the Londoners were treated to "two exceeding great rarities, that is there are two extreme great giants, each of them at least fifteen foot high, that do sit, and are drawn by horses in two several chariots, moving, talking, and *taking* *tobacco* as they ride along, to the great admiration and delight of all the spectators." *

Tobacco had long before this assumed a fixed position as a favourite luxury all over Europe. After its introduction to the East at the close of the sixteenth century, it became a prime favourite there. In Persia it conquered Shah Abbas, who first opposed its use by cruel penalties, and on one occasion threw an unfortunate vendor into the fire with his goods; but the love for the indulgence was too well spread, and he succumbed. The Turks, as .we have noted, had similar persecutions to encounter, after the custom had become all but universal among them, the Sultan, Amurath IV., having taken into his head that smoking made men impotent; an opinion also held by Sir William Vaughan in his *Directions for Health* (1613), and again made the subject of a jocular treatise in 1675, called *The woman's complaint against Tobacco.* Dr. Brown in his *Travels in Germany* (1677), mentions having seen in Vienna the followers of the Cham of Tartary, and says "they took much tobacco in very long pipes; their tobacco not in rolls, but in leaves, and dry." The Chinese obtained the herb from the Portuguese, and often employed it in place of opium. In Russia it was prohibited, because a few instances of fires occurred in Moscow, occasioned by persons dropping asleep with lighted pipes. A law was for a very short

---

* Jordan's *London Triumphant; or the City in Jollity and Splendor*, a pamphlet descriptive of the Lord Mayor's Show in the above year.

time in force in France, prohibiting the sale of tobacco, except by order of a physician,* the supply only
to be obtained of an apothecary. The Dutch have
always been famed for a love of the weed : the pipe is,
and ever was, their great solace. The admirable manner
in which Washington Irving has narrated their smoking
powers in *Knickerbocker*, is no exaggeration ; no one
can travel in Holland in the present day, without
observing the constant use of the pipe. Railway
carriages are expressly fitted for smokers ; and small
metal troughs for tobacco ashes, provided near the
seats. The popular theatres of Amsterdam permit
smoking during the performances, and a Dutch critic
in the pit may see his favourite play, or still more
favourite heroine, through the agreeable medium of
tobacco-smoke. The Germans can, however, rival
them in their powers of smoking.

Barham, in his *Lay of St. Odille* (*Ingoldsby Legends*)
humourously describes

> " ——————— a certain Count Herman,
> A highly respectable man as a German,
> Who smoked like a chimney, and drank like a Merman."

Certainly the Germans' love of beer and tobacco is
unrivalled elsewhere, and enables him to do what none
but those "to the manner born" could do. To drink a
pint of beer at a draught, and several quarts at a
sitting ; and to fill pipes as continually as they are

---

* It was issued by Lous XIII. in 1635.

burnt out, for the best part of a day, is no uncommon thing in Bavaria. It would astonish the weak minds of tee-totallers and tobacco-haters could they take a seat for a day in any *Lustgarten* of this most philosophic nation. After their clear elucidation of the fatal consequences of both habits, it is strange that any Germans are to be found alive after thirty years of age.

The practice of chewing tobacco, recorded to have been used by the Indians to stay hunger in travel, appears to have had no general popularity. Soldiers and sailors adopted it from the same reasons, and from the inconvenience of using the pipe. It was sanctioned by the custom of General Monk at the Restoration, and it was usual with gentlemen to sport silver basins to spit in, something after the American fashion, as represented in an old snuff-box, of the time of James I., published by the Society of Antiquaries,* and copied in our engraving, from which it appears that this questionable custom was " done with a grace," if we may judge from the affected attitude of the cavalier.

Neander, the Dutch physician, whose work *Tabacologia*, published in 1622, we have already quoted, notes

---

* Archæologia, Vol. 23.   Ben Jonson, in his *Every Man Out of his Humour*, notes the custom.

the various kinds of tobacco then used, which obtained their names from the places where they were grown. Thus, Brazilian, St. Domingo, Orinoco, Virginia, and Trinidad tobacco, at once point to well known localities. Of these, the last named was most popular in England, and is frequently named by early authors. Thus the song of the corporal and watch, in Beaumont and Fletcher's play *The Knight of Malta*, has the lines:—

> " To thee a full pot, my little lanceprisado,*
> And when thou hast done, a pipe of Trinidado."

Amazonian tobacco came from the lands on the border of the great river Amazon; and Varinas, called by Brathwait in his *Smoaking Age* (1617), Varina and Varinian tobacco, is named from a town in Columbia, still famed for its tobacco.† Cavendish was named from the great captain, whose voyages made him famous, and was originally cut up from a closely pressed cake of the leaf, for the use of the smoker; it is still the most coarsely cut tobacco of all. *Carotte* was a popular tobacco with Frenchmen, and was formed into long thin rolls, sweetened with treacle, and cut for smoking or chewing like the modern pigtail; it is represented on the table in our cut, p. 57. Roll tobacco was formed in a continuous thin rope of leaf, by aid of a wheel, as twine is made; and

* A lanceprisado is a lance-corporal, the lowest grade of military officer. "A leader or governor of half a file, and therefore is commonly called a middleman, or captain over four."—*Note in Gifford's Massinger.*
† *A Paper of Tobacco*, 1839.

was formed by adding the leaves to each other, and
tightly compressing them as the wheel revolved, a roll
consisting of very many yards was then formed; the
tobacco roll therefore became the favourite sign of
the tobacconist. The process of this manufacture is
exhibited in our cut from the shop-bill of "Benjamin
Parkes, at the Cross, Worcester," temp. Geo. I.

Sometimes this kind of tobacco was twisted in the
manner of coarse cord, into a thick ball larger than a
man's head, which formed a stock from which to "cut
and come again."

During the reign of William the Third tobacco met
with a patronage almost universal. Pipes grew larger
then, and ruled by a Dutchman, all England smoked
in peace. Misson, in his *Memoirs of Travels over
England* (1697), notes "this perpetual use of tobacco,"
among men and women, particularly in country places;
and he thinks that this "makes the generality of
Englishmen so taciturn, so thoughtful and so melancholy;" but as if he agreed with Ben Jonson's Master
Stephen, that "your melancholy is ever the breeder of
your excellent wit," he adds "Tobacco not only breeds

profound theologists, but also begets moral philosophers : witness the following sonnet :—

> " Sweet smoking pipe ; bright glowing stove,
>   Companion still of my retreat,
> Thou dost my gloomy thoughts remove,
>   And purge my brain with gentle heat.
>
> " Tobacco, charmer of my mind,
>   When, like the meteor's transient gleam,
> Thy substance gone to air, I find,
>   I think, alas, my life's the same !
>
> " What else but lighted dust am I ?
>   Thou show'st me what my fate will be ;
> And when thy sinking ashes die,
>   I learn that I must end like thee."

Dr. Henry Aldrich, the musical Dean of Christ-
church Oxford, well known from his popular Glee
"Hark! the bonny Christ-church bells;" was a smoker*
also, and composed the following quaint "*Catch on
Tobacco;* to be sung by four men at the time of
smoaking their pipes ;" which we here reprint, from
The Second Book of the Pleasant Musical Companion,
1687.

> Good ! good indeed !
>   The Herb's good weed ;
> Fill thy pipe, Will, and I prithee, Sam, fill,
> For sure we may smoak, and yet sing still ;
> For what say the learned ?. *Vita fumus,*
> 'Tis what you and I, and he and I, and all of us, *Sumus.*

---

* There is an amusing anecdote related of the Dean's continuous devotion
to his pipe. One of the students betted another that however early, or at
whatever time the Doctor was visited in his own *sanctum,* he would be
found smoking. The bet was taken, and at once the Dean was visited ;
when the reason of the visit was given, " Your friend has lost," said the
Dean, "I am not smoking, only filling my pipe."

But then to the learned say we again,
If Life's a smoak, as they maintain,
If Life's a vapour, without doubt,
When a man does dye,
They should not cry,
That his glass is run, but his pipe is out.
But whether we smoak, or whether we sing,
Let's be loyal, and remember the king ;
Let him live, and let his foes vanish,
Thus like a pipe, like a pipe of Spanish."

Many similar quaint whims were dreamed over a pipe, and occasionally given to the world. In the *True trial of understanding, or Wit newly revived,* a chap-book printed for hawkers in the reign of Anne, is the following riddle :—

" What tho' I have a nauseous breath,
    Yet many a one will me commend ;
I am beloved after death,
    And serviceable unto my friend."

The answer is thus given : " This is tobacco, after cut and dry'd, being dead, becometh serviceable." A much more ingenious "conceit" of the same kind, which requires the name of the herb to be written down letter by letter, in Roman capitals, to fully comprehend it ;—is as follows :—

" To three-fourths of a cross add a circle complete ;
Let two semicircles a perpendicular meet ;
Next add a triangle that stands on two feet ;
Then two semicircles, and a circle complete."

During the reign of Anne, the custom of smoking appears to have attained its greatest height in England —says the author of the excellent little *Paper of*

Tobacco, and "the consumption of tobacco was then proportionably greater, considering the population, than it is at the present time." The golden names of literature patronised the custom. Addison, Congreve, Phillips, Prior, and Steele, consumed tobacco; Pope and Swift, following the favourite example of the Continental clergy, took snuff. In the days of the Regency, no French abbé was without his box, and as the rank of the clergy so was the indulgence in the "pungent dust," rendered more recherché and expensive by the perfection of its quality and scent.

The author of *the Beau in a Wood* (1701), speaks of the enormous wigs then in fashion, as generally "scented with tobacco."

In 1703, one Lawrence Spooner, emulous of the fame of King James or Du Bartas, published some quaint rhymes, which he called *A Looking-Glass for Smoakers;* his rhymes are, as Dogberry would say, "most tolerable, and not to be endured," but his preface (fortunately in prose) lets us into the secret of the very general practice of smoking in England at his period; "in two miles compass may be found a thousand families or persons in country villages, that one with another, do smoak, snuff, or chaw, the year round, one penny a day, and most of these coal or lime-men, firemen, &c." He then goes on to demonstrate that 1525*l.* a year, is the cost of this, which in twenty years would double itself at the interest of a shilling in the pound; but, "if improv'd thriftily, in twenty years it would amount to more than £130,000 to divide amongst the smoakers and their heirs for ever. By which the world may see what mischief this *Land robber* doth amongst them." He adds "The sin of the kingdom in the intemperate use of tobacco, swelleth and increaseth so daily, that I can compare it to nothing but the waters of Noah, that swell'd fifteen cubits above the highest mountains. So that if this practice shall continue to increase as it doth, in an age or two it will be as hard to find a family free, as it was so long time since one that commonly took it." But the author is most pained that the pious should indulge in the habit, and in his horror at recording the fact, he rises so far above himself, that we quote his own words : "But above all, that this practice should overgrow all the powers of reason, religion, and experience amongst most part of the godly, is yet to be admired : * that a thing should grow to that height in their affections (that is not naturally pleasant) is a wonder : that they should suffer such an unnatural fire to be kindled in their nature, that proves in the event to be such a world of iniquity, and puts them in such a ferment and disorder, may make us cry out with the prophet Jeremiah, chap. 2, v. 12, ' Be astonished, Oh ye heavens, at this ! be ye horribly afraid, be ye very desolate, saith the Lord of Hosts ! ' "

Even this did not "put the pipe out" of any faithful lover of the weed ; the clergy were great favourers of

---

* Let no modern reader understand this word in a modern sense ; words change meanings marvellously as times change. Mr. Spooner's *admiration* is a frightened astonishment or holy horror.

the practice, and in no degree diminished the enjoyment of a "cheerful pipe." Hogarth, in his *Modern
Midnight Conversation*, has introduced one in full
canonicals, amid the merry party, smoking like a
steam-engine and carrying a ring tobacco-stopper on
his finger. To be sure, if the parson be the famous

orator Henley (as some
say, but do not *prove**),
it is no very creditable
exemplar of the cloth ;
but that the custom was
common with reverend
sons of the Church appears
from abundant authority ;
and that it still, or till
very lately, was the solace of the country parson
any one acquainted with village life can tell. The
author has known several such smokers ; and can also
instance a London clergyman of much reputation, with
great power in the Arts as well as in literature, who
always smoked in his vestry after Prayers, during the
Psalm, while waiting to begin his sermon.

When Sir Robert Walpole, in 1732, introduced his
excise bill into parliament, the greatest popular hatred
was immediately evinced towards the measure. Tobacco was one of the articles especially "excised," and
the un-English and inquisitorial power ultimately given

---

* Mrs. Piozzi was of opinion that it represented "Parson Ford,"
Dr. Johnson's uncle.

by that measure, has existed as a clog on the trade till
this hour. Sir Robert did not, however, conquer
easily, and an abundance of satire, in picture and
prose, was levelled at him. In one plate, called *The
Triumphant Exciseman,* amid other horrors, trade
droops sorrowfully over a hogshead of tobacco. Another caricature exhibits the Premier drawn in his
chariot by a many-headed
dragon, one of whose mouths
swallows the pipe and pot of
the unfortunate Englishman,
as here represented. The
lieges are flying, deprived of
everything eatable or drinkable, while one of the
monster's heads disgorges into Sir Robert's chariot
an abundant stream of gold. His ravages are thus
predicted :—

> " At first he'll begin ye
> With a pipe of Virginie,
> Then search ev'ry shop in his rambles ;
> If you force him to flee
> From the Custom-house key,
> The monster will lodge in your shambles."

Sir Robert's bill was violently opposed, and his
party endeavoured to turn the tables on their opponents by similar means. A ministerial squib was
published purporting to be " a full and true account of
a curious dialogue between one Mr. D'Anvers, and
one Mr. Cut, a great Tobacco merchant," in which it
was affirmed that the excise was only intended for

the protection of the fair trader, as the tobacconist—

> " Had learnt such a knack
> In the case of *drawback*,
> For each pound of tobacco exported,
> That the custom for *two*
> They draw back as their due,
> By which they are bravely supported."

This way of cheating the customs is thus explained
in a note: "At the lowest computation, the duties
upon tobacco annually imported amount to £800,000.
It is not computed by any one acquainted with that
trade, that in fact there is exported from Great Britain
into all foreign ports, near one half of the whole; but
admitting that a half were sent abroad, in that case
there should remain £400,000 per annum to the revenue; but the truth is the whole duties remaining to
the crown, after drawbacks have been allowed, never
amounted to above £160,000. Whence it is plain the
public must have been cheated of £240,000 per annum
by drawbacks only." Walpole was, however, defeated
in his bill, and "the noble stand, or glorious two
hundred and four" who opposed it, were celebrated in
another caricature, where Britons of all grades are
represented dancing round a maypole garnished with
grapes and tobacco leaves. Liberty, in the foreground,
crushes tyranny; while opposite (to quote the descriptive verse):—

> " Two hogsheads on the right stand side by side,
> This with tobacco, that with wine supply'd;
> On these fair *liberty*, divinely bright,
> And *trade*, with florid looks, your eye delight."

The cut here copied, is a copy of their portion of the
picture. The difference between the tobacco and wine
cask, has been carefully noted
by the engraver. A great opponent of the bill, was the tobacconist Ben Bradley, whose portrait was published by Pond,
with the verse beneath :—

  " Behold the man, who, when a gloomy band
    Of vile excisemen threatened all the land,
    Help'd to deliver from their harpy gripe
    The chearfull bottle and the social pipe.
    O rare Ben Bradley ! may for this the
      bowl,
    Still *unexcised*, rejoice thy honest soul !
    May still *the best in Christendom* * for this
    Cleave to thy stopper, and compleat thy
      bliss ! "

Hogarth decorated this plate
with a minute etching, indicative
of unexcised liberty; in which
the British Lion, pipe in mouth,
makes free with Britannia who
also smokes while seated on a hogshead of tobacco.
This design of Hogarth's was adopted on Bradley's
shop-bill, with the inscription beneath " the best in
Christendom without excise." At this period, when
tradesmen vied with each other in expensive signs,
carved or painted, over their doors, they also rivalled

---

   * Bradley used to wrap his tobacco in papers, thus inscribed. The
noble art of puffing has always flourished in trade.

each other in decorated cards and shop-bills, employ-
ing the best available talent for the purpose. Hogarth,
in his early days, was much employed in designing and
engraving these bills, and Ireland has published fac-
similes of several, among the rest that of "Richard
Lee, at ye Golden Tobacco-roll, in Panton Street, near
Leicester fields," which is remarkable for the general
resemblance the design upon it bears to one of the
best pictures executed in after years by the artist; his
Modern Midnight Conversation.

We may here most conveniently introduce a few notices of the old tobacconists, their "manners and customs" in business, and the minor details of their shops.

The *Signs* of tobacconists' shops in the last century,
usually consisted of a large wooden figure of a black
Indian, decorated with a crown of tobacco-leaves, and
"a kilt" of the same material. He was usually placed
at the side of the door, above which hung three rolls of
tobacco, also cut in wood; and they were never absent,
as the sign of the tobacco-shop, however humble its
owner might be, and unable to afford that higher piece
of art, the blackamoor.

A curious tobacconist's sign
is engraved in an amusing little
volume published in 1840; *
consisting of three hands conjoined to one arm. The first
holding snuff on the thumb, the second a pipe,

---

* It is entitled *A Pinch of Snuff*, and was published anonymously.

the third a quid of tobacco; beneath were the lines :—

> " We three are engaged in one cause ;
> I snuffs, I smokes, and I chaws."

The same distich sometimes appeared on painted signs, beneath figures of a Scotchman, a Dutchman, and a Sailor.

Throughout the seventeenth century, the want of a small copper currency was awkwardly felt by traders ; and the difficulty was met by each man striking small coins for his own use, bearing his name, trade, and address upon them, and sometimes an engraved allusion to his business. Until Charles the Second, in 1672, made the issue of such pieces unlawful, and then provided a royal currency in their place, tens of thousands of these coins circulated in every town in the kingdom. They were tacitly received from trader to trader, " for necessary change," as was sometimes expressed upon them. Evelyn notices their popularity in his time ; and that though sometimes restricted to the immediate neighbourhood of the issuer, they served his purpose as an advertisement, as well as a convenience. We select two thus issued by tobacconists in London : The first is a farthing upon which is exhibited three pipes, it was issued by " Alexander Sharp, in Chick Lane " (West Smithfield); the second is a halfpenny made in the form of a heart, and having upon it a tobacco-roll, and the inscription "John Poyntting, in Cloath-fair (Smithfield), his halfpenny, 1667." Both are in the British Museum.*

There is an anecdote related in *Hone's Table Book*, vol. i. p. 384, of a man named Farr, who opened a tobacco-shop on Fish Street Hill, and attracted customers from an old shop opposite, by writing over his door "The best Tobacco *by Farr*." This attracted the sailors, who deserted the other shop, till the owner put up a new sign, inscribed "*Far better* Tobacco, than the best Tobacco *by Farr*." Now this story, absurd as it may appear, is literally true; his shop-cards are still in existence, in which among rich scroll ornaments and emblematic figures, occur the words "The finest tobacco by Farr."

In the early days of tobacco we have seen that the Apothecary was its salesman; after that the tobacconist combined other trades with his own. He sold liquors, as is proved by the engraving from Brathwait's book, on p. 88, and later he dealt in grocery. Thus the shop-bill of Benjamin Parkes at Worcester, (*temp.* Geo. I.) informs us that he "manufactures all sorts of tobaccos and snuffs; likewise sells coffee, teas, chocolate, lump sugars, and hosiery goods, wholesale and retail." London dealers had the same general

---

* In Bushnell's *Catalogue of American Tokens* (New York, 1858), is one struck in condemnation of tobacco. He describes it as having upon the obverse a figure of a boy trampling upon leaves of tobacco; and the words, "I will never use tobacco in any form." The reverse contains the motto: "Tobacco tends to idleness, poverty, strong drink, vice, ill health, insanity, and death." The metal is, very appropriately, *brass*.

trade, one of the best of the same era, Wimble and
Co., of Fenchurch Street, "sell all sorts of snuffs,
tobaccos, teas, flour of mustard, and Cayenne peppers,
wholesale and retail." Many of these shop-bills are
expensively and carefully engraved, and have furnished
us with a few curious cuts for our volume.

Their tobacco, it is to be hoped, was of better quality
than their poetry: here is a sample from a bill of Von
der Heyde in Bermondsey Street, 1760, representing
the dealer offering two boxes:—

> " Here's two full boxes, taste which you think right,
> The one's to smoak, the other's to clear the sight ;
> I do declare they're both the very best ;
> Then pray confess I'm the Tobacconist."

Such rhymes were frequently printed on tobacco-
papers, which occasionally exhibited an enigma, puzzle,
or charade, for the amusement of the customer; a
custom, that can be traced as far back as the middle
of the seventeenth century. In 1748, an American
printed " choice Pennsylvania tobacco-paper," and
turned to that account some papal bulls captured in a
Spanish vessel ; and he declared his willingness to sell
" at a much cheaper rate than they can be purchased
of the French and Spanish priests, and yet will be
warranted to be of the same advantage to the pos-
sessors." This fashion of giving "something literary"
on tobacco-papers, was very customary about twenty
years ago, and embraced a large variety of topics: they
were printed within a " type-border," in the centre of a

piece of paper, large enough to hold the tobacco.   We
here give an example arranged as in the original:—

Best Tobacco.
LONDON.

ANAGRAM.

MORE ! no fool the play and
 Friend, my and money my keep wou'd I
Before, had have I as
 Friend, a and money both I'd If
Fell ; me from quite away
 Friend, my but money, my had I
Well, very me pleas'd which
 Friend, my came money with length at
Not. would I him sue for
 Friend, my and money my lost I
Got, I words but naught and
 Friend, my of money my ask'd I
Therefore ; word his took and
 Friend, my to money my lent I
Store, great set I both by
 Friend, a and money both had I

This not very difficult puzzle may be solved by
beginning at the end of the rhymes, and reading each
line backward, when " the proceeds of much worldly
wisdom " will be the result.   Another exhibits this
riddle :   " O and P ran a race ; Q backed O, knowing
that P would win.   Why was this like going into a
shop and asking for *shag* and getting *short-cut* ?—
Because it was wrong *to back O*."   Here is a typo-
graphical puzzle on another :—

" Th er ei Sal us tInmann och ainc ant Ame,
O, floUd lypu—Bli, Shin ; gh isn ei gH b(ours's Ha)me ¿
O, Nea, Gles' win " Gsimm, or" ralsc ; an da lsfly,
Whil ? stvi rtu Ou sact (Ion sareb) ut Bor nan d—d ie ! "

Which is a moral apophthegm, a little deranged purposely by the printer, and will read thus :—

" There is a lust in man no chain can tame,
Of loudly publishing his neighbours' shame !
On eagles' wings immoral scandals fly,
Whilst virtuous actions are but born and die ! "

Another gives some original laudatory rhymes called the

CONFESSION OF A CIGAR-SMOKER.

I owe to smoking, more or less,
Through life the whole of my success ;
With my cigar I'm sage and wise—
Without, I'm dull as cloudy skies.
When smoking all my ideas soar,
When not, they sink upon the floor.
The greatest men have all been smokers,
And so were all the greatest jokers.
Then ye who'd bid adieu to care,
Come here and smoke it into air !

Many of these papers are " adorned with cuts," that must have done service for very many years. One, engraved about 1780, is copied in next page ; it represents the three modes of using tobacco, by chewing, smoking, and snuffing, sometimes exhibited in painted signs over tobacconists' doors, as already alluded to. These cuts were printed in the centre of various-sized papers, and used to envelope the weed.

Best Tobacco

The sailor's love for tobacco has always been steady and excessive. It is a most important item in navy estimates, and one of the "greatest necessities" in Jack's estimation; but in this love, he is not without rivals on land, for some few would sacrifice their dinner for their pipe, if the two could not be indulged in.

Spence, in his *Parallel between Magliabechi and Hill* (1757),* declares of the latter, who was a poor Buckinghamshire tailor, "that he has past many and many whole days, in this and the former year, without tasting anything but water and tobacco." The sailor's devotion to tobacco, is amusingly illustrated by

* First printed by Walpole, at the Press of Strawberry Hill, and afterwards by Dodsley, in his *Fugitive Pieces*.

the following letter from a little volume, entitled *Nicotiana*, 1834 :—

"Dear Brother Tom; " GRAVESEND, *March* 24, 1813.

"This comes hopein to find you in good health as it leaves me safe anckor'd here yesterday at 4 P.M. arter a pleasant voyage tolerable short and a few squalls.—Dear Tom—hopes to find poor old father stout, and am quite out of pig-tail.—Sights of pig-tail at Gravesend, but unfortinly not fit for a dog to chor. Dear Tom, Captain's boy will bring you this, and put pig-tail in his pocket when bort. Best in London at the Black Boy in 7 diles, where go acks for best pig-tail—pound a pig-tail will do, and am short of shirts. Dear Tom, as for shirts ony took 2 whereof one is quite wored out and tuther most, but don't forget the pig-tail, as I a'n't had a quid to chor never since Thursday. Dear Tom, as for the shirts, your size will do, only longer. I liks um long—get one at present; best at Tower-hill, and cheap, but be particler to go to 7 diles for the pig-tail at the Black Boy, and Dear Tom, acks for pound best pig-tail, and let it be good. Captain's boy will put the pig-tail in his pocket, he likes pig-tail, so ty it up. Dear Tom, shall be up about Monday there or thereabouts, Not so perticuler for the shirt, as the present can be washed, but don't forget the pig-tail without fail, so am your loving brother."

"T. P."

" P. S.—Don't forget the pig-tail."

Scattered in the Magazine literature of the last century, are some good specimens of what lovers of the weed can do in the way of rhyme. One of the most whimsical of these effusions occurs in the Gentleman's Magazine for February 1857, and is as follows :—

CHOOSING A WIFE BY A PIPE OF TOBACCO.

Tube, I love thee as my life ;
By thee I mean to chuse a wife.
Tube, thy *colour* let me find,
In her *skin*, and in her *mind*.
Let her have a *shape* as fine ;
Let her breath be sweet as thine :
Let her, when her lips I kiss,
Burn like thee, to give me bliss :
Let her in some *smoke* or other
All my failings kindly smother.
Often when my thoughts are *low*,
Send them where they *ought to go*.
When to study I incline,
Let her aid be such as thine :
Such as thine her charming pow'r
In the vacant social hour.
Let her live to give delight,
Ever *warm* and ever *bright :*
Let her deeds, when'er she dies,
Mount as incense to the skies.

One of the best and most curious effusions which tobacco smoke has inspired, was the *Pipe of Tobacco* by Isaac Hawkins Brown.* It is a series of six poems on this theme, written—and admirably written—in the styles of six different authors.† With the selection of one

---

* Born 1705, died, 1760.
† They are Cibber (the Laureat), Phillips, Thomson, Young, Pope, and Swift. They may be seen in Ritson's *Anthology*, and Dodsley.

example we will take our leave of the Nicotian Muse;
this one was, however, according to Ritson supplied to
the series by Dr. John Hoadly. It is in imitation of
Ambrose Phillips, himself the great originator of
burlesque in his *Splendid Shilling*, a copy of the style
of Milton. Thus Phillips is supposed to sing :—

> Pretty tube of mighty power !
> Charmer of an idle hour ;
> Object of my hot desire,
> Lip of wax and eye of fire ;
> And thy snowy taper waist,
> With my fingers gently brac'd ;
> And thy lovely swelling crest,
> With my bended stopper prest ;
> And the sweetest bliss of blisses,
> Breathing from thy balmy kisses ;
> Happy thrice and thrice agen—
> Happiest he of happy men !
> Who, when again the night returns,
> When again the taper burns ;
> When again the crickets gay,
> Little crickets full of play ;
> Can afford his tube to feed,
> With the fragrant Indian weed ;
> Pleasure for a nose divine,
> Incense of the god of wine !
> Happy thrice and thrice agen—
> Happiest he of happy men !

Notwithstanding the restrictive policy of the English
Laws to benefit colonial growers, efforts were made to
cultivate it in Great Britain. Prior to the year 1782
it was extensively grown in the vale of York and Rye-
dale in the North Riding of Yorkshire. In the latter
district it did not excite the notice of regal authority,
and it was cured and manufactured by a man who had

formerly been employed upon the tobacco plantations
in America; who not only cured it properly, but gave
it the proper cut, and finally prepared it for the pipe.
But in the vale of York the cultivators met with less
favourable circumstances. Their tobacco was publicly
burned, and themselves severely fined and imprisoned.
Penalties, it was said, were paid to the amount of
£30,000.* In Scotland it was successfully cultivated
during the American war in the neighbourhood of
Kelso, Jedburg, and a few other places, and succeeded
so well that the produce of thirteen acres at Crailing
realised £114 at the low rate of four pence a pound,
which only was allowed to be charged for it to Government, to whom only by Act of parliament were the cultivators allowed to sell the leaf, or they might have
obtained treble the price. The Act of the 19 Geo. 3
permitted Ireland to grow tobacco free of duty for
home consumption; but it was never cultivated there
to any great extent, and in 1828 its cultivation was
entirely prohibited. It was a piece of jocularity among
the lower classes in Ireland, about a century ago when
transportation to " His Majesty's plantations in North
America " was a punishment, to term it " being sent to
His Majesty's tobacco manufactory."

The pipe may be useful to the Sportsman; for Dr.
Forster, in his *Kalendar of the Months*, says when
tobacco smoke hangs lazily in the air, scarcely moving,
and preserving a strong aroma, " it is almost an

---

* Brodigan, *Treatise on the Tobacco Plant.*

infallible method of judging of good scent " for that
day ; as he observed from his own habit of constantly
amusing himself with a pipe early in the morning.
Another mode of using tobacco smoke—to " throw off
the scent " of the worst kind of animal, a cruel Jailor
—occurred in the Paris prisons during the Reign of
Terror, when commissaries searched even there for
plots and implements, depriving the unfortunate of
"a needle to darn hose with." " Two shifty citizens,"
says Carlyle—" determined to defend themselves by
tobacco; they light their pipes to begin smoking.
Thick darkness envelopes them. The red nightcaps
opening the cell, breathe but one mouthful; and burst
forth into chorus of barking and coughing. ' Quoi!
Messieurs,' cry the Citizens, 'You dont smoke? Is
the pipe disagreeable? Est-ce que vous ne fumez
pas ? ' But the red nightcaps have fled, with slight
search : ' Vous n'aimez pas la pipe ? ' cry the Citizens
as their door slams-to again." *

Cowper the Poet entertained a similar dislike to
tobacco ; in one of his letters he descants in the
highest terms of his friend the Rev. Mr. Bull, and
ends his eulogium with these words :—" Such is Mr.
Bull—but—*he smokes tobacco.* Nothing is perfect ! "

His other clerical friend, the Rev. John Newton, did
the same. It may be doubted if the Poet might not
have been improved by taking a pipe as well as a

* Maison d'Arrêt de Port-Libre, par Coittant (Mémoires sur les Prisons,
ii.)—Carlyle's *French Revolution*, vol. iii., p. 336.

sermon from either. "In many cases of religious melancholy, where long prayers are ineffectual, great relief may often be expected from a pipe. The late Rev. Robert Hall of Leicester, a truly pious man, and from his talents an honour to the religious community to which he belonged, found in a pipe a remedy for the melancholy with which he was afflicted in his younger years." *   The celebrated Dr. Parr is the greatest modern example of an excessive smoker. He smoked continually in season and out of it, even in company of ladies, and in their drawing-rooms ; he insisted in the indulgence wherever he went, and generally picked out some young lady to light his pipe after dinner. He sometimes smoked twenty pipes in an evening, and he never wrote well without tobacco ; he describes himself as composing his works "and rolling volcanic fumes of tobacco to the ceiling." Dr. Richardson, in his *Recollections of the last Half-Century*, tells us that Dr. Parr, at the dinner given at Trinity College to the Duke of Gloucester as Chancellor of the University of Cambridge, upon the removal of the cloth, indulged in his eternal pipe, "blowing a cloud into the faces of his neighbours, much to their annoyance, and causing royalty to sneeze by the stimulating stench of mundungus." This is certainly no example for a decent smoker to follow ; but as Parr lived to the ripe age of seventy-eight, it is a pretty good proof that the *immoderate* use of tobacco is not very fatal.

* *A Paper of Tobacco*, p. 74.

Another and a greater philosopher, Thomas Hobbes of Malmesbury, smoked to excess, and he lived to the age of ninety-two. Aubrey tells us that he always took a pipe of tobacco after dinner as a digestive, a custom held to be of " a rare and singular virtue " in his day. Sir Isaac Newton was also a great smoker, and as if to show the fallacy of many objections to tobacco, one being that it injures the teeth, though he lived to a good old age he lost but one tooth.*

Of royal symposiums where the weed was largely indulged in, perhaps the most remarkable was that of the first Frederick of Prussia, whose " Tabaks Collegium " was the cabinet council of the country. It is vividly described by Carlyle, who slyly remarks, in contrasting it with our parliament, " the substitution of tobacco-smoke for Parliamentary eloquence, is by some held to be a great improvement." †

Of literary men Goethe hated tobacco, a very extraordinary thing for a German to do. Heinrich Heine had the same dislike. Of French littérateurs Balzac, Victor Hugo, and Dumas, did not smoke ; but the smokers are Alfred de Musset, Eugène Sue, Merimée, Paul de St. Victor, and Madame Dudevant, better

---

* Tobacco in powder was formerly used as a dentifrice. In *Tobacco, a Poem*, 1669, we are told :

" At Celia's toilet dost thou claim a right—
The nymph so famed for teeth, like ivory white,
For breath more fragrant than the vernal air,
Blest with thy aid, makes every swain despair."

† Carlyle is himself a smoker, a becoming qualification in such a distinguished German scholar.

known by her soubriquet George Sand, who often
indulges in a cigar between the intervals of literary
labour; as the ladies of Spain and Mexico delight in
doing at all other intervals.

Charles Lamb, " the gentle Elia," was once a great
smoker. In a letter to Wordsworth he says : " Tobacco has been my evening comfort and my morning
curse for these five years. I have had it in my head to
write this poem for these two years (*Farewell to
Tobacco* *); but tobacco stood in its own light, when it
gave me headaches † that prevented my singing its
praises." Lamb once, in the height of his smoking
days, was puffing coarsest weed from a long clay pipe
in company with Parr, who was careful in obtaining
finer sorts, and the Doctor in astonishment asked him
how he acquired this " prodigious power ! " Lamb
answered, "by toiling after it, as some men toil after
virtue." Of other literary smokers in England we may
note Sir Walter Scott, who at one time carried the
habit very far. So did the Poet Bloomfield. Campbell,
Moore, and Byron delighted in its temperate enjoyment,
as does our present Laureat Tennyson, who has
echoed its praises with Byron in immortal verse.

---

* This elegant little poem is too well known to require us to do more
than allude to it. It is remarkable for its vituperation as well as its
praise. The former is insincere ; but it is difficult to doubt the sincerity
of such words as
            " For thy sake, tobacco, I
            Would do anything but die."

† Tobacco does not induce headache ; but beer, spirits, and wine will.
Lamb records that he drank freely.

Robert Hall, when at Cambridge, acquired the habit of smoking from being in Parr's company ; and being asked why he had commenced, answered " I am quali- fying myself for the society of a Doctor of Divinity, and this (holding up the pipe) is the test of my admission." When presented with Clarke's pamphlet on *The Use and Abuse of Smoking,** he said, " I can't refute his arguments, and I can't give up smoking."

The " learned in the law " as well as the dignitaries of the Church have smoked.† Lords Eldon and Stowell, and Lord Brougham in early life, indulged thus. The late Duke of Sussex and the Duke of Devonshire gave it aristocratic sanction, and George IV. royally patro- nised it. Thus, from the throne to the cottage the pipe has been a solace ; it has aided soldier and sailor in bearing many a hard privation. Many would rather go without their rations than their pipe, and endure any hardship with it. Here is a modern instance from the late Crimean war :—" A lady told me a story of a man, M——, in her division, which shows how much some of them will venture for a smoke. He had just had one of his toes taken off, under the influence of chloroform. It bled profusely ; and the surgeon, after binding it up, went away, giving her strict injunctions not to allow him to move, and ordered him some medicine, which he would send presently. She was

---

* This was one of the most bitter attacks on the habit, and became the text-book of the oppositionists.

† It is recorded that Bishop Fletcher (of London), died in 1596, "while sitting in his chair taking tobacco."

called away to another patient for a few minutes, and went, leaving M—— with strict orders not to put his foot down. On her return to his bedside, to her astonishment he was gone; and after some searching she discovered him, by the traces of blood on the stairs and corridor, sitting down in the yard, smoking his pipe with the greatest *sang froid*. She spoke to him seriously about disobeying orders and doing himself an injury; but he was perfectly callous on the subject of his toe. She succeeded, however, in working on his feelings at having disfigured the corridor with blood, and he came back, saying, ' Indeed, ma'am, I could not help going to have a pipe, for that was the nastiest stuff I ever got drunk on in my life '—alluding to the taste of the chloroform." *

Powerful as may be the objection made by the " softer sex " to smoking, backed by some few of that other sex " softer " still, who so vapidly denounce what they cannot enjoy; two popular writers of the day are inclined to doubt the success of either assailant. Thackeray, in his *Fitz-Boodle Papers*, jocularly says, ladies cannot expect to succeed in conquering the practice. He asks, " What is this smoking, that it should be considered a crime? I believe in my heart that women are jealous of it, as of a rival. The fact is, that the cigar *is* a rival to the ladies, and their conqueror too. Do you suppose you will conquer? Look over the wide world, and see that your adversary

* *Ismeer, or Smyrna, and the British Hospital in* 1855. By A LADY.

has overcome it. Germany has been puffing for three-score years ; France smokes to a man. Do you think you can keep the enemy out of England? Pshaw! look at his progress. Ask the club-houses. I, for my part, do not despair to see a Bishop lolling out of the Athenæum with a cheroot in his mouth, or, at any rate, a pipe stuck in his shovel hat." And thus Bulwer discourses :—" He who doth not smoke hath either known no great griefs, or refuseth himself the softest consolation next to that which comes from heaven. ' What, softer than woman ? ' whispers the young reader. Young reader, woman teases as well as consoles. Woman makes half the sorrows which she boasts the privilege to soothe. Woman consoles us, it is true, while we are young and handsome ; when we are old and ugly, woman snubs and scolds us. On the whole, then, woman in this scale, the weed in that : Jupiter, hang out thy balance, and weigh them both ; and if thou give the preference to woman, all I can say is, the next time Juno ruffles thee—O Jupiter, try the weed !"

CHAPTER IV.

THE "Fairy pipe" of Ireland may be safely accepted
as the most ancient form of the tobacco-pipe used in
the British Islands. This popular name with the
Irish peasant is sometimes changed for that of "Danes'
pipes." The Scottish peasantry, with the same feeling, term these minute receptacles for tobacco "Elfin
pipes;" and with equal desire to antedate their history, call them also "Celtic pipes." This popular love
for associating old things with the most ancient times,
or with supernatural beings, is equally the result of a
love of the marvellous, inherent in vulgar minds. There
are also persons of poetic temperament, who by no
means deserve to be classed among these; but who,
from their mental conformation, prefer poetic dreams
to prosy realities, and who find no difficulty in believing an assertion that upsets a generally received fact,
in preference to the fact itself if supported by a hundred proofs, any one of which is stronger than those
on which they build their theories. Such persons have

not scrupled to do battle for vulgar tradition ; and
have fought lustily for the Celtic and Danish origin of
tobacco-pipes; and might, with equal consistency, have
asserted their superhuman origin, as the works of the
Irish Fairies. Why make possibility the limit for
ingenious speculation, which has outstripped all probability ? Once " out of bounds," the poetic tendencies of some Irish antiquaries carried them to the
goal of their wishes with a wondrous, and to them, a
satisfactory rapidity. In 1784, a short pipe was
asserted to have been found sticking in the mouth of
the skull of an ancient Milesian, at Bannockstown in
Kildare. A learned paper at once appeared in the
Anthologia Hibernica, parading it as a relic proving
the use of tobacco ages before Ireland was invaded by
the Danes. Fortunately a representation of the pipe
has been preserved, and in structure it is identical
with the Elizabethan pipe. Only those persons who
are conversant with the singular idiosyncrasies of some
writers, can form an idea how far they allow their
imaginations to carry them away, and fortify their
theories by a display of misplaced erudition which is
but a *reductio ad absurdum* after all. It is precisely
thus, with the pipe theory.* There is no doubt that
tobacco-pipes have been found in connection with
early remains in England, Ireland, and Scotland;—
but so have many other things of undoubtedly recent

---

* Dr. Cleland dismisses the subject at once by saying "the absurdities
written about pipes found in Ireland need not be adverted to."

origin. We may not be able to account for the fact, but the fact remains—

> " The thing we know is neither rich nor rare,
> But wonder how the devil it got there."

Tobacco-stoppers of the age of George II. have been found with Roman remains in England, and engraved as Roman bronzes. Copper coins, from Charles II. downwards, have been found at great depths in the ground, and mixed with Roman remains. One mode of accounting for this may be in the facilities afforded for burial by deep fissures in seasons of drought, or holes of rabbits, rats, or moles; another in the results of the constant turning of the earth by the plough; and the fact that Roman antiquities are sometimes a very short distance below the surface; and another, and probably the best solution, that in all excavations the ground from the sides rolls down to the centre, and reveals for the first time, at the bottom of a hole, that which came from the top. We may be certain, that no authenticated discovery of Celtic or Roman antiquities, where the ground has been entirely undisturbed, includes tobacco-pipes.

Sometimes these advocates for ancient smoking prove too much. Thus when the Turkish traveller Eulia Effendi assures us he found a tobacco-pipe imbedded in the wall of an edifice constructed before the birth of Mahomet; his desire to " make assurance doubly sure " by declaring it still retained the smell of tobacco smoke, leads us to conclude with the author of a paper in the *Quarterly Review*, No. XXV., "that smoking, having at first been prohibited to the Mahommedans as an innovation, and contrary to the principle of their law; the pipe had probably been inserted in the wall by some lover of tobacco, in order to furnish an argument for the antiquity of the custom, and therefore of its lawfulness." Attempts of another kind have been unblushingly made. "The *Koran* has been appealed to, and its modern versions even furnish the American name. A traditional prophecy of Mahomet is also quoted by Sale, which, while it contradicts the assumed existence of tobacco in his time, foretells that:—' in the latter days there shall be men bearing the name of Moslem, but not really such, and they shall smoke a certain weed which shall be called tobacco!'* If the prophecy did not bear on the face of it such unmistakeable evidence of being the invention of some Moslem ascetic of later times, it would furnish no bad proof of Mahomet's right to the title of false prophet; for Sale quotes in the same preliminary discourse to his edition of the *Koran*, the Persian proverb, ' Coffee without tobacco is meat without salt.' " Such are the words of Dr. Wilson,† who, with Dr. Bruce, seems at one time to have been somewhat doubtful of the origin of the pipes found in Scotland and England,‡ but which doubts both gentlemen have dispelled by

---

* Sale's *Koran*, 8vo, Lond., 1812, p. 164.

† In his pamphlet already alluded to, p. 34.

‡ See Dr. Bruce's volume, descriptive of the Roman Wall extending from the Tyne to the Solway. 2nd edition, 1853, p. 441.

further investigation. The former considers, and with reason, that the reference to classic authorities, such as Herodotus, Strabo, and Pliny, to prove the antiquity of tobacco-smoking, " is nothing more than a proof of the antiquity of the process of applying the fumes or steam of certain plants for medicinal purposes.* So far, however, is this ancient process from indicating a mode of inhaling herbs in any sense equivalent to the American luxury by which it may be supposed to be superseded, that it is by no means banished, even now, from the practice of ancient female herbalists and domestic mediciners, whom I have known recommend the inhalation of the fumes of various plants, not by means of a tobacco-pipe, but through the spout of a tea-pot ! "

There is also good proof that much of this plant-smoking has been introduced *since* the use of tobacco has made it a necessity with the poor, who have been driven to the usage by economic reasons ; in the same way as *herb-tea* has been employed, when the genuine leaf has been too expensive.

The wild assertions of some Eastern travellers we have already alluded to in p. 43 and its foot-note. Dr. Cleland, in his *Essay on Tobacco*, has disposed of some others,† coming from writers " of so comparatively

---

* Dioscorides says the Greeks smoked the fume of dried leaves of colts-foot through a funnel for difficulty of breathing ; and Pliny notes that the Romans inhaled the same "through a reed, for relief of old coughs."

† This, one of the best works devoted to the history of tobacco, was published in 4to, at Glasgow, 1840.

recent a date as to preclude their evidence being considered in any other point of view than as mere traditions of the people among whom they travelled—a proof obviously of no conceivable weight, from the love of antiquity which is so well-known a mania of the inhabitants of Oriental countries."

E. W. Lane, whose long residence and intimate acquaintance with the Eastern nations makes his opinion of the highest value, gives the weight of his authority to this view, both in his translation of the *Tales of a Thousand and One Nights*, and in his *Manners and Customs of the Modern Egyptians*. In the latter work he says :—

" The most prevalent means, in most Moos'lim countries, of exciting what the Arabs term ' *keyf*,' which I cannot more nearly translate than by the word ' exhilaration,' is tobacco. It appears that tobacco was introduced into Turkey, Arabia, and other countries of the East, soon after the beginning of the seventeenth century of the Christian era : that is, not many years after it had begun to be regularly imported into Western Europe, as an article of commerce, from America. Its lawfulness to the Moos'lim has often been warmly disputed; but is now generally allowed. In the character of the Turks and Arabs who have become addicted to its use, it has induced considerable changes; particularly rendering them more inactive than they were in earlier times ; leading them to waste over the pipe many hours which might be profitably employed; but it has had another and a better effect ;

that of superseding, in a great measure, the use of wine, which, to say the least, is very injurious to the health of the inhabitants of hot climates. In the *Tales of a Thousand and One Nights*, which were written before the introduction of tobacco into the East, and which we may confidently receive as presenting faithful pictures of the state of Arabian manners and customs at the period when they appeared, we have abundant evidence that wine was much more commonly and more openly drunk by Moos'lims of that time than by those of the present day. It may further be remarked, in the way of apology for the pipe, as employed by the Turks and Arabs, that the mild kinds of tobacco generally used by them have a very gentle effect: they calm the nervous system; and, instead of stupifying, sharpen the intellect. The pleasures of Eastern society are certainly much heightened by the pipe; and it affords the peasant a cheap and sober refreshment, and probably often restrains him from less innocent indulgences."

This view of the case has been completely established by the researches of Dr. Mayer of Königsberg, who discovered in the works of an old Hindostanee physician, a passage in which tobacco is distinctly stated to have been introduced into India by the Frank nations in the year 1609.* This completely coincides with the records of early travellers, who state what they saw in the way of punishment awarded

* Vide Geiger's *Handbuch*.

in the East to natives who indulged in the habit, in
opposition to the royal edicts against the Frankish
novelty ; as well as with the records of the nations
themselves.* Some sectarians, of an austere piety,
have denounced the use of tobacco and coffee, as
unlawful to the true believer, and still hold that faith.

To deduce therefore the modern custom of tobacco-
smoking from the ancient herb-smoking is clearly
illogical ;—the one being used in sickness as a remedy,
and in occasions of necessity ; the other by persons
in perfect health, at all times, and as a pleasurable
gratification. No instance can be quoted of the ancient
use of any herb in the modern way tobacco is taken—
that is, as a luxury, and not as a physical necessity or
an intoxicating agent.† How prone some persons are
to jump to conclusions—and more particularly if those
conclusions are startling, and upset all previously
believed historical assertions—must have frequently
astonished or amused all investigators. The conclusions drawn from the finding of tobacco pipes are perhaps the most remarkable of all ; had one been found
on Mount Ararat, it might have been affirmed to have
been smoked by Noah ! ‡

* See chap. iii. p. 121.

† We purposely leave China out of the argument. Tobacco is asserted
to have been anciently smoked there ; but their annals do not give it a
very remote date, and as we are, from the nature of their policy, restricted
from a proper investigation of the truth of much that they assert, we
cannot be sure that some of their remote pretensions are not the results of
the Eastern love of exaggeration. See also p. 213.

‡ This is not too absurd an assumption, and might be fortified by a
reference to the authority of Eastern sages. See p. 43. Such an assertion

Leaving therefore any further consideration of this
question, really not worth the time bestowed upon it,
but rendered necessary by being forced in our way;
we may proceed to examine the pipes themselves and
what they tell us of their own history, and the modes
adopted for the consumption of the herb by the world
of Smokers.

In the collection of the Society of Antiquaries of
Scotland is an old wooden tobacco-pipe, the spur of
which projects considerably, and the bowl has been
much burnt away in smoking.* It is stated to have

been found in Gould Scalp mine, in the ball of New-
lands, the first copper vein discovered in England, and
claimed as a Royal Mine by Queen Elizabeth. It was
worked by Dutch miners in 1582, but tempting as this
specimen might be to found a presumption upon, a
much more recent date than that must be given to the
pipe, for the form of the stem belongs to the middle of
the seventeenth century, as a glance at our engraving,

would be quite in accordance with the usual style adopted ; and quite as
worthy to be received as evidence.

* In the Museum of the Department of Science and Art at Kensington
is a very beautiful pipe, procured from the collection at the Collegia
Romana. It is elaborately carved in box-wood in the style of the Renais-
sance, and is an exquisite example of the applicability of ornamental art to
general uses. It was probably made in the seventeenth century.

p. 63, will show. This may serve as an instance of the mode in which subjects are occasionally "anti-quated." Some other instances will occur in the course of our narrative.

The smaller pipes, termed "fairy-pipes" in Ireland, correspond with the oldest American ones in their capacity for containing tobacco, for it was not the original custom of the Indians to take the weed in large quantities, hence the European imitated his savage instructor. The excessive cost of tobacco when originally imported to Europe, has been adduced as the true reason for this smallness of bowl.* In the middle of the seventeenth century the capacity of the pipe increased with the increased duties on tobacco, and, until the era of Dutch William, kept on enlarging until it appears to have satisfied the most inveterate smoker, though by no means holding so much as the modern Meerschaum.

The late Thomas Crofton Croker, Esq., author of the *Fairy Legends of Ireland*, devoted much attention to this subject, and formed a very large collection of pipes, by which he was enabled to generally *date* them from their form. The very smallest he had obtained

---

* On this subject see p. 70. The quantity a pipe would contain may be gathered from a story told of Dr. Butler, temp. Jas. I., by Sir Theodore Mayerne: "A person applying to him who was tormented with a violent defluxion of his teeth, Butler told him 'a hard knot must be split by a hard wedge,' and directed him to smoke tobacco without intermission till he had consumed an ounce of the herb. The man was accustomed to smoke : he therefore took twenty-five pipes at a sitting, which had the effect of curing him."—Aikin, *Biographical Memoirs of Medicine in Great Britain*, 1780, p. 19.

M

is here engraved.   It was brought up from the bed of
the Thames, near Kingston.   It is formed of very fine
close clay, and there is a polish on the outer surface
as if it was thinly enamelled.   We have depicted it the
full size of the original; it held a very small quantity.
Our second example is somewhat larger, and the dots
within show the capacity of the bowl.   The edge has a

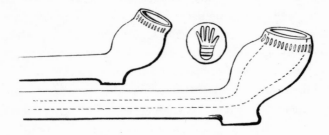

milled or indented pattern round it, the heel is broad
and marked with an open right hand.*   The early
pipes of Ireland are precisely like this, and their
fairy origin has been believed in England as well
as in the more poetic sister-island.   "These pipes are
believed by the peasantry to belong to the Cluricaunes
(a sort of mischievous fairy-demon), and when discovered are broken or otherwise treated with indignity,
as a kind of retort for the tricks which their supposed
owners had played off." †   A quantity of pipes of this

---

* Aubrey describes such pipes as made by one Gauntlet, "who markes
the heele of them with a *gauntlet*, whence they are called *gauntlet-pipes*."

† Croker's *Fairy Legends of Ireland*.   It was made one of the articles
of impeachment against the Earl of Strafford, in 1640, that he had, when
in Ireland, monopolised the trade in tobacco and pipes.

kind were found in the parish of Old Swinford in
Worcestershire, and the country folks there had a
tradition that it was a favourite spot for the resort
of Queen Mab and her court, and that among other
appendages of royalty was a fairy pipe-manufactory, of
which these were the remains. Nearly all of them
had initials or maker's marks on the broad stem, which
was formed to allow the pipe to be laid on the table in
an upright position for the temporary convenience of
the smoker, a fashion now " gone out," but which
might be revived with advantage.

The result of Mr. Croker's unremitting attention to
the age of pipes and their forms, he obligingly communicated to the author of this volume, before his
death; and a selection carefully made from many
hundreds, gave the varieties here engraved, from the

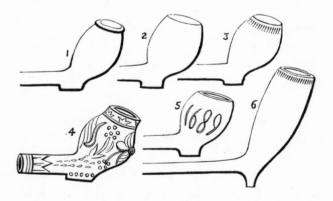

era of Elizabeth to that of William the Third:—Fig 1
was found at Dundanion Castle (between Innishannon
and Bandon), Ireland; it is chiefly remarkable for a

narrow fillet round the mouth of the bowl.   This, and
all the others in this group are engraved exactly one
half the size of the originals.   Fig. 2 was found in the
Roman amphitheatre at Dorchester, and is a good example of the pseudo-Roman pipes; it is nearly identical
with Fig. 3, which was found beneath the foundation
of the house No. 319, Strand, which was considered to
be about two hundred years old, it has a flat spur, and
is capable of resting unsupported.   Fig. 4 was dug
up in 1814, at Thomond Gate Bridge, Limerick, while
sinking a well.   It was the only one ever seen by Mr.
Croker of that early form bearing any ornament, but
that ornament evidently belongs to the latter half of
the seventeenth century, for one with the date 1689
scratched on it, was found at Fulham in 1829, and is
engraved Fig. 5; it was found in conjunction with
many others of the Dutch form, Fig. 6, with very
capacious bowls, and short spurs incapable of being
used for support.

The inferences to be deduced from these facts may
be thus given in extracts from authors describing
such "finds" :—

"On the ridge which commands the fort (Dun-
cannon to Wexford), and on which two martello towers
now stand, tobacco-pipes with exceedingly small bowls,
and which the peasants call *Cromwellian pipes*, are
frequently found.   They plainly indicate the position
occupied by Ireton." *

* Hall's *Ireland*, ii., 143.

" Dr. Wilson communicated a notice of the discovery of various of the small tobacco-pipes popularly termed ' Celtic ' or ' Elfin pipes,' in digging the foundation of a new school-house at Bonnington, in the immediate vicinity of Edinburgh. Along with them were found a quantity of bodles or placks of James VI., which he exhibited with the pipes,* and at the same time expressed his belief that they probably supplied a very trustworthy clue to the date of this somewhat curious class of minor antiquities.† "

Pipes, exactly similar to Figs. 5 and 6, were found at Hoylake, Cheshire, " on the site of the camp where the troops of King William III. were located, previous to their embarkation for Ireland ; and also on the battle-field of the Boyne, at Dundalk, and in other parts of Ireland where the troops were quartered. In the pictures of Francis van Mieris, who flourished during the latter half of the seventeenth century, such pipes are delineated.‡ "

Such are the pipes which have been found in close contiguity with Roman relics, and have occasionally puzzled persons to know the period they should assign

---

* In the *Sussex Archæological Collections*, vol. ii., is an engraving of an andiron or fire-dog, "the upper portion in the costume of temp. Jas. I. (6th of Scotland), holding a tobacco pipe in the right hand, and in the left a jug or tankard. It is of use as an authority for the form of tobacco pipes at that era."

† *Proceedings of the Scottish Antiquaries*, 1853, vol. i., p. 182. Dr. Wilson has since incorporated this in his excellent *Ethnographical Sketch of Pipes and Tobacco*, carrying out and enforcing the idea.

‡ *Proceedings of the Historic Society of Lancashire and Cheshire*, vol. iii.

to their fabrication. Some of the Low Country antiquaries have boldly termed them Roman,* and as the
demand now-a-days for " curiosities " is always met by
a full supply, pipes have been fabricated in red clay to
imitate the so-called Samian pottery, so abundant in
Roman localities, and offered to such " collectors " as
may wish for them.

Ben Jonson notes that the best pipes of his time
were made at Winchester. He has a curious jest on the
form of the old tobacco-pipe, in the comparison whimsically made by *Saviolina*, in his *Every Man out of his
Humour* :—" Your pipe bears the true form of a wood-
cock's head,"—a simile illustrated in Gifford's edition
by an engraving of an old English pipe, which if
reversed, and with a short stem, bears some resemblance to the head of that bird ; which was also the
type of folly !

The early period at which tobacco-pipes were first
manufactured, is established by the fact that the in-
corporation of the craft of tobacco-pipe makers took
place on the fifth of October, 1619. " Their privileges
extending through the cities of London and Westminster, the kingdom of England and dominion of Wales.
They have a Master, four Wardens, and about twenty-
four Assistants. They were first incorporated by King
James in his seventeenth year, confirmed again by

---

* They are so exhibited in the Antwerp Museum, merely from the fact
of being found in Roman localities, regardless of the old Irish postulate :
" though born in a stable a man is no horse."

King Charles I., and lastly on the twenty-ninth of
April in the fifteenth year of King Charles II., in all
the priviliges of their aforesaid char-
ters. The annexed device is given
by this company on all their publick
occasions."* Arms which simply exhibit a tobacco-plant flourishing in
full vigour. Allen in his *History
of London*, describes them more
fully :—"*Argent* on a mount in base
vert, three plants of tobacco, growing and flowering,
all *proper*. Crest.—A Moor, in his dexter hand a
tobacco-pipe, in his sinister a roll of tobacco, all *proper*.
Supporters.—Two young Moors *proper*, wreathed about
the loins with tobacco-leaves *vert*. Motto.—' Let
brotherly love continue.'"

For the introduction of this art the Dutch are
indebted to this country ; in proof of which, Mr.
Hollis, who passed through the Netherlands in 1748,
mentions that, having visited very extensive pipe-
works in Gouda, he was informed by the master of
them, that even to that day their principal working
tools bore English names.† Hentzner, who visited us
in the reign of Elizabeth, was surprised to see the
English " draw the smoke into their mouths (through
pipes made of clay), which they puff out again through
their nostrils, like funnels ; " and Dr. John Neander
says, that the English are to be praised for their mode

* Strype's edition of Stowe, vol. ii., p. 247.
† Marryat's *History of Pottery and Porcelain*, p. 65.

of smoking through fictile tubes, if indeed the habit
was not introduced from that of the savages, for he
also notes that our Captain Greenfield says the Virginians used tubes of clay for smoking. Le Sieur Baill-
lard, in his *Discours du Tabac* (12mo. 1668), says of the
English : " Ces derniers ont inventé les pipes de terre
cuite, qui ont cours aujourd'huy par tout le monde."

In p. 120 of the previous chapter we have noted the
large increase of tobacco-smoking during the Great
Plague of London.* Pepys notes in his curious *Diary*,
another use he made of the herb. He says the 7th
of June, 1665, was "the hottest day that ever I felt in
my life. This day, much against my will, I did in
Drury Lane see two or three houses marked with a
red cross upon the doors, and ' Lord have mercy upon
us ! ' writ there ; which was a sad sight to me, being
the first of the kind that to my remembrance I ever
saw. It put me in an ill conception of myself and my
smell, so that I was forced to buy some roll tobacco,

---

* Dr. Willis, who constantly visited the sick during the Great Plague,
and has left us a treatise upon it, says, p. 18, that the virtue of tobacco as
a preventive was so great, that no tobacconist's houses were infected, "nor
indeed those who smoaked tobacco, especially if they smoaked in a morning,
for the smoak of this plant secures those parts which lie most open (*viz.*
the mouth, nostrils, &c.), and at once intercept and keep the contagion that
floats in the air from the brains, lungs, and stomach. It also stirs the
blood and spirits all over, and makes them shake off any contagion that
may adhere to them." Diemerbroeck, the Dutch physician, in his *Essay
on the Plague*, relates that he smoked for his own preservation whilst he
attended the sick at Nimeguen ; about 10 o'clock in the morning he smoked
a pipe of tobacco, and after dinner two or three more, and the like again
after supper ; and if at any time he found himself affected by the sick
people, he had immediate recourse to his pipe of tobacco, which he always
found an effectual preservative.

to smell to, *and chaw*, which took away my appre-
hension."

The larger number of pipes discovered in and about
London, belong to this era.   Mr. Crofton Croker had
come to similar conclusions, and he says "the reason
why so many of the barrel-shaped pipes (Figs. 3 and 5,
p. 163) are found is obvious. I need hardly say I allude
to the increased use of tobacco as a disinfectant during
the plague years of 1644 and 1666.   Very many such
were found in 1825, at Battle Bridge, London, where
it is traditionally said the persons who died of the
plague were buried."   The places where the Dutch
troops of William were stationed also produce evi-
dences of their occupancy in pipes of the forms here

engraved, and which continued to be a favourite till
the middle of the last century.

Before dismissing the old English pipe, we must
devote a few words to the marks found upon their
bases.   We have given one example of a hand thus
impressed; sometimes a star or other mark is found,
at other times the initials of the maker's name, after

the fashion of the specimens here engraved from pipes
found at Kilmallock, formerly in the collection of Mr.

Croker.   In 1854 there was exhibited at the meeting
of the Archæological Institute at Shrewsbury, part of
a large collection formed by Mr. Thursfield of Broseley
in Shropshire ; the clay of which they were made came
from Shirlett, about two miles from Broseley, where a
large pipe-factory existed.   One of them was particu-

 larly interesting, as it had a very
broad spur, which was stamped
with a hollow square, having
within it, in raised letters, the
name of the maker and the date—
JOHN   LEGG, 1687 ; another
bore the same name and the date
1696.   The clay of which they were formed was very
pure and hard.

Aubrey, writing about 1680, tells us that tobacco-
smokers at first sported silver pipes, "but the ordinary
sort made use of a walnut shell and a straw." The
clay pipe soon became cheap and common. "I have
heard my grandfather say that one pipe was handed
from man to man round the table." This exactly
accords with what the dramatists of the age of Eliza-

beth and James I. describe.* In the reign of William
III., they were occasionally made of iron and brass.†
Mr. Croker had one precisely like the Battle Bridge,
an iron specimen, which was found at Limerick.

The old Dutchmen had an affection for their pipes,
and carried them in wooden cases more or less ornamented. Horace Walpole possessed that which belonged to the famous Admiral Van Tromp, it was
similar in form to that here engraved, which is also

Dutch, formed of mahogany inlaid with brass, and
having the pious inscription "When man has the
right way taken, death has no fears for him." ‡ It
opens with a spring on the heel, having a hinge at the
upper part. The pipe became the mark of a Dutch
engraver, M. Martini, at the commencement of the
seventeenth century; it was placed above the double

* See p. 61.

† The *Albany Journal, U.S.*, in 1858, speaks of the pipe of the famed
Miles Standish, "which came over with him in the Mayflower, and was
smoked by him to the day of his death," as "a little iron affair of about
the size and shape of a common clay pipe."

‡ This love of scriptural allusion is strongly indicative of the Low
Countries, and was perhaps one result of their long religious wars. Drinking cups, beer jugs, pipes, and tobacco boxes, are alike covered with
religious sentences and exhortations.

M of his initials, and is here copied, Fig. 1, from
Heller's *Monogrammen-Lexikon*, published at Bam-
berg in 1831. The company of
goldsmiths of Narbonne, had the
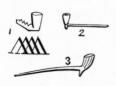
pipe, Fig. 2, for their mark : they
were founded in 1669. In the
Journal of Timothy Burrell, Esq.
(published by the Sussex Archæolo-
gical Society, vol. iii.), we get the form of the tobacco-
pipe of the same era, that gentleman having a curious
habit of marking passages by a drawing of a tobacco-
pipe. This, Fig. 3, occurs to an entry in 1696.

That the short Irish pipe termed the *dudeen*,* and
similar to the *cutty-pipe* † in Scotland, was known
about the same era; and valued for its exhibition of
the prowess of the smoker in darkening it, seems to be
inferred from a passage in one of Radcliffe's *Poems*
(1682), termed a *Call to the Guard*, in which he
describes the soldiers :

> " With pipes black as their mouths,
> And short as their pay."

From a passage in Phillips' *Splendid Shilling*, we
may infer that the Welsh at his era indulged in the
short pipe. His poor author:

> " ———— from tube as black
> As Winter's chimney, or well-polished jet,

---

* "Dudeen," says Croker, "means a little stump of a pipe ;" it is
sometimes not three inches long, and keeps the smoker's nose warm.
† *Cutty* is Scottish for *short*.

Exhales *mundungus*, ill-perfuming smoke ;
Not blacker tube, nor of a shorter size,
Smoaks Cambro-Britain."

The form of pipe which found favour in the eyes of
the smokers of the reign of Anne and George I. may
be seen in our cut on p. 130, or studied in the works
of Hogarth. Ben Bradley, the tobacconist, whose portrait was published in 1737, with the
commendatory verses beneath it, printed
p. 133, is represented holding the
pipe we here engrave. It is of the
genuine Dutch form, with a long straight
stem, tipped with red wax to prevent the
porous clay adhering to the lip. Such
long pipes were reverently termed *alder-*
men in the last age, and irreverently
yards of clay in the present one.*
Pipe-makers seem to have discarded the
long Dutch bowl by the middle of the
eighteenth century, and to have recurred to the older
form ; but adapted it to the increased capacity of the
smoker for quantity of tobacco.

Tobacco-pipes have contributed to amuse non-
smokers, by being subservient to ingenious tricks. We
are told in the *Spectator* of "a tavern-keeper who
amused his company with whistling of different tunes,

---

* Pipes of this kind allow the arm of the smoker to rest with perfect
ease on the arm of his elbow-chair, without lifting the hand to steady the
bowl. The *curved* form of the bowl is worth noting as a very distinct
feature of the older English and Dutch tobacco-pipe.

which he performed by applying the edge of a case-knife to his lips; upon laying down the knife, he took up a pair of clean tobacco-pipes, and after having slid the small ends of them over a table in a most melodious trill, he fetched a tune out of them, whistling to them at the same time in concert. In short the tobacco-pipes became musical pipes in the hands of our virtuoso, who confessed ingenuously, that he broke such quantities of pipes that he almost broke himself, before he brought this piece of music to any tolerable

perfection." Balancing tobacco - pipes was a novel feat introduced for London's amusement: in 1743 a Turk named Mahommed Caratha, performed on the slack-rope at Sadler's Wells, firing pistols from each hand as he stood upon it, and balancing at the same time seven tobacco-pipes on a ring held in his mouth; as shown in our cut, copied from a rare engraving published at the time. He performed for some years, and was succeeded by an Englishman named Maddox, who flourished from 1753 to 1770, balancing the same number of pipes on his chin, "two pipes crossways on a hoop," holding also in his hands a chain and a coach wheel! Powel, the fire-eater, in one of his advertisements (*circa* 1770), notes among his other performances, that " he licks with his naked tongue, red-hot tobacco-pipes flaming with brimstone."

In 1787 John Frederick Bryant, " late tobacco-pipe maker at Bristol," published a few " Verses " to which he appended a memoir of his own vicissitudes " while I went about the country with a hamper of pipes upon my shoulder, in that manner travelling ten, fifteen, and often twenty miles out." Such were the difficulties of a small country trader, half a century ago. In these weary and solitary excursions the poor traveller amused himself with composing his " Verses," and as one of these relates to his own trade, and is probably unique as a specimen of a poem by a pipe-maker, it is here reprinted :—

ON A PIECE OF UNWROUGHT PIPE-CLAY.

Rude mass of earth, from which with moiled hands
　(Compulsive taught) the brittle tubes I form,
　Oft listless, while my vagrant fancy warm
Roves (heedless of necessity's demands)
Amid Parnassian bow'rs, or wishful eyes
　The flight of Genius, while sublime she soars
　Of moral truth in search, or earth explores,
Or sails with science through the starry skies :—
Yet must I own (unsightly clod) thy claim
　To my attention, for thou art my stead,
　When grows importunate the voice of need,
　And in the furnace thy last change I speed :
Ah ! then how eager do I urge the flame,
How anxious watch thee mid that glowing fire,
That threats my eye-balls * with extinction dire !

---

* The last lines allude to the damaging effect produced on the eyes by watching the " burning," or baking the pipes in the kilns. The author notes " the tobacco-pipe trade being greatly on the decline " when he published his book, which was chiefly to aid him in his poverty.

The manufacturers seem to have rested content
with the fabrication of pipes after one fashion for a
very long period. We trace no attempt at fanciful
decoration or quaintness of form until within the
last twenty years. Before that time, the tobacco-pipe
makers only showed their ingenuity in occasionally
twisting their stems into convolutions and knots, such
pipes being hung in tobacconists' windows almost as
signs of their trade. The ingenuity of the French
artisans first exhibited the vast variety of design a
pipe-bowl might display; and the higher artistic taste
of the Germans made their Meerschaums articles of
vertu. But before we take their works into consideration, let us bestow a little thought on the manufacture
of the ordinary English article, which has thus been
excellently described by a writer in *Chambers' Edinburgh Journal*, and to which we add a cut and some
further explanatory details.

The clay from which pipes are manufactured comes
principally from Purbeck, in Dorsetshire, whence it is
transported to all parts of the kingdom. The first
process is the breaking and pounding the clay with a
wooden rammer, and mixing it with water to a consistency similar to that of putty. The clay, at the requisite
consistency, then passes on to a man who pulls, twists,
rolls, thumbs, and kneads it out, with astonishing
celerity, into small separate long-tailed lumps, each
large enough, and to spare, for a single pipe. These
he lays loosely together in a heap, ready for the
moulder. The moulder, a skilled artisan in his way,

dexterously draws the long tail of the lump over a fine
steel-rod which he holds in the left hand; performing
in less than half a minute what seems a miracle of skill,
by embedding the rod in the exact centre of the clay
through the whole length of the pipe. He then lays
the rod in the lower section of the mould, represented
at A in our cut; the upper portion is precisely similar

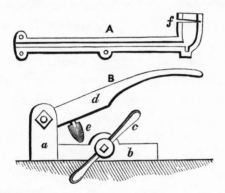

and is shut down upon it, and secured by a projecting
pin in one mould fitting into cavities in the other. It
is then placed in the press B fixed to a bench by a
strong beam *a*, with which is connected an iron plate *b*,
having a screw turned by a handle *c*, which presses
toward it another iron plate; between the two the
mould is placed and squeezed tightly together, the
handle *d* is then brought down upon it, the projecting
rounded cone at *e* entering the mass of clay destined
to form the bowl of the pipe; the clay is thus squeezed
upward, and all that is superfluous is cut away by a
knife, a passage for which is made in the mould at *f;*

and when the mould is opened, the pipe is turned out complete as to form, In this state, the pipes are passed to the trimmer, generally a young lad or a female. The trimmer, with a sharp steel instrument, first pares away the thin protuberances on the stem formed by the junction of the two sections of the mould; then dresses the bowl to a neat shape; then cuts the mouth piece smooth; then draws out the steel-rod and blows down the pipe, to be sure that it has a free passage for the smoke; and, lastly, lays it on the frame to dry, previous to burning in the kiln. A pipe-kiln is more or less capacious, in proportion to the exigencies of the establishment; but an enormous number of pipes may be burned in a comparatively small kiln, as they are ingeniously packed on frames so that little space is lost, and are sufficiently fired in a short time. On inquiry, we are informed that the number of pipes made in an establishment when trade is prosperous and the demand brisk, is about forty-five gross a day; which gives an average of nearly five hundred pipes *per diem* for each of the hands employed. With the exception of a fractional proportion, the whole of them find their way into the tap-rooms and parlours of the publicans and the shops of the tobacconists. When sent to a distance, they are packed as carefully as possible; but the loss consequent on breakage is borne by the consignee, not by the maker. Countless numbers of them are sold in London by pipe-hawkers, who carry them about by hand, and each of whom cultivates a " pipe-walk," or a

connection with publicans and tobacconists, whom he
supplies from year to year. The profit these men
derive from their merchandise is exceedingly small;
but they have an allowance for breakage which, being
a careful race, they contrive to avoid, and thus
increase their percentage.*

The same author observes: The commonest French
pipe is a well-finished article, with a graceful bowl
and a well-proportioned stem; its owner keeps it in a
case, and reveres it for its blackened hue and pungent
odour, and grows attached to it from long use. Numbers of the better class of French pipes are manufactured of porcelain, and some are adorned with
enamelled portraits and beautiful heads, executed in a
style that puts to shame the works of our average
miniature painters. Others are formed of various
kinds of earth or earthy compounds, compressed in
moulds by the potter, and afterwards cut in deeper
relief by hand. Some are made of rare kinds of wood
turned in the lathe or artistically carved, and lined
with clay or earthen bowls to resist the fire. Again,
they are fashioned in elegant shapes from masses of
agate, amber, crystal, carnelian, and ivory, as well as
the various kinds of pure or mixed metals. Pipes

* The price wholesale for these pipes is astonishingly low, about 1s. 4d.
per gross. They are bought retail (allowing a profit to the vendor) at the
rate of four for one penny ! It is the custom to collect the dirty tobacco-
pipes of the *parlour* customers of public-houses, and purify the bowls by
burning in the kilns for the use of the *taproom* customers ; for this a very
small charge is made by the pipe-makers. Poor people frequently clean
a pipe when foul, by thrusting the bowl into the fire until it is red hot.

fashioned of every practicable material, and upon which
unwearied labour and exquisite taste have been bestowed, are to be met with in the stores of the Parisian
dealers; and yet it is a rare thing to see in a
Parisian's mouth anything more costly than the
simple nine-inch pipe of soft porous clay, which, with its
case, fitting it almost as closely as the mould in which
it was pressed, may be bought for twenty-five sous.
The magnificent pipes of the French market are got
up for the delectation of the foreigners with whom
the capital abounds, and for the pipe-collector, a
being who rides a hobby liable to become franticly
extravagant.

An illustrated volume might easily be composed on
the subject of French and German pipes, so extensive
is the variety, and sometimes the beauty, of the form
and design they exhibit.   Ingenuity, so far from
exhausting itself, absolutely seems to revel over the
production of new and uncommon forms.   Not only
are they beautiful in design and lavish in enrichment,
but they occasionally are exceedingly quaint and grotesque; at times they exhibit the features of some
popular personage, at other times they picture some
great event.   Throughout the two last Revolutions in
France, the cheap clay pipe embodied the struggles of
the people for their liberty; honoured those who fell
in its defence, or who triumphed as leaders in the
fray.   One of the best of these designs is exhibited in our cut.   A figure of Liberty has fallen on the
tricolor flag; she holds a wreath of *immortelles* in

her hand, and clasps an urn enwreathed with funereal drapery inscribed *Morte pour la Patrie*. It was executed by Fiolet of St. Omer, one of the best designers

of pipe-bowls. In another we see a Paris *ouvrier en blouse* reposing along the pipe-stem, and pointing to the bowl inscribed *Suffrage universel*.* Two really good designs exhibit French and Italian liberty ; the former

has a noble figure supporting the Victor's wreath in the right hand, and the flag inscribed *Liberté* in the left,

* Dumeril of St. Omer issued a black pipe at this time. On one side of the bowl is the capped flag inscribed *Liberté, Égalité*, 1848. On the other, a barricade, surmounted by cannon, barrels of gunpowder, &c., inscribed *République Française*, 23, 24 *Février*.

beside her stands a lion, and she is supported by the *fasces* of Justice, which form the bowl of the pipe. Italia is in the costume of a Roman warrior, her right hand directs the sword to the neck of the Austrian Eagle, expiring beneath her feet. The papal arms are upon the shield, and the *fasces* again form the bowl.

Cavaignac, Changarnier, and Louis Napoleon have in turn had the honour to exhibit their busts " in little," as pipe-heads. One by Gambier, of Paris, commemorates the establishment of Louis Napoleon's Empire ; a figure of France, robed in an imperial mantle sprinkled with bees, rests her right hand on a shield inscribed *L'Empire c'est la Paix*, the famous enunciation of the new ruler; a sheaf of cereals spring up to support her, and cornucopias pour fruits in abundance at her feet.

Others have been constructed for such as care less for politicians : thus the artists have been supplied with a head of Rubens; the literati, with that of Victor Hugo ; and such as admire the " pastoral simplicity " of the *Régence* may have Corydons and Sylvias in all the glories of straw hats and powdered hair, worthy to have come forth from the atelier of Watteau. A *Vieux Militaire*, with a fiercely cocked hat, ferocious moustache, and love-locks arranged in plats on each side his face (Fig. 1), may gratify the soldier ; while the satirist may be charmed with a grotesque German Professor in his flat university cap, with a profusion of hair, a lengthiness of beard, and a shortness of vision (Fig 2) ; or the medical student may outrage a natural

repugnance by sticking a skull in his mouth (Fig. 3).*
If he chooses to be hard on the Church, a sleek *abbé*
may appear to laugh and talk as his brain seems to
evaporate in smoke; or an old Turk may excogitate
till his turban is on fire. A wreath of glory in the
form of tobacco smoke may encircle the head of some
prima donna, almost as evanescent as the fame or the
flower wreath of the theatre; a bent leg may call forth

remembrances of some beauty of the ballet; a dog's
head, or that of an elephant or camel, will suit the
naturalist. The sportsman may be gratified by the
hound and horn (Fig. 4),† or by the wild boar's head;
or the smoker may again "drink tobacco" from the
jug held in the hand which stretches forth from his
pipe-stem (Fig. 5).

Satan, Sin, and Death have each been typified in

* The eyes are sometimes hollow, and filled with green or red glass,
glaring hideously as the tobacco burns.

† The head of the hound holds the tobacco, the pipe-stem is inserted in
the mouth of the horn, and a small aperture through the dog's nose gives
the necessary draught in smoking.

characteristic heads by the artists of Gambier's manufactory. * The "Prince of Darkness" assumes various
forms, as he seems to be a favourite. Sin appears as a
lady of advanced years, with a tendency to *embonpoint,*
her hair flows into flame, horns bud from her forehead, and her necklace is composed of the skull and
crossbones; the eyes are coated with glossy green
enamel.†

Death we have already seen under one form; but
there is a long pipe, stem and all of clay, where the
vertebræ are elongated down the stem, and the eyes
filled with a mass of glittering green glass; the broken
teeth are covered with white enamel, and when the
skull is browned by use, nothing can be conceived
more ghastly than this pipe. Another, devoted to the
same grizzly subject, is termed the Car of Death; in
which the "King of Terrors" is taking his onward
course in a chariot, whose wheels are winged, the
postilion being a smartly dressed skeleton also.

Satirical pipes have been already alluded to. Gambier
has published an excellent one, in which a solemn old

---

* He has produced the best and the largest works; some of them are
admirably modelled, and deserve preservation as art-manufactures. A head
of Silenus is particularly good. Fiolet of St. Omer is his only legitimate
rival, and he has executed a vast variety of designs, many exceedingly good.
Dumeril, who also has his works at St. Omer, has produced some characteristic things, particularly some cheap pipes in red clay, covered with a
glaze which seems to have been suggested by the old Roman red pottery,
so constantly found wherever that ancient people stationed themselves.

† Enamel glazes of various colours are sparingly introduced in most of
these pipes, a general tinge of brown pervades the clay from the tobacco
oil in smoking, but the part coated with the colours is preserved from its
effects. A white enamel is constantly used for the eyes of these figures.

owl is decorated with the riband and star, and looks
quite as important as any high official need do. Fiolet
has one pipe that might delight Landseer, who sees in
the canine a type of the human countenance (Fig. 1); but
certainly the *Dames de la Halle* would feel no pleasure
if this typification were "translated in the vernacular."
John Bull appears *in propriâ personâ* in one instance,

which we exhibit to our readers (Fig. 2). The beetle-
browed Dutchman (Fig. 3), with his chin thrust into a
wooden shoe, is another queer impersonation; so is
the Jew "bonneted," by having his hat knocked over
his eyes; the frog in the costume of Abd-el-Kader,
kneeling for mercy; the advocate roaring in defence
of a bad cause, &c.

England has occasioned the production of one satirical pipe for sale among ourselves. The late Duke of
Wellington, toward the close of his life, took a strong
dislike to the use of tobacco in the army, and made
some ineffectual attempts to suppress it. Benda, a
wholesale pipe importer in the city, employed Dumeril,
of St. Omer, to commemorate the event, and the

result was the pipe-head we engrave, in which a subaltern, pipe in hand, quietly "takes a sight" at the

great commander, who is caricatured after a fashion
that must have made the work a real pleasure to a
Frenchman.*

Quaint inventions abound in these French clay
pipes.   One is formed like a carrot, the top forming a

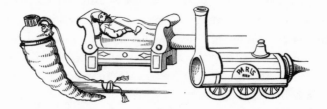

cover; the root of the leaves being a funnel for the
smoke. A cucumber covered with bright green varnish
is a varied example of the powers of adaptation possessed by the artists who design for the French pipe-

* The duke's hat receives the tobacco; the hat of the subaltern, the
pipe-stem.

makers. Another may be considered as a satire on smoking in bed, a frequent practice with smokers on the Continent; another is whimsically formed in the fashion of a steam-engine, the funnel with perfect propriety carrying-off the smoke. A grotesque head, in one instance, lolls out a long red tongue, to attract

a green lizard, which creeps along the stem, unaware of the " ant-eater " trick about to be played on it. In another instance the denizens of the woods are enjoying themselves with a dance under the trees; the Monkey who has seen the World being arrayed in the last French fashion, and capering to the music of the hare seated on the stem, who plays his clarionet with much *gusto.* *

When a nation is so much enraptured by *La Gloire militaire* as France, we must expect to find the popular taste catered for. Hence pipes founded on military subjects abound. *Napoléon le Grand* of course appears, and so do popular commanders. Many

* These figures on the stem are ''contrived a double debt to pay," they are useful as well as ornamental, and afford finger-hold to the smoker, and prevent the pipe from slipping.

of the grades of the army also decorate pipe-heads,
and the caps of the Hussars and Grenadiers have presented a tempting opportunity for being filled with
tobacco. The soldier's drum and trumpet, and the
casque of the cavalry have all been adapted to the
same use. An arm firing a pistol makes an entire
pipe; a mortar does duty for the bowl of another;
while one formed like a cannon, with two bombs

placed upon it, allows the smoker to fill both of them,
and, with one "draw," smoke two pipes at once; a
pertinent illustration "of the economy of time and
labour," so much desired by some philosophers !

The Naturalist may rejoice with a figure of a butter-
fly or a duck, both brilliant in natural colours, or a green
frog from the atelier of Dutel, which is so humourously

expressive that it carries the mind to the marshes of
St. Omer and Holland, and "the most sweet voices"
which greet the stranger from their myriad inhabitants.

A negro carrying a basket affords a very simple and pleasing *motif* for one design from Fiolet's establishment; and appears to have originated in a desire to give the smoker a share in spreading the universal popularity of the American novel by Mrs. Beecher Stowe —*Uncle Tom's Cabin*—whose principal character is thus impersonated at his labour. We end our notice of French clay pipes (of which there are more than 200 varieties), by recording the recent introduction of those which are formed from a warm-tinted modelling clay, and are worked upon by hand, after being roughly turned from the mould; they generally are extremely vigorous and artistic. One representing an old birch broom is so good for its truthful character and fitness of form for the smoker's use, that we engrave it for our final ex- 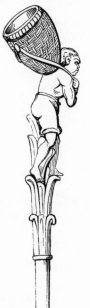 ample. These pipes, though involving manual labour

of a superior kind, are to be purchased for sixpence each in London.*

* It is calculated that more that 5000 persons are employed in the pipe manufacture of France.

English pipe-makers have made few attempts to
rival the artistic powers of the Continental *fabricants;*
but they may be fairly said to beat them in grotesque
design.   Some few years ago the seaport towns exhibited several of these quaint imaginings, which almost
equal German *Diablerie.*

They are covered with varnish colour.   One of these
represents a horrible blue
demon, whose wooden leg
forms the funnel for smoking, the bent leg acts as a
handle for the smoker to
hold the pipe; the same office being performed by the
leg of the other figure, who receives the tobacco in his
wide mouth.   Another English pipe, carefully coloured

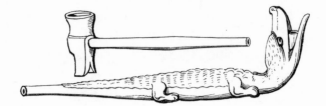

throughout, is made in the form of a crocodile, and
is fit for the mouth of any imitative demon at a masquerade.   Another is ingeniously made in the form of
a hammer, and its perfect truthfulness may rival the
French broom.   Others of English manufacture, but
much ruder in style, have grotesque heads turning at

right angles from elongated bodies, or heads alone, demoniacal or canine, affixed to the tube. They are generally covered with a bright green or yellow-red glaze. The late war originated a pipe formed from a gun, upon the stock is placed a soldier's cap, it is stamped with its designation, "Sebastopol pipe," on one side, and the maker's name, "Longworth, London," on the other. The rarity of an original design among ourselves, has induced the engraving of this specimen.

In Ireland, some few years ago, pipes of a very whimsical form were common. Hone, in his *Table Book*, vol. ii. has engraved two which we here copy.

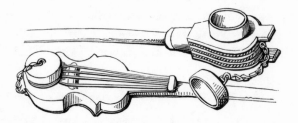

One is shaped like a fiddle; the other, like a pair of bellows. He accompanies his cut with this explanation: "A young friend brings me from Ireland, a couple of pipes in common use among the labouring people in Dublin and Clonmel. Their shape and materials being wholly different from any in England, they are represented in the above engraving. The bowl part, formed of iron, like the socket of a candle-stick, is inserted in a piece of mahogany carved into some whimsical form, and the mahogany is securely bound and ornamented with brass wire; to a small brass chain is attached a tin cover to the bowl. The tube is of dogwood, such as butcher's skewers are made of, or a similar hard wood; and, being moveable, may be taken out for accommodation to the pocket, or renewal at pleasure. These pipes cost sixpence each." * It was in 1828 that Hone published these cuts, but the use of such pipes ceased in Ireland before the first visit there of the author of this work in 1841, to assist in the illustration of Hall's book on Ireland, and this has been an inducement to him to devote so much space in the present work, to the forms assumed by pipes, as they exhibit fashions almost as evanescent as the fumes they emit.

In the Far North tobacco seems naturally welcome. We have already noted the severity with which the

---

* A pipe, evidently of the same workmanship, having an iron bowl inserted in a wooden stock of less artistic workmanship, but also bound  with brass wire, was very care-fully drawn by an Irish artist, under the superintendance of an antiquary, and sent to Mr. Crofton Croker as a great curiosity, "having been found in a Danish Rath (or Hill Fort), in the county of Waterford, Nov. 1839." This was in perfect good faith, with no attempt at imposition; and is a curious proof of the value of this kind of evidence. The note fortunately made by Hone at once clarifies the obscurity; and is also a proof that these pipes were compara-tively unknown out of the Irish capital.

Russian autocrats opposed its introduction. The am-
bassadors of the Duke of Holstein, who visited Moscow
in 1634, relate that they saw eight men and a woman
publicly knouted for selling brandy and tobacco ; the
restriction against tobacco was severe, whipping for
the first and death for the second offence ; those who
used snuff had their nostrils split. It was not till the
close of that century
that restrictions were
removed. But then
the custom became
universal. We give a
cut of the common
Russian pipe. It is
of wood, tipped with
the red copper of the
Ural mountains, and
lined with a thin sheet
of tin, rudely nicked

and turned over at the rim. The stem is of dogwood,
and is tied to the pipe by a rough thong of leather, to
which is affixed a pick, made of copper wire, to clear
out the pipe when necessary. It was taken from the
pocket of a Russian soldier killed at Sebastopol, and
may have cheered a brave poor man, sacrificed with
many other " good men and true," to the selfish
injustice of kings.

Many modes have been adopted to drain the essential oil of tobacco, so that it be not inhaled by the
smoker. Sometimes we find in French pipes a false

bottom of clay, star-shaped, to allow this drainage
through the points; at other times a small receptacle
below the bowl of the pipe receives the oil exuded in
smoking. A glass tube to the pipe has recently been
introduced, which occupies the centre of the stem,
and swells to a considerable size in the midst for
the same purpose. Since then an improvement has
been invented in what is termed the *diaphragm* pipe,
 the enlarged centre of the glass
tube being divided longitudinally
by a glass partition (*a*), against
which the smoke beats, the oil
descends, and the regurgitating smoke is drawn in a
purified state through the smaller tube (*b*), which
projects from the centre of the division. A glass
worm is sometimes made to encircle this central pipe,
and so give condensation to the smoke.

The German pipe is the most important, for the
art-workmanship it occasionally exhibits; and the
Meerschaum is the king of European articles of the
kind. The name, which literally signifies *sea-foam*,
is a simple translation of the term *keff-kill*, applied
to it by the Tartars. It is found in various parts of
Asia Minor. Constantinople is the great mart for its
sale. Its component parts are chiefly silica, magnesia,
carbonic acid, and water; and it occurs chiefly in
veins or lumps among serpentine rocks. When first
obtained it is capable of forming a lather like soap,
and is used by the Tartars for washing linen. Its
name (which the French also adopt in *Ecume de Mer*),

is obtained from its softness, lightness, and purity; but in manufacturing it into good pipes a large proportion of the material is useless, as it is liable to crack when heated, owing to the air it contains. The Turks use it for tobacco pipes, which are made in the same way that pottery is fabricated, and then soaked or boiled in tallow or wax; it is considered the best material for pipes, as it heats slowly, and is capable of great absorption; and a smoker therefore darkens his *meerschaum* with the essential oil of

tobacco as he smokes, until it reaches a rich deep brown tint; well-coloured pipes are consequently treasured as triumphs of smoking feats. The care and devotion requisite to colour a pipe properly, assumes the character of an "amiable weakness" among tobacco-lovers, but might excite the worst feelings of tobacco-haters. The pipe is carefully swathed in folds of flannel, that the line of mark between the tints of yellow and brown be well-defined, and the perseverance of many months is devoted to obtaining the rich tint so much prized by connoisseurs. There is a legend of one who determined to have a perfect meerschaum,

o 2

and it must be understood that perfection cannot be attained if the pipe once lighted be allowed to cool; so an arrangement was made that it should pass from mouth to mouth of a regiment of soldiers, the owner of the pipe paying the bill. After seven months a most perfect pipe was handed to the "fortunate" proprietor, with a bill for more than one hundred pounds sterling, which had been the cost of the tobacco sacrificed in the feat.* Meerschaums are frequently mounted in silver, and have sometimes been decorated with jewels, so that their cost has been excessive. They are generally enriched with ornaments in high relief, executed with much beauty, and embracing a vast variety of design. The care with which this material may be moulded and fashioned by the artist (for such he is), who decorates the bowl, allows the greatest ingenuity and elaboration of design to be exhibited in this branch of art-manufacture. Most pipe-sellers and tobacconists can exhibit specimens which are perfect miracles of patience and labour, and are worth forty or fifty pounds each. They are generally enshrined in velvet, and shown like the jewels of a Marchioness.

Dr. Dibdin, in his *Bibliographical Tour in France and Germany*, speaks of Vienna as a city characterised by a love of smoking—" a good Austrian thinks he can never pay too much for a good pipe," and he instances

---

* This is an "extreme case," but many tobacconists are conversant with customers willing to pay for a due amount of smoking in new pipes.

a gentleman he met " who drew forth from his pocket
a short pipe which screwed together in three divisions,
and of which the upper part of the bowl—made in the
fashion of a blackamoor's head—near the aperture
was composed of diamonds of great lustre and value.
Upon inquiry I found that this pipe was worth about
£1000 of our money."

Schwind of Vienna, an artist who received much
praise from Goethe for his powers of fanciful invention,
etched a series of small plates, designs for pipes of
this class,* two of which we here copy. The first is

a winter scene, and the time may be evening, when, the
day's labour over, the farm servants sleep on the bench
which surrounds the large porcelain stove; and the
aged boor lights his pipe, and dozes beside the mistress
of the mansion, who also nods over her knitting. The
icicles hang from the roof, and a figure of winter
wrapped in a capacious mantle, floats gloomily below,

* They are published in the *Almanach von Radierungen*, Zurich, 1844,
but they are rarely to be met with now upon the Continent, though highly
prized by collectors for their great merit.

as a support to the whole. The second is a still more
ingenious design, admirably adapted to its purpose,
without the least violation of natural arrangement.
Two monks in a railed garden, well stocked with
cabbages, are employed in their sacred duties. The
one reads in the sunshine ; the other enters the little
chapel constructed principally from the stems of trees.
The deep roof forms a capital cover for the pipe,
beneath the eaves is a pigeon house ; the whole scene
is a pleasant picture of seclusion, well fitted to the
contemplation of the thoughtful smoker—and few
smokers are other than thoughtful men.

    " The Germans have perhaps experimented more
profoundly in pipes than any other European people.
They long used a beautiful pipe, carved by the herds-
men and peasants of the Black Forest from the close-
grained and gnarled root of the dwarf-oak. The wood
is hard enough to resist the action of the fire, becoming but slightly charred by years of use. The carvings
represented sylvan scenes—boar-hunts, rencontres with
wolves, sleigh-driving, fowling, and ·the exploits of
robbers. Not unfrequently the subject was an illustration of ancient German literature, as a scene from the
story of Reynard the Fox—or of the works of Goethe
or Schiller, in which Karl, or Faust, or the Satanic
leer of Mephistopheles, was sure to figure." [*]

    Wooden pipes of this kind have been introduced in
England ; and pipes made of briar root are now
common in our shops, but expensive, the bowls costing

    [*] *Chambers' Edinburgh Journal.*

about three shillings each. The Potato-pipe has also been largely imported, and first became known here by a notice in that amusing little book, *The Log of the Water Lily*, whose crew first saw it on the banks of the Maine: "while here, a native addressed us, who was smoking a very singular looking kind of pipe (we saw many of them afterwards), which is said to be made of potato; but whatever they may be made of, their properties are peculiar: when new they look like china, but when smoked they rapidly colour in wavy lines all round, and present an appearance like the landscape bottles of Alum-bay sand."

The ordinary German pipe of porcelain consists of a double bowl, the upper one containing the tobacco,

which fits into a spout or socket, and allows the oil to drain into the lower bowl, which is generally held in the hand of the smoker; the tube of wood, usually formed of cherry-tree,* is easily moved, by which it

---

* This custom of using some odorous wood for the stem is of Eastern origin; it is noted by Baillard, in 1668, as used "to add to the vapour a particular virtue." A flavour like that of the cherry kernel is given by this means to the tobacco-smoke.

may be cleaned. These bowls are sometimes very beautifully painted, and a dealer's stock exhibits a vast variety of subjects, sacred and profane, religious and historic, varying in price according to quality of workmanship. They are painted by the artists who are employed in china factories, and are afterwards baked in the same way as the painted porcelain for the table.* This kind of pipe is similar to the Dutch one, which is known by its long straight stem; a qualification always considered a necessary requisite by the Dutchman, and adopted in the common clay pipe; it saves him all

trouble in holding it seated in his chair; and our cut, copied from the picture of a Dutch inn, showing one of the windows, happily occupied by a traveller in repose, will testify to the lazy convenience thereof. It is the custom in some public gardens to insist on the bowl of the pipe being covered to prevent accidents from the fall of lighted tobacco ash,† and these coverings are of perforated metal in a gentleman's pipe, or a wire lattice in that of the peasant. In that model village Broeck, near Amsterdam, celebrated

---

* A vast variety of subjects is chosen for the decoration of such pipes ; from the freest illustration of amatory lyrics to the most spiritual works of Raphael. Hood has noted of the Continental galleries, "instead of a catalogue *raisonnée*, you may go to any pipe shop to know which are the best, or at any rate the most popular pictures, by the miniature copies on the bowls."

† A Hungarian village, not far from Vienna, was almost entirely consumed a few years ago by such an accident.

even in Holland for its cleanliness, a public notice is affixed to the bridges which lead across the
canals to it, requesting all visitors to prevent the fall
of tobacco-ashes on the gravel or grass; and not to
knock out their pipes anywhere within bounds of this
Dutch Paradise. In Amsterdam the managers of the
"people's theatre" are not so particular, but allow
smoking in pit and boxes; and the spectator may see
the tragic or comic scenes of his native poets, through
the fumes of a hundred pipes. The railway trains are
all fitted with conveniences for smoking : and small
trays to receive the ash of pipe or cigar are fitted to the
elbow of each seat. It is the land of smoke. To use
the words of Washington Irving, " the pipe is never
from the mouth of the true-born Nederlander. It is
his occupation in solitude, the relaxation of his gayer
hours—his counsellor, his consoler, his joy, his pride;
in a word, he seems to think and breathe through his
pipe."

We engrave a pleasing specimen of
a German pipe, in coloured porcelain, representing a dog begging; his
body forms a capacious receptacle for
tobacco, the collar round his neck
opens with a spring, to allow the pipe
to be filled; when lighted it is again
closed, and the smoke finds vent at
each angle of the dog's mouth. The
scroll upon which he is seated is hollow, and forms a
capacious drain for the oil condensed in smoking; it is

gaily coloured in green and gold. A rim of metal with
a loop, allows a silk cord to secure it to the stem.

In the pages of Irving's *Knickerbocker*, and Hood's
Up the Rhine, are many humorous notes of the smoke-
loving Hollanders and Germans. They are generally
looked upon as pleasant exaggerations; though they
are solemn facts. So necessary is the pipe, that Hood
says " I should be loth to trust a sentimental Prussian
with himself, with his pipe out, and an empty tobacco-
bag ;" and he adds, " I can quite believe the story of a
Prussian doctor, who recommended to a consumptive
countryman to smoke Virginia tobacco, just as an
English Physician in the like case, would advise a
change of air." There is a sentimentalism in the pipe
also, and Schwind's etchings already alluded to, depict
many " touching scenes," with pipe and cigar ; such as
the exchange of each made by parting friends ; the
associations connected with an old pipe, &c. He has
also depicted the young Fraulein busily employed in
embroidering a tobacco bag for her lover, a very common gift of affection from ladies, who are as " well
seasoned " to tobacco in Germany as Hood has assured
us that they are, in the capital tale he narrates on that
subject in the book just quoted.

Noel Humphreys' clever descriptive letter-press to
Cook's *Views in Rome* contains an amusing analysation
of the German smokers among the artists there, " and
their never idle pipe, which is the medium through
which a German introduces the external air to his
breathing apparatus." At the Cafe Greco, the celebra-

ted rendezvous for artists of all countries in the Via Condotti, he says: " The Germans say little, but are attentive observers, and signify their assent or dissent, or doubt by a puff; they have the puff acquiescent, the puff dissentient, and the puff doubtful. The puff acquiescent is given downwards, from a small round aperture formed in the centre of the lips accompanied by a slight inclination of the head forward; the puff dissentient on the contrary, is given upward; the body thrown slightly back, the chest expanded, and the column of smoke broader and somewhat more vehement. For the puff doubtful, the head is slightly inclined toward the right shoulder, and from the left corner of the mouth curls gently upwards, as fine as a cobweb, this dubious whiff." He concludes that the character of a German may be understood from his mode of smoking, as well as by his phrenological development.

One of the popular songs, the *Volks-Lieder*, of Germany, is devoted to the praises of the pipe in the following strain:—

> When my pipe burns bright and clear,
> The gods I need not envy here;
> And as the smoke fades in the wind,
> Our fleeting life it brings to mind.
>
> Noble weed ! that comforts life,
> And art with calmest pleasures rife;
> Heaven grant thee sunshine and warm rain,
> And to thy planter health and gain.
>
> Through thee, friend of my solitude,
> With hope and patience I'm endued,
> Deep sinks thy power within my heart,
> And cares and sorrows all depart.

Then let non-smokers rail for ever ;
Shall their hard words true friends dissever ?
Pleasure's too rare to cast away
My pipe, for what the railers say !

When love grows cool, thy fire still warms me.
When friends are fled, thy presence charms me ;
If thou art full, though purse be bare,
I smoke, and cast away all care !

The Persians speedily invented the luxurious mode
of drawing the tobacco-smoke through water, and so

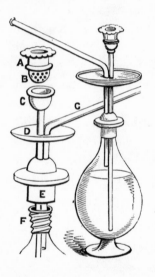

cooling it, before it was inhaled.   It is to smoking what
ice is to Champagne.   Neander in his *Tabacologia* (1622)
engraves two specimens of
these pipes, one of which we
copy. The tubes, he says, are
made of gold or silver for
the rich, and of ordinary
metal for the poor.   The tobacco is burned in the cup A;
the smoke drawn through the
perforations at B ; the cup is
fitted in another at C, to which
is attached a hollow tube
which descends to the bottom of the glass vase ; a broad
saucer, D, prevents ashes or sparks falling on carpets or
the floor ; E is the cap which fits over the mouth of the
glass, and is held firm by a screw F. The pipe G is used
for inhalation ; it does not quite touch the water, and
as it is used it produces a vacuum, which induces the

smoke to rise through the water, and find its way
through the other pipe to the mouth.

The luxuriousness of Eastern taste has far outshone
all other nations in the costly character of the pipes
used by the nobles there. The hookah is capable of
more lavish outlay than the Viennese meerschaum,
and usually receives it. There is no such costly and
elaborate mode of enjoying the weed as this. Taking
a pipe with the Grand Turk is a truly regal solemnity.

The hookah is a ponderous piece of machinery, and it
owns proper attendants sacred to its necessities; their
business being to bear the pipe wherever it may
be required, and all the articles used therewith by
the smoker. The receptacle for the water is usually
formed of glass richly cut, or engraved and gilt, sometimes of the precious metals, decorated with enamels.

The tobacco is lighted in a receptacle at the summit
of the tube, generally formed of gold or silver, and
often studded with precious stones ; and the smoke is
drawn into the water by means of the long smoking
tube, which is made of leather, covered with velvet,
and enriched with threads of gold and silver wire.
These tubes vary in length from five to ten yards, and
the hookah is sometimes borne behind a nobleman on
horseback, who can by this means continue to enjoy
the luxury.* A considerable exertion of lung is requisite to draw the smoke through the water ; and the
use of the hookah is said to have induced consumptive
tendencies in some persons. The clay pipe used by
the lower orders is formed of a deep red earth, decorated with indented ornament produced from a mould,
and sparingly decorated with rude gilding. The long

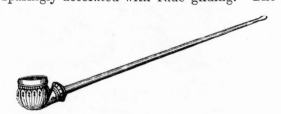

straight stem is made from a branch of jasmine, cherry-
tree, or maple; it is long enough to allow the bowl to
rest on the floor when a Turk seats himself.

* The construction of this instrument is elaborately described in *Du
Royaume de Siam, par Mons. De La Louvere*, Envoy from Louis XIV. to
the King of Siam, in 1687 and 1688, who saw it in use at the court of that
king, and seems to have been much impressed with its novelty and
splendour. He describes them as provided with many pipes, through which
persons might smoke in company from one hookah.

The tobacco smoked in Turkey is of a light kind, and therefore allows a continuous inhalation with an impunity not accorded to our stronger sort. So completely have the Turks become identified with smoking, that one cannot imagine how they existed before tobacco was introduced. That quaint illustrator of books, Gustave Doré of Paris, in his pictorial *History of Russia,** has represented every Turk  with a pipe in his mouth, whatever his occupation; and he has reached the highest point of burlesque in depicting the Moslem nurse with a baby provided with a long pipe.

We engrave two specimens of modern Egyptian pipes, made of a peculiarly fine clay, of a delicate red

tint; and with a surface as smooth and polished as agate. These pipes are made at Osioot on the Nile, and sent thence to Cairo; whence they are afterwards exported in large quantities. The smallest is the new-fashioned style. The larger with the broad base is the old style. They are very cheap. The best kind

* *Histoire de la Sainte Russie*, Paris, 1854. A severe satire on Russia in past and present time, produced at the commencement of the last war in the East.

of pipe-bowl is made there, but other inferior factories
are established at Keneh and Assoum.   Lane, in his
Modern Egyptians, describes with his usual accuracy
the smoking practices of that people.   He says :—

"The pipe and the cup of coffee are enjoyed by almost
all persons who can afford such luxuries, very early in
the morning, and oftentimes during the day.   There
are many men who are scarcely ever seen without a
pipe either in their hand or carried behind them by a
servant.   The smoker keeps his tobacco for daily use
in a purse or bag made of shawl-stuff, or silk, or
velvet, which is often accompanied with a small pouch
containing a flint and steel, and some agaric tinder,
and is usually crammed into his bosom.

"The pipe (which is called by many names, as *shib'-
ook*,* *'oo'd*, &c.) is generally between four and five feet
long: some pipes are shorter, and some are of greater
length.   The most common kind used in Egypt is
made of a sort of wood called *gur'mush'uck*.†   The
greater part of the stick (from the mouth-piece to
about three quarters of its length) is covered with silk,
which is confined at each extremity by gold thread,
often intertwined with coloured silks, or by a tube of
gilt silver ; and at the lower extremity of the covering
is a tassel of silk.   The covering was originally designed to be moistened with water, in order to cool the
pipe, and consequently the smoke, by evaporation :
but this is only done when the pipe is old, or not

---

* From the Turkish *chiboock'*.
† I believe it is maple.

handsome. Cherry-stick pipes, which are never covered, are also used by many persons, particularly in the winter. In summer, the smoke is not so cool from the cherry-stick pipe as from the kind before mentioned. The bowl (called *hhag'ar*) is of baked earth, coloured red or brown.* The mouth-piece (*foom'*, or *turkee'beh*) is composed of two pieces or more of opaque, light-coloured amber, interjoined by ornaments of enamelled gold, agate, jasper, carnelian or some other precious substance. It is the most costly part of the pipe : the price of one of the kind most generally used by persons of the middle order is about from one to three pounds sterling. A wooden tube passes through it. This is often changed, as it soon becomes foul from the oil of the tobacco. The pipe also requires to be cleaned very often, which is done with tow, by means of a long wire. Many poor men in Cairo gain their livelihood by going about to clean pipes.

" The tobacco smoked by persons of the higher orders, and some others, in Egypt, is of a very mild and delicious flavour. It is mostly from the neighbourhood of El-La'dickee'yeh, in Syria. The best kind is the 'mountain tobacco' (*dookh'kha'n geb'elee*). A stronger kind, which takes its name from the town of Soo'r (*dookh'kha'n Soo'ree*), sometimes mixed with geb'elee, is used by most persons of the middle orders.

---

* To preserve the matting or carpet from injury, a small brass tray is often placed beneath the bowl ; and a small tray of wood is made use of to receive the ashes of the tobacco.

P

In smoking, the people of Egypt and of other countries
of the East draw in their breath freely; so that much
of the smoke descends into the lungs; and the terms
which they use to express 'smoking tobacco' signify
'*drinking* smoke,' or '*drinking* tobacco:' for the
same word signifies both 'smoke' and 'tobacco.'
Few of them spit while smoking: I have very seldom
seen any do so.

"Some of the Egyptians use the Persian pipe, in
which the smoke passes through water. The pipe of
this kind most commonly used by persons of the
higher classes is called *na'rgee'leh*, because the vessel
that contains the water is a cocoa-nut, of which '*na'r-
gee'leh*' is an Arabic name. Another kind, which has
a glass vase, is called *shee'sheh*.* Each has a very
long, flexible tube. A particular kind of tobacco,
called *toomba'k*, from Persia, is used in the water-pipe :
it is first washed several times, and put into the pipe-
bowl while damp; and two or three pieces of live
charcoal are placed on the top. Its flavour is mild
and very agreeable ; but the strong inhalation necessary in this mode of smoking is injurious to persons of
delicate lungs.† In using the Persian pipe, the person
as freely draws the smoke into his lungs as he would
inhale pure air. The great prevalence of liver-com-
plaints in Arabia is attributed to the general use of

---

* A Persian word, signifying "glass."
† It is, however, often recommended in the case of a cough. One of my
friends, the most celebrated of the poets of Cairo, who is much troubled by
asthma, uses the nárgeéleh almost incessantly from morning till night.

the na'rgee'leh ; and many persons in Egypt suffer severely from the same cause. A kind of pipe, called *go'zeh*,* which is similar to the na'rgee'leh, excepting that it has a short cane tube, instead of the snake (or flexible one), and no stand, is used by men of the lowest class, for smoking both the toomba'k and the intoxicating *hhashee'sh*, or hemp."

The ruder smoking luxuries of the South Africans in humble imitation of this, have been thus amusingly described :—

"A party of *headmen* and older warriors, seated cross-legged in their tents, ceremoniously smoked the *daghapipe*, a kind of hookah, made of bullock's horn, its downward point filled with water, and a reed stem let into the side, surmounted by a rough bowl of stone, which is filled with the *dagha*, a species of hemp, very nearly, if not the same, as the Indian *bang*. Each individual receives it in turn, opens his jaws to their full extent, and placing his lips to the wide mouth of the horn, takes a few pulls and passes it on. Retaining the last draught of smoke in his mouth, which he fills with a decoction of bark and water from a calabash, he squirts it on the ground by his side through a long ornamented tube in his left hand, performing thereon, by the aid of a reserved portion of the liquid, a sort of boatswain's whistle, complacently regarding the soap-like bubbles, the joint production of himself and neighbour. It appeared to be a sign of special

---

* " Gózeh " is the most common name.

friendliness and kindly feeling to squirt into the same hole. "*

Tobacco is extensively used by the Chinese; the pipe resembles the Turkish pipe, having a straight stem from three to five feet in length; the bowl holds but a very small quantity of tobacco. To the stem of

the pipe is sometimes attached tassels, and silken pendent ornaments. The cut here given exhibits one of these pipes (Fig. 1). The stem is usually made of bamboo; and as they are in constant demand by both sexes, the pipe-seller may be seen with long bundles of pipes tucked

under the arm, or held in the hand, in all the " celestial " cities. Ladies and gentlemen wear at the girdles pouches for tobacco, embroidered with all that beauty and brilliancy of effect for which the silk-workers are deservedly celebrated. Fig. 2 represents another kind of Chinese pipe, made of brass, and constructed on the principle of the hookah, described p. 205, and the large trumpet-shaped receptacle is filled with water; above is the cup for tobacco; it is provided with a base to stand upon a table, and the smoke is drawn through water; only a few whiffs are taken at a

* *Campaigning in Kaffir Land.* By Capt. R. W. King, 74th Highlanders, 1825.

time, the tobacco used being cut into very fine shreds, and sometimes supplied by a servant at every inhalation. The Chinese have a tradition that tobacco was introduced with the Yuen dynasty, A. D. 1300. But most things connected with China are difficult of substantiation, and ask for a large amount of faith.* The only country of the Indian Archipelago, in the annals of which any direct mention is made of the date in which tobacco was first introduced, is Java. This refers to the year 1601, or one hundred and eighteen years after the discovery of America, and ninety years after the first appearance of the Portuguese in the waters of the Archipelago. It was therefore most probably introduced through them to the Chinese.

We conclude our specimens with a Japanese pipe of silver, inlaid with flowers and insects in enamelled

copper; the central portion is formed of cane, for convenience of holding.

Cigars are of comparatively recent use in England. Heavy duties, and absolute prohibition, helped to keep a knowledge of cigars out of the country. America and Spain indulge freely in their use: in the former country leaves of pure tobacco are rolled into the

---

* It is asserted by some writers that the plant anciently smoked by the Chinese was not tobacco, but a different herb, smoked in a similar way, and that they were led to the substitution of tobacco by the example of the Europeans.

proper form; but in Spain " the people generally
make their cigars at the time they smoke, by wrap-
ping up some tobacco in thin paper, but the inner
leaf of the Indian corn is preferred."* Cigarettes
are much indulged in by ladies of South America and
Spain.

A reference to p. 16 of the present volume, will
show that this mode of taking tobacco is derived
from the aborigines of America. The cigar, though
more delicately manufactured, is essentially the same
as smoked by the Red Man when first visited by
Columbus. We may here describe an Indian mode of
tobacco-taking, not yet given in this volume, but which
is evidently the origin of the cigar. It is told by
Lionel Wafer, in his account of his *Travels in the
Isthmus of Darien* in 1699. He says that when the
tobacco-leaves are properly dried and cured, the natives
"laying two or three leaves upon one another, they roll
up all together sideways into a long roll, yet leaving a
little hollow. Round this they roll other leaves one
after another, in the same manner, but close and hard,
till the roll is as big as one's wrist, and two or three
feet in length.

" Their way of smoking when they are in company
together is thus : A boy lights one end of a roll, and
burns it to a coal, wetting the part next it to keep it
from wasting too fast. The end so lighted he puts into
his mouth, and blows the smoke through the whole
length of the roll into the face of every one of the

† Inglis's *Rambles in the Footsteps of Don Quixote*, p. 67.

company or council, though there be two or three
hundred of them. Then they, sitting in their usual
posture upon forms, make with their hands held together, a kind of funnel round their mouths and noses;
into this they receive the smoke as it is blown upon
them, snuffing it up greedily and strongly, as long as
ever they are able to hold their breath, and seeming to
bless themselves, as it were, with the refreshment it
gives them."

Lieutenant Page, who commanded the American
expedition to La Plata, speaks of the universal custom
of smoking in Paraguay and inviting visitors to join.
The servants, as a matter of routine, bring in "a small
brass vessel, containing a few coals of fire, and a plate
of cigars. This last hospitality is offered in every
house, however humble its pretensions in other
respects; and all men, women, and children—delicate
refined girls, and young masters who would not with
us be promoted to the dignity of pantaloons—smoke
with a gravity and *gústo* that is irresistibly ludicrous
to a foreigner. My son sometimes accompanied me
in these visits, and was always greatly embarrassed by
the pressing offer of cigars. I made his excuse by
saying 'Smoking is a practice we consider injurious
to children.' 'Si, Señor,' the Paraguayan would
reply, 'with all other tobacco, but not with that of
Paraguay.'" With both sexes tobacco is a constant
passion. At all hours, and in all places, smoking goes
on—in the office, the drawing-room, at the dinner-
table, and even at balls and theatres. On the subject of

ladies smoking, Stephens, in his *Incidents of Travel in
Central America*, says : " I am sorry to say that,
generally, the ladies of Central America, not excepting
Guatemala, smoke — married ladies, *puros*, or all
tobacco ; and unmarried, cigars, or tobacco wrapped
in paper or straw. Every gentleman carries in his
pocket a silver case, with a long string of cotton, steel,
and flint, and one of the offices of gallantry is to strike
a light ; by doing it well, he may kindle a flame in a
lady's heart ; at all events, to do it bunglingly would
be ill bred. I will not express my sentiments on
smoking as a custom for the sex. I have recollections
of beauteous lips profaned. Nevertheless, even in this
I have seen a lady show her prettiness and refinement,
barely touching the straw with her lips, as it were
kissing it gently and taking it away. When a gentleman asks a lady for a light, she always removes the
cigar from her lips."

The *puros* mentioned is, as its name implies, a cigar
entirely formed of the tobacco leaf. The *papelotos* is
wrapped in paper, and sometimes in the thin dry leaf
of maize. The modern Spaniards are quite as fond
of cigars, and in the *Album d'un Soldat pendant la
Campagne d'Espagne en* 1823 (Paris, 1829), is an
amusing picture of a ball-room scene at Ecisa, in
which a fat Spanish countess is performing a fandango
while she smokes her cigar, of which she is reported to
have consumed several during the evening.

The Spaniards have a proverb' to this effect :
" A paper cigarette, a glass of fresh water, and the

kiss of a pretty girl, will sustain a man for a day without eating." So constant is the cigar in Spain that it has banished the pipe from genteel society. Muleteers and persons of that class occasionally indulge in a short pipe; but it is seldom used even by the lower orders.

Cigars are classified into *white* (Tabaco Blanco), made from the Havanna and Virginia leaf; and *black* (Tobaco Negro), made from Brazilian tobacco. The paper of which cigarettes are made is of a peculiar structure, porous like India paper, and smouldering without smoke. The best is made at Valencia, and is sold for the use of such persons as may wish to cut up their own tobacco and form cigarettes, in small books, bound in a coloured or plain· cover, and from which a leaf, sufficient to form a cigarette, may be torn as wanted.

The Havanna cigars have been justly famed as the finest made. The best tobacco leaves for their fabrication grow in the Island of Cuba; and the primest were formerly reserved for the King of Spain, who used them as presents for his officials. The finest leaves are carefully culled for the cover or outside, in which are rolled the smaller or torn leaves. The exportation of leaves unmanufactured was once forbidden, nor could the planter manufacture for himself; he was compelled to give up his growth to the government commissioner, who allowed him its value, and manufactured them in the Royal Warehouse. The Havanna cigars vary in size and thickness; one par-

ticularly large and fine kind is to be obtained from
the priests; such being made from the picked leaves
which are presented to the Church, and manufactured
by the monks themselves. A smaller kind of excellent cigars is made for the use of ladies, and are
termed *Queens*. Straw cigars are also made here for
ladies' use; the straw being inserted as a mouth-piece;
a few years ago they were the only ones smoked in
London, but are now seldom seen.

Spanish cigars are those which are made in the
King's factory at Seville (Cigarros Sevillanos); they
are generally sold in *atados*, or bundles containing
fifty-one. The Virginian leaf is only used, and the
difference in make between these and Havanna cigars
is that the outer leaf or covering of the Havanna cigar
is wound from right to left; that of the Seville from
left to right.

American cigars are those manufactured out of
Havanna, in Caraccas, Buenos Ayres, Porto Rico, &c.
They vary in size and quality, "taking all shapes
and bearing many names." Cheroots are peculiar in
their manufacture, not made by hand, but wound on
a wire, both ends being cut flat. They are made from
the mildest Maryland tobacco, and are extensively
imitated in France and Germany.* They are sometimes sold for Turkish cigars.

The manufacture and consumption of cigars in

---

* Sometimes mustard seed is rolled in with them, to strengthen the
flavour; and they have been made to order in Hamburg with carraway and
anise-seed.

Northern Europe only dates from the close of the last century. It was in 1796 that the fashion began in Hamburg, and soon spread; leading to the establishment of native manufacturers in that town, and in Altona.* Bremen is now one of the principal towns in Germany, both for manufacture and export. Scented cigars were at one time fashionable, and were perfumed with *vanille;* but all such tastes lead to the substitution of bad tobacco in their construction, and the ruin of the flavour of good tobacco, if such should be used. The cigars of Germany are greatly inferior to those of America, but are very mild. In Austria and the Italian States they are a government monopoly; hence pipe-smoking is sometimes looked on as a disaffection toward the ruling powers if indulged by any but the poorest class ; and a determination to really injure the revenue has been plotted more than once by a general disuse of cigars; enthusiastic opponents dashing cigars from the mouths of smokers, to the great increase of street rows, as was recently the case in Milan.

The duty in England was originally as high as eighteen shillings a pound for foreign cigars, after the general Peace of 1815 threw open ports for their admission. The great increase of the cigar trade is very clearly shown in the tables of the consumption of tobacco in England, published in the *Encyclopædia*

* Some of these ingenious men sent their home-made cigars to Cuxhaven, and so brought them back again to Hamburg in American vessels lying there, for the benefit of smokers who were particular in obtaining the "genuine" article.

Metropolitana. In 1823, 26 lbs. only of manufactured cigars were imported; the duties were then reduced, and the return for 1824 showed 15,380 lbs., sinking the next year to 9569 lbs., but steadily increasing till 1830, when they reached 253,882 lbs., and have now vastly increased. In 1830 the duty was reduced to nine shillings a pound. Cigars were quite an aristocratic luxury then; but the taste for them has so greatly increased, that fully half the quantity of tobacco smoked in our large towns is in the form of cigars. The best kinds come from Havanna, though the Cuban are much valued when old. The large variety of cigars now traded in may be understood by the subsequent list, published by an importer and manufacturer in the city of London :—

Cabanas.	Emperors.	La Flor de Cabana.
Woodvilles.	La Famas.	La Martinez.
Silvas.	La Unions.	Panetellas.
Dos Amigos.	Ingenuidads.	Figaros.
Pellons.	Laranagas.	Tomecos.
Purezas.	Kings. Queens.	Yaras.
Riondas.	Dukes.	La Lealtads.
Estrellas.	Patrons.	Cacadores.
Integridads.	Recompenzas.	Planters.
Lopez.	Cavallos.	Cubas.
Manillas.	Fragancias.	Bengals.
Principes.	Isabellas.	Pilots.
Trabucas.	Lord Byrons.	Trinidads.
Royals.	Prensados.	Gondolas.
Britannias.	Gems.	Mexicans.
Alberts.	Medianas.	Favorites.
Esculapias.	La Normas.	Eldorados.
Pedro Acostas.	La Presidents.	Albonias.
Imperials.	La Primeras.	Elections.
Regalias.	La Esperanzas.	Wellingtons.
Claro Ferias.	La Esparteros.	Crusaders.
La Fidelidads.	Garantizados.	Alhambras.

Long as this list appears, it does not contain *all* the varieties of name attached to cigars. Thus, the "Bengal Cheroot" is not named, or the more humble "Penny Pickwick," a cigar christened after the hero of Mr. Dickens's first and most-celebrated work, and from which low price the cigar smoker may rise until a shilling be given for a really fine cigar, though amateurs have paid even higher prices.

Byron has immortalised his love of the cigar ; when praising tobacco, he exclaims—

> " ——— thy true lovers more admire by far
> Thy naked beauties—Give me a cigar !

The clever authors of *Odes and Addresses to Great People* (Thos. Hood and G. Reynolds) exclaim—

> " A few more whiffs of my cigar
> And then in Fancy's airy car,
>   Have with thee for the skies :
> How oft this fragrant smoke upcurl'd
> Hath borne me from this little world,
>   And all that in it lies ! "

A modern German poet (Friedrich Marc) has signalised his attachment in the following pleasing little poem, which has not before appeared in an English dress :—

TO MY CIGAR.

> THE warmth of thy glow,
> Well-lighted cigar,
> Makes happy thoughts flow,
> And drives sorrow afar.

The stronger the wind blows,
    The brighter thou burnest !
The dreariest of life's woes,
    Less gloomy thou turnest.

As I feel on my lip
    Thy unselfish kiss ;
Like thy flame-colour'd tip,
    All is rosy-hued bliss.

No longer does sorrow,
    Lay weight on my heart ;
And all fears of the morrow,
    In joy-dreams depart.

Sweet cheerer of sadness !
    Life's own happy star !
I greet thee with gladness,
    My friendly cigar !

Cigars are sometimes asserted to have a superiority over pipes, because they consume the oil of tobacco ; but this is a fallacy, inasmuch as the oil is no more burnt away or evaporated than in a pipe ; it is, in fact, drawn to, and condensed in, that part of the cigar between the lips of the smoker ; hence cigars, though mild in smoking, contract a rankness of flavour when consumed to the last inch, which is generally thrown away.   This has led to the invention of cigar-tubes, or holders, by which they are kept at a distance from the lips, and may be entirely consumed.   These are sometimes made of meerschaum clay, and occasionally decorated with sculptured figures, as in the example engraved, where a lion is baited by dogs.   Such sculpture serves another purpose than mere ornament, as it gives the smoker's fingers a firmer hold, for which reason the scroll of foliage beneath has also been introduced. A very cheap holder has been made of pipe-clay, and is not deficient in quaint fancy. The example we select comes from the prolific pipe-factories of France, and costs but a penny.

In Berlin, a few years ago, an ingenious pocket-knife, entirely of steel, was fabricated for the use of cigar-smokers, of which we here give an engraving.

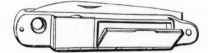

It had all the strength of the usual knife, but the spring was so constructed that it did not shut down to the edge of the blade; the cigar-end being placed through the aperture at the end, the point of the knife, on being pressed down by the finger, cut off the end of the cigar. On one side of the handle was a thin flat box, with a division; the longer one (open in the cut) contained fusees, the smaller (represented closed) held German tinder; the fusee was lighted by rubbing along the rough edge of the lower part of this shallow box, which did not give more weight or thickness to the handle than a strong pocket-knife usually exhibits. A smaller knife has since been made on the same principle, without the box, and with a sharp point, or bodkin, closing down beside the knife, to open the cigar if better draught be required. It may be conveniently placed in the waistcoat pocket.

Another simple little implement, to act as cigar-cutter and holder, is here represented, the size of

the original. The double cutter at one side takes off the end of the cigar, and, when closed, acts as a hold for the finger and thumb, the opposite arms closing round the cigar and securing it very firmly. A small loop on one of the cutters allows it to be attached to the watch-chain if desired.

The luxuries of the cigar-smoker, in the way of ornamental receptacles for cigars, need not here be descanted on. Some, in their elaboration and costliness, belong to the wealthy, and are merely to be considered as the vanities of selfish pride. When men enshrine cigars in pearl cases, elaborated with metal work, that make them seem only fitted for the scent-cases of a lady's boudoir, they may be looked upon

with due contempt, not only by ladies, but by those of
their own sex who adhere to the honest useful case of
plain russia leather.

Tobacco when carried about the person for use, if
not placed in a metal box, is held in a pouch or bag;
both being generally formed of leather. German ladies
think it no unfit employ to devote much time and
attention in embroidering tobacco-bags for favoured
swains; they are too inured to smoking to think
otherwise of it, than of beer-drinking, as the natural
habit of the male part of the creation; which they
may look forward to enjoy themselves in their old age,
with as little chance of cavil or interruption. Gentlemen hang the tobacco-bag on the arm, as ladies used
the reticule some time ago.* The pouch is for the
pocket, and is made of soft leather, frequently with the
hair outside; a favourite substance for this purpose is
moleskin, the thick soft down making it a mere pad in
the pocket. The tobacco is closely packed in a receptacle in the lower part, and lapped round with the
outer skin, and tied together; it is thus kept duly
moist, as it is protected from evaporation.

The tobacco-box is of course the oldest invention.
Ralph Thoresby the antiquary of Leeds, preserved in
his museum at the early part of the last century, a
tobacco-box traditionally said to have been that used

* At Constantinople " Among the more prominent but less valuable
articles of embroidery for sale, are the *dookauny*, or *toutoon kesscssy*
(tobacco bags), made of different coloured stuffs, generally cut in an oblong
square form, and embroidered with coloured silks and gold." For Chinese
tobacco pouches, see p. 212.

by Sir Walter Raleigh. It was of sufficient capacity
to hold a pound of tobacco, which was placed in the
centre, and surrounded by holes to receive pipes. It
was thirteen inches high, and seven in diameter;
formed of leather, and decorated with gilding. I am
indebted to J. Y. Akerman, Esq., secretary of the
Society of Antiquaries of London, for permission to
engrave an old wooden carved tobacco-box, also traditionally said to have belonged to Raleigh; and which

has the initials W. R. conjoined within the lid. If
not Raleigh's box, it is of his period, and is decorated
with figures on one side in the costume of the end of
the sixteenth, or beginning of the seventeenth century.
On the opposite side is a hunting scene. The lid
slides out; the head of the figure who supports the
anchor forming a convenient projection to aid its
course. The English rose is below; and at the bottom
of the box a mariner's compass is engraved.

Expensive tobacco-boxes were part of the outfit of
Elizabethan dandies. Simplicus, an upstart in Marston's play *What you Will* (1607), says: "I'le go to
the half-crown ordinary every meale, I'le have my
ivory box of tobacco." Henry Fitz-Geffery in his

satirical *Notes from Blackfriars* (1617), speaks of a
" spruce coxcomb : "—

> " That never walkes without his looking-glass,
> In a tobacco-box or diall set,
> That he may privately conferre with it."

There is a good satirical description of the smoker
and his paraphernalia, in *The Man in the Moone*,
1609, (a pamphlet levelled at the fashionable follies of
the day) in which one person questions another as to
who one of the company present may be, and he is
answered; "I know not certainly, but I think he cometh
to· play you a fit of mirth, for I behelde pipes in his
pocket ; now he draweth forth his tinder-box and his
touchwood, and falleth to his tacklings : sure his
throate is on fire, the smoke flyeth so fast from his
mouth; blesse his beard with a bason of water, lest he
burn it : some terrible thing he taketh, it maketh him
pant and look pale, and hath an odious taste, he
spitteth so after it."

The pedlar, in his song given in the Duke of Newcastle's play, *The Triumphant Widow* (1677), enumerates pipes and tobacco-boxes among his wares ; and a
silver tobacco-box of thirty shillings value is mentioned
in an inventory of the time of James II.; as well as
a tobacco-box of tortoise-shell.

The old tobacco-box was generally capacious, and
made for the pipe as well, which was laid in one
compartment of the interior. Such large brass boxes
were generally carried by sailors, particularly Dutch

ones, and were covered with rudely executed ornaments and inscriptions. Pictured semblances of their
own good ships were common on the lids, and Dutch
tobacco-boxes, or boxes in their style, were common to
English sailors. They were the love-gifts of sweet-
hearts, who :

> " Gave them the 'bacca box mark'd with her name,"

and were kept as sacred memorials of those " on
shore." Tobacco-boxes were bequeathed to "mess-
mates " as parting gifts of friendship in death, and
such souvenirs were as affectionately esteemed as if
they had been formed

> " Of one entire and perfect chrysolite."

A certain Mr. Pynsent who left all his estates in
Somersetshire to the great Lord Chatham (the father
of Pitt), in admiration of his talents and patriotism,
possessed a tobacco-box on which, under a skull, was
engraved :—

> " Mens Ignis, Tubulus corpus, mihi vitaque fumus.
> Herba Panis, Clavus fata, suprema Cinis."

Which has been thus "rendered into English : "—

> Of lordly man, how humbling is the type,
> A fleeting shadow, a tobacco pipe !
> His mind the fire, his frame the tube of clay,
> His breath the smoke so idly puffed away,
> His food the herb that fills the hollow bowl,
> Death is the stopper, Ashes end the whole."

It is not uncommon to find the old Dutch tobacco-box engraved all over with quaint pictures and inscriptions, sometimes allusive to life in a similar strain.

The old brass tobacco-box was generally oblong, and contained all the smoker required, including materials for lighting the pipe, consisting of tinder, flint and steel, all packed in proper divisions. The round tobacco-box belongs to the last century. Tin and horn were both used as material for their fabrication; and there is a horn tobacco-box preserved in London, which worthless in itself, is enshrined in so many valuable cases, that it is the most remarkable tobacco-box existing. It belongs to a club consisting of the past overseers of the parishes of Saint Margaret and Saint John the Evangelist, Westminster, who venerate it highly, and have published a curious illustrated volume devoted to its history. Mr. Henry Monck, one of the parishioners, purchased at Horn Fair * in 1713, the original box, which cost him four-pence; this he presented to his parish club, and they kept it in memory of a worthy associate. Seven years after the gift, the lid of the box was decorated with a silver rim; and it was placed in the care of the senior overseer of the parish, (the club consisting of such persons as were serving, or had served the office, or

---

* At this ancient fair, held at Charlton, in Kent, it was customary to sell all kinds of articles manufactured from horn. It was also usual for persons to wear horns on the head, and for men to go disguised in female attire; the fair was, in fact, a complete Saturnalia.

paid the fine in lieu of doing so) and it became an
object of interest to all. A silver side-casing and
bottom was added in 1726; the defeat of the Pretender
was commemorated in 1746 by a portrait of the Duke
of Cumberland, with allegorical accessories, the work
of Hogarth, which is placed within the lid; and various
other additions made until the year 1765, when the old
four-penny horn box was completely hidden by deco-
rative silver work. It having become a sort of custom
with each senior overseer, to add something to the
box, and there being no longer a chance of doing it, a
case was prepared for it; and this received a series
of silver plates, the gifts of different members, which
generally commemorated some historic event which
happened in their own time. When the case became
covered with these ornaments, a fresh outer case was
provided; and now there is a series of four embel-
lished cases to fit over each other, until the whole has
become of greater bulk and worth, than any tobacco-
box in the kingdom.* Many of these engravings are
curious; and a detailed history of the box and its
cases, was published by subscription in 1824; it forms
a goodly quarto volume, and is decorated with many
engravings, fac-similes of those on the silver plates
which ornament the cases. In the title-page is a

* One recreant overseer refused to return the box to the Society, and
even threatened its destruction; it took three years of a weary Chancery
Suit to settle the question; but it was decided in favour of the Society;
and it has since been delivered to its keeper on condition that it be pro
duced on all necessary occasions, and ultimately delivered to the Society
under the penalty of two hundred guineas.

vignette, representing the box and its cases arranged on a table, with the various accessories of a social meeting, from which our cut is copied.*

It was the custom during the last century, to present country churchwardens with tobacco-boxes, after the faithful discharge of their duties.

There is a simple and ingenious tobacco-box used frequently in country ale-houses, which "keeps its own account," with each smoker, and acts also as a money-box. It is kept on parlour tables for the use of all comers; but none can obtain a pipe-full, till the money is deposited through a hole in the lid. A penny dropped in causes a bolt to unfasten, and allow the smoker to help himself from a drawer full of tobacco. His honour is trusted so far as not to take more than his pipe-full, and he is reminded of it by a verse engraved on the lid :—

> " The custom is, before you fill,
> To put a penny in the till ;

* The volume is of course a rarity ; but those who desire more details of this curious work will find an abundance in Hone's *Year Book*, where five closely printed pages are devoted to its description.

> When you have filled, without delay,
> Close the lid, or sixpence pay."

Tobacco jars of porcelain are a comparatively modern invention, and exhibit a large variety of design. Many are costly, none are cheap. We select three examples, sufficient to display the whim and fancy they occasionally exhibit. The first represents a fat cook bearing

two horns to hold cigars, the body of the figure contains the tobacco; the line formed by the tucked-up sleeves and the apron conceals the juncture of the lid, which is converted into the upper half of the figure. The second represents a fool who has broken his way through a large drum, the head of the fool is a convenient handle to remove the lid, which fits into the top of the drum where the tobacco is placed. The third, which has enjoyed the most general popularity, represents a young girl in the dress of the *Regencé* smoothing the folds of her ample petticoat. The festoons of her dress conceal, at their edges, the junction of the upper and lower portion of this convenient and pretty tobacco-box.

Tobacco-stoppers have exhibited as much variety of design as pipes have done; but while the decoration of the pipe is a comparatively modern thing, the tobacco-stopper engrossed a large share of the attention of the fanciful workman of the last century. The author of the very clever *Paper of Tobacco*,* says—" This was the only article on which the English smoker prided himself. It was made of various materials—wood, bone, ivory, mother of pearl, and silver ; and the forms which it assumed were exceedingly diversified. Out of a collection of upwards of thirty tobacco-stoppers of different ages, from 1688 to the present time, the following are the most remarkable : a bear's tooth tipped with silver at the bottom, and inscribed with the name of Captain James Rogers of the Happy Return whaler, 1688; Dr˙ Henry Sacheverel in full canonicals carved in ivory, 1710 ; a boot, a horse's hind leg, Punch, and another character in the same Drama, to wit, his Satanic majesty; a countryman with a flail; a milkmaid, an emblem of Priapus, a bottle, Hope and Anchor, the Marquis of Granby, a greyhound's head and neck, a paviour's rammer, Lord Nelson, the Duke of Wellington, and Bonaparte." To this long list I am enabled to add a few others, of which I offer engravings. Fig. 1, is the earliest in point of date I have ever met with, and represents a soldier in the half armour of the time of James or Charles I., consisting of a cuirass with shoulder-pieces and tassets, as worn in the

---

* Published anonymously in 1839.

last era of plate armour. Fig. 2, has evidently belonged
to some devoted royalist, and represents the bust of
Charles I. crowned and decorated with the collar of
the Garter. Fig. 3, belonged to one of "the Opposition," and is surmounted with a bust of Cromwell in
a richly decorated cuirass; it bears on the reverse the
lion shown in Fig. 4, which supported the Arms of
England during the Protectorate. Both appear to
have been cut from a medal, or a thin plate of silver,
and soldered back to back; the shaft of the stopper is
hollow, unscrewing at the neck, and allowing the pick
to be taken out (as shown in Fig. 4), to clear the pipe
of ashes. Fig. 5, is a ring-stopper, to be worn upon
the finger as an ordinary ring, the stopper concealed in
the hand; it can thus be easily turned round for use
when required, and does not run the risk of being lost
or mislaid by the smoker. The clergyman in our cut
p. 130, carries one on his finger; and there is a
humorous allusion to them in *Hudibras* (Part. ii.
canto 3), and to the symbol which astronomers use to
denote one of the planets.

> " ———— Bless us ! quoth he,
> It is a planet now I see ;
> And, if I err not, by his proper
> Figure, that's like tobacco-stopper,
> It should be Saturn ! "

Fig. 6, is of silver, and ingeniously formed of two
pipes braced together, and serving as a holder to a
stopper and pick, which screws between them. The
stopper is formed of a twopenny piece of Queen Anne.

Fig. 7, is the device of an old sailor, delineating the real and imaginary denizens of the sea with an equal amount of exactitude. Fig. 8, is the Pierrot of the old French stage, and is apparently a work of the latter part of the seventeenth century. Fig. 9, has its handle

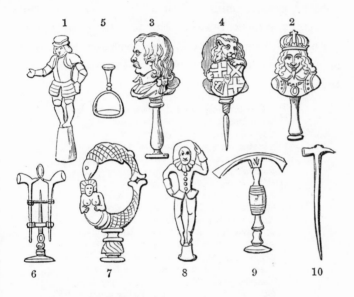

formed like the head of an adze, to be used in clearing the pipe; in the centre of the stem is the rude representation of a barrel. Busts of a grotesque kind were general favourites, or figures of a jolly sailor; but a very large number took the form of the human leg or arm, which was fabricated as if bent, and made a very useful implement. Fig. 10, is a copper pick of the simplest and cheapest form; it was dredged from the Thames, and may be the oldest of our series. Many

cheap tobacco-stoppers were cut in hard wood, some
few in mahogany; but by far the greatest number were
cast in brass, like the specimens we engrave, which are
all in that material, with the exception of Fig. 3.

In the *Shrubs of Parnassus*, a small volume of
poetical essays, published in 1760 (under an assumed
name), by James Boswell, the famous biographer of
Johnson; is one devoted to the tobacco-stopper, which
is curiously descriptive of those in ordinary use at
that time :—

> " O ! let me grasp thy waist, be thou of wood,
> Or lævigated steel, for well 'tis known
> Thy habit is diverse.   In iron clad
> Sometimes thy feature roughens to the sight ;
> And oft transparent art thou seen in glass,
> Portending frangibility.   The son
> Of labouring mechanism here displays
> Exuberance of skill.   The curious knot,
> The motley flourish winding down thy sides,
> And freaks of fancy pour upon the view
> Their complicated charms, and as they please,
> Astonish.   While with glee thy touch I feel
> No harm my finger dreads.*   No fractured pipe
> I ask, or splinter's aid, wherewith to press
> The rising ashes down.   Oh ! bless my hand,
> Chief when thou com'st with hollow circle, crown'd
> With sculptured signet, bearing in thy womb
> The treasured Corkscrew.   Thus a triple service
> In firm alliance may'st thou boast."

It was a not unfrequent desire with the old smoker
to associate his tobacco-stopper with some great person
or thing.   A tree planted by a great man, a fragment

* It is recorded of Sir Isaac Newton that on one occasion he used the
finger of the lady he was courting for a stopper, as he sat and smoked in
philosophic abstraction beside her.

of a celebrated ship, a beam of an historic mansion, were each taxed for a tobacco-stopper. The custom is very old, for Taylor, the Water Poet, notes, in his *Wandering to See the Wonders of the West*, 1649, that he saw a sprig of the famous Glastonbury thorn, which the monks at that place had celebrated for its miraculous flowering at Christmas, and which was cut down by the parliamentary soldiers. He says : " I saw the sayd branch, I did take a dead sprigge from it, wherewith I made two or three tobacco-stoppers, which I brought to London."

The reader of the *Spectator* will remember the remark made by Sir Roger de Coverley, when viewing the coronation chairs in Westminster Abbey : " If Will Wimble were with us, and saw those two chairs, it would go hard but he would get a tobacco-stopper out of one or t'other of them."

The flint and steel and tinder, which the old smoker was necessitated to carry on a journey, has been superseded in our days by many ingenious inventions. German tinder first took the place of the old rag-tinder and dried moss; and this is still used, separated into thin strips, but coated at top with an explosive composition, which ignites by friction ; small boxes will contain a packet of this tinder, a part of the case being rough to ignite it. Matches, headed with a lump of combustible matter, which burns long enough to light any pipe or cigar thoroughly, are also to be obtained in boxes which occupy very small space in the pocket. Those who are fond of a display of showy materials for obtaining a light, are provided with an elaborate apparatus of silver tubing, through which a smouldering cord of coloured cotton can be drawn, lit by means of a flint, elegantly fashioned from the purest stone, struck against an equally tasteful steel; the whole process being an elegant and costly realisation of " much ado about nothing," chiefly patronised by "heavy swells," who take tobacco more for the sake of ostentation than pleasure.

There is no indulgence that more completely equalises itself to all classes than that of tobacco. It is possible, as we have seen, to make it a very expensive taste; but it is equally possible to make it a cheap one. Tobacco will give as much enjoyment to the poor man in his clay pipe, as to the nobleman in his jewelled Meerschaum. Indeed, it may be doubted if the pleasures of the poor are not greater; and there is much truth, as well as sound philosophy, in the *morale* of tobacco-smoking, which we have seen enforced by many whose opinions are of value, and whose indulgence has been limited to temperate and wholesome enjoyment.

CHAPTER V.

SNUFF AND SNUFF-BOXES.

WHEN tobacco was originally recommended to the attention of the Old World, its claims as a curative agent were strongly asserted; one mode of using the leaves was to pulverise them, and inhale the powder by the nose : this custom, as well as all others connected with the European form of using the plant, was adopted from the Indians. We have quoted, in p. 16, the description given by the Friar who accompanied Columbus in 1494, of their mode of inhaling it for medicinal purposes. It was consequently recommended for all diseases of the head brought on by colds; and particularly that one popularly termed the *pose*, a dry stoppage which much troubled our ancestors. Physicians had, on the faith of old Indian usages, on which they seem to have implicitly relied, recommended it. Catherine de' Medicis was the first so to use it, within a short period after the introduction of the tobacco-plant by Jean Nicot; and the new sternutatory was first handed about in the Court of France about 1562. This Queen's patronage decided the success of the plant, which was called *Herbe à la*

Reine ; and snuff was for a long time a fashion with the court-party, held in abomination by the Protestants. The literary controversy was violent; some physicians contended that, if it concealed a vicious odour of the breath, it also injured the digestive power: while some theologians affirmed that it inspired contemptuous feelings, by inducing indolence.

Examples of recipes used by old physicians, when tobacco was considered in the light of a medicinal herb, may be found in Neander: we have given some specimens, in our quotations from the English Doctor Edmund Gardiner's *Triall of Tobacco* (1610), see p. 49; we will now quote from the latter what he recommends in the way of snuffs. He prefaces his remarks by saying :—

" Sternutatories, especially those which are made of tabacco, being drawne up into the nostrels, cause sneesing, consuming and spending away grosse and slimie humors from the ventricles of the braine. These kind of remedies must needes doe good where the brain is repleat with many vapours, for those that have a lethargy, or vertiginy, in all long griefes, paines and aches of the head, in continuall senselesses, or benumming of the braine, and for a hicket that proceedeth of repletion."

The following is one of his specifics :—

> *Rec.* Piperis,
> Zinziberis, ana Ði.
> Pyrethri,
> Foliorum siccorum tabaci Ðij.
> Trita naribus inspirentur ante cibum.

"Another Sternutamentorie :—

Rec. Foliorum siccorum tabaci ℈ijss.
Zingiberis.
Pyrethri, ana ℈iss.
Radicum Hellebori albi, grana 6
Pulverisata commisceantur, et fiat sternutamentorium
Ex fistula naribus parum infletur.

" These sternutatories which are very forcible, vehement, and strong ; as Euphorbium, Helleborus albus,
and the like to these, must not be blown up into the
head, but rather put into a boxe, the same being a
little shaken, and so holding it to the nose, to draw up
a little at once. But Tabacco is not so violent, and
therefore may in my judgment bee safely put in
practise. Thus then you plainely see that all medi-
cines, and especially tobacco, being rightly and ration-
ally used, is a noble medicine, and contrariwise not in
his due time with other circumstances considered, it
doth no more than a nobleman's shooe doth in healing
the gout in the foot."

One other, and less pleasant mode of using the herb
as a sternutatory is thus described by a later author :
—" It is sometimes taken in little longish pellets put
up the nose, where it is found to produce very good
effects, to attract a deal of water, unload the head,
resolve catarrhs, and make a free respiration ; for the
subtile parts of the tobacco in inspiration are carried
into the trachea and lungs, where they loosen the
peccant humours adhering thereto, and promote ex-
pectoration. Some have left this tobacco in their

R

noses all night; but this is found to occasion vomiting usually on the next morning. Another thing charged on this way of application, is, that it weakens the sight."

Though thus originally recommended for adoption as a medicine, it soon became better known as a luxury, and the gratification of a pinch was generally indulged in Spain, Italy, and France, during the early part of the seventeenth century. It was much patronised by the clergy, and led to the Anathema of Urban VIII. in 1624 against any person who took snuff in a church, as mentioned in p. 78. The author of *Le Bon Usage du Tabac en Poudre*, Paris (1700), says it is "the passion of Prelates and Abbés, the religious community generally are fond of it, and in spite of the Pope and his ordinances, the Spanish Priests will not scruple to place their snuff-boxes on the altar for their use."

Butler has noted that the Saints of the Cromwellian era were not averse to its use; he says of one :—

> " He had administered a dose
> Of snuff mundungus to his nose ;
> And powdered the inside of his skull
> Instead of the outward jobbernole." *

In that scandalous satire on the ladies of the puritanic party called *Newes from the New Exchange* (1650), they are frequently accused of a love of tobacco,

* *Hudibras,* pt. iii, cant. 2.

and particularly one Mistress Cambell, whose maxim is
said to be :—

> " She that with pure tobacco will not prime
> Her nose, can be no lady of the time."

It was the grandees of the French Court who " set
the fashion" of snuff, with all its luxurious additions
of scents and expensive boxes. It became common in
the Court of *Louis le Grand*, although that monarch
had a decided antipathy to tobacco in any form.* He
endeavoured to discourage the use of snuff, and his
valets-de-chambre were obliged to renounce it when
they were appointed to their office. One of these gentlemen, the Duc d'Harcourt, was supposed to have died
of apoplexy in consequence of having, in order to please
the king, totally discontinued the habit which he had
before indulged to excess. Other grandees were less
accommodating : thus we are told that Marechal d'Hux-
elles used to cover his cravat and dress with it. The
Royal Physician, Monsieur Fagon, is reported to have
devoted his best energies to a public oration of a very
violent kind against snuff, which unfortunately failed
to convince his auditory, as the excited lecturer in his

---

* Louis was ungrateful in his dislike, if tobacco enabled his soldiers to
support themselves in their arduous campaigns as described by Le Sieur
Baillard, in his *Discours du Tabac*, 1668, who says :—"Ce que a été
verifié dans le vieux et le nouveau monde, par l'expérience de plusieurs
soldats, qui sans boire, et sans manger, et sans prendre autre chose qu'une
demi-once de tabac en vingt-quatre heures, soutenoient toutes les fatigues
de la guerre ceux-cy pendant trois ou quatre jours, et ceux-là même une
semaine entière."

most enthusiastic moments refreshed his nose with a pinch. The daughters of Louis were no enemies to tobacco, as we have seen in our anecdotes in p. 69, and they doubtless had their private snuff-boxes, for the fashion became very general in France by the middle of the century; and a snuff-box of an elegant material, sometimes decorated with paintings, or resplendent with precious stones, was part of the necessities of a beauty of ton.

Molière, in the opening speech uttered by *Sganarelle* in his *Don Juan*, makes him laud snuff in a strain of eulogy bordering on hyperbole, as " la passion des honnêtes gens."

Tobacco was reduced to a rough powder at this time by pounding, or by grating, and was known as *tabac en poudre* or *tabac râpé*; the latter term we still retain in the name of one kind of snuff—*rappee*—long after it has ceased to bear its legitimate sense of *grated tobacco*. The outfit of a snuff-taker was at this period a costly thing, and the tobacco-grater formed of ivory was richly carved with a variety of scroll ornament, enclosing fanciful scenes of various kinds. Our cut opposite is copied from a finely sculptured ivory specimen of French manufacture; it represents Cupid instructed by Venus, whose costume indicates the date of its fabrication to have been about 1680. Above the figures ornamental scroll-work supports a canopy.

The form of this implement is semicircular; the flat side discloses the grater of brass fitted into a groove, and having a receptacle at each end for the tobacco-

powder, which passes from beneath the grater, through
a small aperture into each.   If the snuff-maker wished
to fill his box, he rasped a sufficient quantity to fill the
large receptacle at the bottom ; if he wished for a pinch

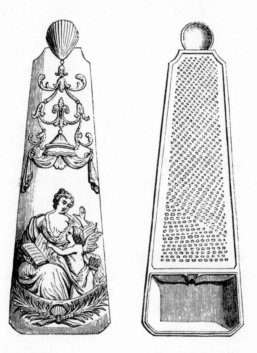

" fresh and fresh," he shook out a small quantity into
the little shell at the top, which was not large enough
to admit the fingers for a pinch, it was therefore turned
out upon the back of the hand, and so snuffed up
the nose.

A similar snuff-rasp to this, with figures precisely
the same, proving the popularity of the design, is

engraved in Du Sommerard's *Arts du Moyen Age.**
It has a cover for the larger receptacle, into which the
snuff falls in grinding; which is also ornamented with
carving. Du Sommerard had several such implements
made in wood, ivory, and bronze, and they are now with
his other collections in the Hotel Cluny, Paris. In the
work just quoted he has engraved five other specimens.† One sculptured in wood bears the title and
arms of Gaston d'Orleans, the brother of Louis XIII.
Another has upon it a figure of Sganarelle, rasping
the tobacco and singing his celebrated couplet "Le
tabac est divin," &c. Another represents Lot and his
daughters, and the destruction of Sodom. Another the
rape of Proserpine ; thus proving that as much variety
of subject and decoration was adopted for these implements, as for the more modern snuff-box.‡

It was the custom at this time to half ruin the
tobacco by "purifying" it in water. It was for two or
three days washed in a clay vessel and strained, then
washed again, dried in the sun, and finally coloured to

---

* Album, serie iii. pl. 29.

† In the plate above referred to, and in serie x. pl. 35.

‡ The engraving on p. 123, of a man chewing tobacco, is copied from
the top of one of these rasps ; it has been thus described in vol. xxiii. of
Archæologia :—It is six inches in length and two in breadth, about
half an inch deep, composed of several ornamental woods inlaid with ivory.
It contained a perforated grater of blue steel, and a small compartment
was left uncovered at the upper end to receive the snuff and admit the
fingers. On the sliding lid is an inlaid ivory figure of a man. This lid
protected the grater, and converted it into a sort of snuff-box. The custom
of chewing tobacco is alluded to in early medical works, as well as in the
earliest accounts we have of the Indians. But it met with most disfavour
at the hands of physicians, and only achieved its great popularity in the
British Navy.

fancy; the colours were produced from red or yellow ochre, which was mixed on a slab of marble with oil of almonds, and the grains of tobacco incorporated there-with. After all this was done, the last flavour of tobacco was destroyed, by various perfumes mixed with it. We give two recipes for the practice from a curious little French book printed in Paris in 1700, entitled *Le Bon Usage du Tabac en Poudre* : —

" *La manière de parfumer le Tabac.*—On prend du Tabac de Virginie six livres, de S. Christophe trois livres, ces tabacs sont les plus communs, et les moins âcres de tous ; on les lave dans l'eau de Melilot, et on les fait ensuite sécher à l'ombre, et puis on les pulver-ise dans un mortier pour le sasser ou tamiser ; on lave la poudre sèche dans les eaux de Santal, de fleurs d'orange, et de bois d'Inde mêlées ensemble ; on la met ensuite sécher sur une claye couverte d'une toile forte, la remuant à mésure qu'elle sèche, et l'arrosant souvent d'eau d'Ange ; enfin on la fait sécher à l'ombre ; étant sèche, on la sasse, et on l'expose quelque tems à l'air, et on la parfume plusieurs fois et successivement avec des fleurs d'orange, et des fleurs de jasmin, enfermant le tout pour cet effet dans une boîte de plomb assez haute, où les fleurs et le tabac soient disposés lit sur lit.

" *Autre manière de parfumer le Tabac.*—On prend plusieurs feuilles de papier, chacune de la grandeur de la caisse, on les fait sécher au feu, et on les pique par tout avec une grosse épingle ; on met dans le fond de la caisse une couche de tabac épaisse d'un doigt, et une feuille de papier par dessus, sur laquelle on met une

couche de fleurs, et sur les fleurs une autre feuille de
papier sur laquelle on étend un pareil lit de tabac,
continuant ainsi jusqu'à ce que tout soit employé ; de
cette manière la poudre de tabac n'est point mêlée
parmi les fleurs que l'on change de 12 heures en 12
heures, si on a beaucoup de fleurs, si non de 24 en 24
heures pendant quatre ou cincque jours, et ensuite on
retire les feuilles de papier, et on met les fleurs et le
tabac dans un sas dont la toile de crin soit assez fine,
pour retenir les fleurs et laisser passer le tabac."

Spanish snuff was flavoured with musk, civet, and
essence of millefleurs. Essence of cedar and bergamot was also used for snuffs bearing the name of each.
Neroly was named from the essential oil distilled from
orange-flowers. A snuff called "Odeur de Rome,"
probably from being a favourite with prelates, was
made by adding to one pound of snuff six ounces of
musk, and five of civet, mixed with a little sugar.
Another termed "Odeur de Malthe," had to the same
quantity of snuff, six grains of civet and sugar, five
grains of amber, and orange-flower water. Baillard *
notes that snuff was also mixed with ginger, cubebs,
cummin, mustard, hellebore, spirits of wine, &c., to
make what he terms, and we may fairly believe to be, a
" puissant sternutatoire."

This abominable mode of making snuff by destroying tobacco, was also common in England. Thus in
John White's *Art's Treasury of Rarities and curious*

---

* In his *Discours du Tabac*, 12mo, 1668.

Inventions (circa 1700), we get this recipe: " To make
snuff, and how to cleanse it.   Put your tobacco-dust in
a strong linnen cloth, soak your tobacco-dust in a pail
of water, only once in twenty-four hours ; then let the
water out, and squeeze the snuff well in the cloth, then
dry it on wicker hurdles in the sun, stirring it carefully whilst it's a drying ; being dry, pour sweet water
over it, as rose-water, or any other you like best, and
make it as a paste ; dry it again, and pour more rose-
water to it, and dry it again, and it's fit to receive what
smell you please.   Mint dry'd and powdered, makes a
pleasant snuff; or some rose-leaves and cloves distilled and powdered, and put to your snuff; or what
herb or flower you please."

The shop-bills of the old manufacturers (*temp.* Geo.
I.) give us representations of these modes of manufacturing snuff.*   We find
the curious engraving here
given, on that of John L.
Hullier, who calls himself
" French manufacturer of
Rappée Snuff, formerly in-
spector-general of all the
manufactures of snuff in
France," and who then lived
" at the corner of Little
Newport Street, by Castle

Street, Leicester fields, London."   The bill is sur-

* I am indebted for my copies of this, and all others from shop bills, to
the curious collection of J. J. A. Fillinham, Esq.

rounded by a rich scroll border, within which are introduced figures of men unloading snuff-casks, pounding leaves, and rasping carottes ; while the enjoyment of snuff-taking is depicted in a fourth figure, dressed in the extreme of fashion.

This mode of making snuff by grating the twisted tobacco is excellently shown in the cut. Carver, in his *History of the Tobacco-plant* (1779), thus describes the mode of preparing this roll tobacco and snuff, as he saw it in America :—" Being possessed of a tobacco-wheel, which is a very simple machine, they spin the leaves, after they are properly cured, into a twist of any size they think fit ; * and having folded it into rolls of about twenty pounds weight each, they lay it by for use. In this state it will keep for several years, and be continually improving, as it every hour grows milder. When they have occasion to use it, they take off such a length as they think necessary, which, if designed for smoking, they cut into small pieces, for chewing into larger, as choice directs; if they intend to make snuff of it they take a quantity from the roll, and laying it in a room where a fire is kept, in a day or two it will become dry, and being rubbed on a grater will produce a genuine snuff. Those in more improved regions, who like their snuff scented, apply to it such odoriferous waters as they can procure, or think most pleasing." As the tobacco-roll and the Indian became the sign of the tobacconist ; so the

---

* See a cut of the process, p. 125.

tobacco-rasp was that of the snuff-maker.   From a bill
of 1768 we gather this : it is that of "John Saullé and
Pontet, successors to the late James Fribourg, French
manufacturer of Rappée Snuff, ready rasp'd or un-
rasp'd, at the Crown and Rasp in Pall Mall near the
Haymarket, where is sold the right Clerack, St. Domingo, Scotch and Spanish Snuff."   The sign is given
on this bill (which is for "six pounds of Dutch bran at
five shillings per pound"*), and is considerably older
than the date of the bill.   We copy it as a
curious specimen of a snuff-shop sign.   The
Highlander taking a pinch seems to have
been introduced about 1745, when the English
were attracted to Scottish events; and the
fondness of the nation for snuff was noticed.
The Irish were equally remarkable in the previous century, for the translator of Everard's *Essay on
Tobacco* (*De Herba Panacea*, 1659), informs us that :
" The Irish are altogether for snuff tobacco to purge
their brains."

The process of pounding snuff is
represented in our cut, copied from a
shop-bill of Abraham Delvalle of Bury
Street, St. Mary Axe, (*temp.* Geo. II.),
who tells us that "he makes and sells
at his manufactory in Featherstone
Street, Bunhill fields, fine Scotch, Rap-
pee, Spanish, and Havannah Snuffs."

* This "bran" was a coarse kind of snuff made from tobacco leaves
pounded in a mortar, but not ground to dust; see p. 258 ; in Wimble's
list, p. 286, several of these snuffs are noted.

In this instance the manufacturer is depicted pounding the leaves in a mortar, the pestle being of peculiar form to allow the more perfect mixing of the scents so commonly used.

The popularity of snuff in England increased after the Great Plague, which gave fresh impetus to the consumption of tobacco.* When William ascended the throne the prevalence of the Dutch taste confirmed its general use, and it was the fashion to be curious in snuffs; valuable boxes of all kinds were sported, and the beaux carried canes with hollow heads, that they might the more conveniently inhale a few grains through the perforations, as they sauntered in the fashionable promenades. Rich essences were employed to flavour it, and a taste in such scents was considered a necessary part of refined education.

In Southerne's *Wives' Excuse* (1692), at a fashionable party in an after-dinner scene, the following dialogue occurs :—

"*Wild.* Yours is very good snuff, Mr. Friendall.

"*Mr. F.* Yes, truly, I think 'tis pretty good powder.

"*Wild.* Pray your opinion of mine, you are a critick.

"*Mr. F.* This is Havanah indeed; but then 'tis wash'd. Give me your dry powders, they never lose

* Dr. Henry Stubbe, of Warwick, the formidable opponent of the Royal Society in the reign of Charles II., and whose career is noted in D'Israeli's *Quarrels of Authors*, was a great snuff taker. He was drowned after paying a night visit to a patient, when—to use the cynical language of Anthony Wood—"his head was intoxicated with bibbing, but more with talking and snuffing of powder."

their scent:—besides yours is made of the leaves of
the tobacco.

" *Wild.* Why, what the devil's yours ?

" *Mr. F.* Mine, Sir, is right Palillio, made of the
fibres, the spirituous part of the plant; there's not a
pinch of it out of my box in England; 'twas made, I
assure you, to the palate of his most Catholick Majesty,
and sent me by a great Don of Spain, that's in his
Prince's particular pleasure."

Dryden used to frequent Will's Coffee-house in
Bow street, Covent Garden ; and it hence became the
great resort of the wits of his time. Ned Ward
relates, in his *London Spy*, that "a parcel of raw,
second-rate beaux and wits, were conceited if they had
but the honour to dip a finger and thumb into Mr.
Dryden's snuff-box."

In the *Cornish Comedy* (1696), mention is made of
" a gay modish spark, with a long beau peruke, and
gawdy snuff-box."

In *Oldham's Poems* (1682), a hanger-on of a foolish
nobleman is satirised :

> " There's nought so mean can 'scape the flattering sot,
> Not his lord's snuff-box, nor his powder pot."

Misson, in his *Travels in England*, 1697 (already
quoted for his account of the use of tobacco), speaks of
the beaux who frequented our public places. He describes them somewhat contemptuously as " creatures,
compounded of a periwig, and a coat laden with powder
as white as a miller's, a face besmeared with snuff, and

a few affected airs." Tom Brown, in his *Letters from the Dead to the Living*, speaks of "a flaming beau of the first magnitude," whose long lace cravat, reaching down to his waist, "was most agreeably discoloured with snuff from top to bottom." In Congreve's *Love for Love*, Mr. *Tattle* commences his advances to *Miss Prue* by the present of a snuff-box; and she exclaims joyously, "Look you here what *Mr. Tattle* has given me! Look you here, cousin, here's a snuff-box; nay, there's snuff in't: here, will you have any? Oh, good! how sweet it is!" In the *Pleasant and Comical History of Scaramouch* (1698), is given an amusing account of his shifts for a living (afterwards made the

subject of a paper in the *Spectator*), one of which consisted in obtaining large handfuls of snuff from the boxes of friends who "obliged him with a pinch." Among the varieties of snuff named, is Orangery, Neroly, Bergamota, and Jassamena; which when he resold to the dealers, was necessarily mixed and called "snuff of millefleurs." To take snuff and offer a box gracefully was one part of a beau's education. There is a curious wood-cut of a full blown exquisite thus employed, on the title-page of a rare pamphlet of four leaves, published in

1703, called *The Beau's Catechism;* which is here copied. He is accused in the text of having "more Periwig than Man," with " the necessary additions of Vigo Snuff; " and his employment in the theatre is defined to be, "to chat an hour with a mask in a side box, then whip behind the scenes, bow to a fool in the pit, take snuff, and talk to the actresses." In Baker's comedy, *Hampstead Heath* (published 1706), a song describing "the Beau's character," commences with these peculiar details :—

> " A wig that's full,
> An empty skull,
> A box of burgamot."

Tom Brown, who drew his highly coloured pictures from nature, speaks of one, "whose periwig was large enough to have loaded a camel, and he bestowed upon it at least a bushel of powder;" he adds other details equally confirmatory of the general satire. Misson was just in saying, "They are exactly like Molière's marquises, and want nothing but that title, which they would assume in any other country but England."

In the *Spectator*, No. 43, this question is very reasonably asked :—" Would it not employ a beau prettily enough, if, instead of playing eternally with a snuff-box, he spent some part of his time in making one ? "

Scented snuffs were sometimes made the recipients of poison. In 1712 the Duke de Noailles presented the Dauphiness of France with a box of Spanish snuff in which she delighted ; she kept it for a few days pri-

vately; it was charged with poison, which she inhaled;
and five days after the present, died of it, complaining
of sharp pain in the temples. This excited much
attention, and great fears of "accepting a pinch," on
the one hand, or offering it on the other. It became a
general belief that such poisoned snuff was used in
Spain, and by Spanish emissaries to clear away political opponents, and that the Jesuits also adopted it for
the purpose of poisoning their enemies. Hence it was
termed "Jesuits' snuff," and a great dread of it was felt
for a considerable time.

One instance of the dangers inseparable from scented
snuff is given in an anecdote of the Duc de Bourbon,
grandson of the great Condé; who took Santeuil the
poet to a great entertainment, compelled him to drink
a large quantity of champagne, and ultimately poured
his snuff-box, filled with Spanish snuff, into his wine.
This produced a violent fever, of which Santeuil died,
amid excruciating agonies, within fourteen hours after.

The general use of scented snuffs at this time is
noted in a little pamphlet published in 1710 called
*The Travels and Misfortunes of the Enchanted Snuff-
box*, which appears to be a satire on Dr. Sacheverel,
whose box is described as filled with a snuff called
Orangery: after dinner "the ladies all impatient for
the first pinch, put in their fingers almost all at once;
the gentlemen with some respect after." Agreeable as
all these scents may be, they are generally unwhole-
some, and the "disguise" in the true flavour of the
tobacco produced by such means, gives the dishonest

trader much power of adulteration, or at least of mixtures of bad and inferior tobacco. It is not unusual to
save the sweepings of tobacco-shops and warehouses
for the purpose of mixing in snuff. Of course in all
such establishments tobacco is scattered and falls upon
the floors in the warehouse ; portions of leaf adhere to
the shoes, which are scraped in receptacles for the
purpose; it is never wasted, but is dried and ground
down with all extraneous matter, to put into dark
coloured highly scented snuffs. This cannot be done
with light-coloured pungent snuffs, like high-dried
Scotch, which is made from the central stalk of the
tobacco, cut fine and ground, and is one of the purest
snuffs manufactured.

Rappee may be considered as the parent of all other
snuffs : its name smacks of a genuine origin. *Carotte,*
in the same way, carries the mind back by its name to
the early part of the seventeenth century, when tobacco
was rolled into the *carrot* form, and the end of the lump
rasped as the snuff was wanted; according to the
arrangement already described on p. 249, and further
illustrated in our cut of the decorated ivory rasper,
p. 245, one of which was an essential piece of fur-
niture to the pocket of the beau, or the boudoir
of the belle, in the days of the *Grande Monarque.*
The *Carotte* was sometimes steeped in wine or sweet
liqueurs to give it flavour.

Palillio, mentioned in Southerne's play, quoted in
a previous page, was properly termed *pulvilio,* and is
frequently mentioned by other authors of that era.

It was Portuguese snuff: in considerable favour. The
Orangery, Bergamotte, and *Jassamena,* took their
names from the scents they indicate as adopted to
flavour them. During the reign of Anne, snuff-taking
increased to a great extent, and so did the varieties of
mixtures, flavours, and names. Chambers, in his
Enclyclopædia of 1727, says : " The kinds of snuff and
their several names are infinite, and new ones are
invented ; so that it would be difficult, not to say
impossible, to give a detail of them. We shall only say,
that there are three grand sorts, the first granulated,
the second an impalpable powder, and the third the
bran, or coarse part remaining after sifting a second
sort." We may here note a few of the principal old
court favourites : *Étrenne* obtained its name from the
custom of presenting Louis XV. with choice specimens
of snuff, as a New Year's offering from the various manufacturers : his selected choice being adopted as the
fashionable stimulant for the noses of courtiers for the
year. *Bureau* is a snuff of the same character, and
was one of the selected favourites of the sovereign,
which being of peculiarly good flavour, achieved a less
fleeting popularity, and being pretty generally used in
the cabinet of the politician, became known by the
French name thereof.

A great impetus to the habit of snuff-taking was
given in 1702. The fleet under the command of Sir
George Rook captured at Port Saint Mary near Cadiz,
several thousand barrels of very choice Spanish snuff,
along with the plunder. On returning by Vigo

they also obtained native snuff from the Havanna destined for the Spanish market. This very large quantity of snuff was sold at the principal seaports, as " prizes," for the benefit of officers and crews, with the usual carelessness of sailors in bargaining with Jews and " Land sharks," to the quickest purchasers ; and waggon loads were parted with at the rate of four-pence per pound! It was christened " Vigo snuff;" and the popularity of the war, the name of the snuff, and the novelty of excessive cheapness, combined to induce a very general use of it.*

Pope in his *Rape of the Lock* notes the use of the *Snuff-box* as a luxurious appendage to the *bon ton* :—

> " Sir Plume of amber snuff-box justly vain,
> And the nice conduct of a clouded cane ;
> With earnest eyes, and round unthinking face,
> He first the snuff-box open'd, then the case."

This nobleman's habit of " tapping the box," in the pauses of his speech, is very characteristic of the habit of the beau snuff-taker, whose mental powers are satirically hinted at by the poet's mention of " the lunar sphere ; " where—

> —— "hero's wits are kept in ponderous vases,
> And beaux in snuff-boxes and tweezer cases."

It is said of Prince Eugene in Pope's *Key to the Lock* that " 'tis remarkable the General is a great taker of Snuff as well as Towns."

---

* One of the dealers of the day advertises "Fine Seville Snuff from the Pearl Prize, sold by Jas. Healey at the Black boy, without Bishopsgate."

Gold, silver, and precious stones were frequently adopted as the materials from which snuff-boxes were manufactured. Agate, pietra dura, rare woods, or mosaics, were used for such persons as could not " sport " gold and diamonds. The following is a good description of the snuff-boxes of Queen Anne's era :—

> For females fair, and formal fops to please,
> The mines are robb'd of ore, of shells the seas,
> With all that mother earth and beast afford
> To man, unworthy now, tho' once their lord :
> Which wrought into a box, with all the show
> Of art the greatest artist can bestow ;
> Charming in shape, with polish'd rays of light,
> A joint so fine it shuns the sharpest sight ;
> Must still be graced with all the radiant gems
> And precious stones that e'er arrived in Thames.
> Within the lid the painter plays his part,
> And with his pencil proves his matchless art ;
> There drawn to life some spark or mistress dwells,
> Like hermits chaste and constant to their cells. *

Enamelled boxes, looking like porcelain and covered with painted ornaments, were manufactured in fanciful variety. Our engraving represents a curious box of this

kind, which has no doubt been the treasured " pocket companion" of some devoted musician. It is formed

* *Pandora's Box ; a Satyr against Snuff*, 1719.

like the old harpsichord, and withinside the lid is a
Sonata; the outside is painted with groups of musical
instruments, and it is dated 1723, being of German
manufacture. Subjects from Watteau were favourites
on such painted boxes; and the famous Dresden China
Factory at Meissen produced some exceedingly
beautiful boxes in that brittle material, which are now
treasured within the cabinets of wealthy collectors, they
were mounted in metal, and were perfectly tight at all
junctures, the whole of the metal work being fabricated
with exceeding care. The hinges of all old boxes are
generally exquisitely made. Very frequently these boxes

assumed fanciful forms, so that they became part of the
decoration of a lady's boudoir. In Cibber's comedy
of *The Careless Husband*, Lord Foppington declares
"Lady Betty was just upon the wing, but I caught her
by the snuff-box, and she pretends to stay to see if I
will give it her or no." To which an equally foppish
rival Lord replies, "Death! 'tis that I gave her, and
the only present she would ever receive from me."
Two examples of these toy-boxes for Ladies are here

engraved. The one formed like a hen and chickens;
the other, like a Shepherdess with a pet lamb; both are
enamelled on a thin piece of copper, and are highly
coloured with great delicacy and finish; the lid is at
the base, and the figures which might repose on the
toilette table, or in the boudoir of a beauty, must be
reversed when the contents are used. When not in
use they would scarcely be taken for *tabatières*.
Newly fledged "poets" of the smaller kind, indulged
their wits in tributes to the Ladies, when such presents
were made. Here is a sample from "Poems on
several Occasions," appended to a play called the
Intriguing Milliners (1738):—

> Dear Jenny, if this snuff shou'd want
> Such odours as your breath bestows,
> Your touch will give 't a sweeter scent
> Than quintessence of fragrant rose.

The fashionable mode adopted by Lady snuff-takers
at this period, is thus narrated in the same volume:—

> From agate-box, the newest mode,
> Her snuff Miss Bid takes in a shell :
> A thousand times to me sh' has vow'd,
> Tis faint, 'tis languid, has no smell.
>
> The reason's plain ; her rosy hand,
> Its fragrance to the snuff denies ;
> The rival shells triumphant stand,
> The snuff with envy pines and dies.
>
> These guilty shells if you'll but throw,
> Dear Bid, like others, in the streets,
> Your snuff with finest scents will glow,
> And vie with bless'd Arabia's sweets.

Snuff-takers were not permitted to indulge their favourite mode of taking tobacco, with an impunity disallowed by the strict to their brethren the smokers. A journalist thus quietly descants on the habit: Snuff-taking is an odd custom. If we came suddenly upon it in a foreign country, it would make us split our sides with laughter. A grave gentleman takes a little casket out of his pocket, puts a finger and thumb in, brings away a pinch of a sort of powder, and then with the most serious air possible, as if he were doing one of the most important actions of his life (for even with the most indifferent snuff-takers there is a certain look of importance), proceeds to the thrust, and keeps thrusting it at his nose; after which he shakes his head, or his waistcoat, or his nose itself, or all three, in the style of a man who has done his duty, and satisfied the most serious claim of his well being. It is curious to see the various modes in which people take snuff; some do it by little fits and starts, and get over the thing quickly. These are epigrammatic snuff-takers, who come to the point as fast as possible, and to whom the pungency is everything. They generally use a sharp and severe snuff, a sort of essence of pins' points. Others are all urbanity and polished demeanour; they value the style as much as the sensation, and offer the box around them as much out of dignity as benevolence. Some take snuff irritably, others bashfully, others in a manner as dry as snuff itself, generally with an economy of the vegetable: others with a luxuriance of gesture, and a lavishness of supply, that announce a

moister article, and shed its superfluous honours over
neckcloth and coat.   Dr. Johnson was probably a
snuff-taker of this kind.   He used to take it out of his
waistcoat pocket, instead of a box.   There is a species of
long-armed snuff-takers, that perform the operation in
a style of potent and elaborate preparation, ending with
sudden activity.   But a smaller and rounder man sometimes attempts it.   He first puts his head on one side;
then stretches forth the arm, with pinch in hand; then
brings round his hand, as a snuff-taking elephant
might his trunk; and finally, shakes snuff, head and
nose together, in a sudden vehemence of convulsion.
His eyebrows all the while lifted up, as if to make
room for the onset; and when he has ended, he
draws himself back to his perpendicular, and generally
proclaims the victory he has won over the insipidity
of the previous moment, by a sniff and a great
" Hah ! "

There were others by no means satisfied with such a
quiet satire on the habit.   By them it was declared:
"physicians observe that more people have died of apoplexies in one year since the use of snuff has come up
than before in one hundred; and indeed most, if not all,
of those who die of apoplexies and other such sudden
deaths, upon inquiry will be found to have been great
snuff-takers; as it happens usually in Spain and Portugal, where of late years the common disease that carries
people off is apoplexy."*   Death was in fact paraded as

* A Treatise of the Use of Tobacco, &c., 1722.   The Edinburgh Encyclo-

freely, to act as a bugbear for snuffers, as for smokers; and grave doctors were not wanting to declare that the brains of snuff-takers were found after death, dried to a sort of dirty membrane, clogged with soot.* Cancer of the nose was another pleasant threat held out as the goal to which all snuff-takers must arrive; but the threats of the medicals had no effect on snuff-takers, because they found very many doctors of an opposite way of thinking, who used snuff in their gold-headed canes, as a disinfectant, and believed in its utility when used in moderation.

The author of the *Toilette des Dames, ou Encyclopédie de la Beauté*, published in Paris about 1760, is very hard on his fair countrywomen who take snuff. He says : "Everything in France depends upon *la mode ;* and it has pleased the *mode* to patronise this disgusting custom, and carry about with them small boxes, which they term *demi-journées.*" He declares that it "deforms the nose, stains the skin, taints the breath," and asks what would be thought of Venus or the Graces, if all were engaged in snuff-taking.† But, as every medal has its reverse, Arbuckle, in his *Poem*

pædia ends a short but severe article on snuff with the significant reference, *See Poisons.*

* Hoffman says that the heads of some executed criminals (who had been great snuffers) being dissected, the *patera* of the brain was black with snuff; and he was informed that of the heads of the English soldiers who were killed in the Bohemian war, all who snuffed had their brain in that condition.—T. SHORT's *Discourse on Tea and Tobacco.* 1750.

† Those who may be curious to see the lengths to which coarse attacks on the lady snuff-takers were carried, may refer to Henry Season's *Almanack* for 1743 : the passage cannot now be reprinted *pro causâ pudoris.*

on Snuff, 1719, absolutely holds up the custom as one
which adds a new charm to beauty :—

> " With Snuff the beauteous Celia shades her face,
> And adds a foil to every obvious grace.
> Her lips o'erspread with dusky Vigo, speak
> The brighter colour on her lovely cheek ;
> Nay, underneath the tawny shade they wear,
> The lips themselves more beautiful appear.
> For beauty mask'd, like the great few who shun
> The praise and honour by their merits won,
> By how much it denies its own applause
> Or seems but so to do, a greater draws.
> For, apt to imagine more than is conceal'd,
> The fancy heightens every charm that's veil'd."

In the same year appeared an opposition poem, entitled, *Pandora's Box ; a Satyr against Snuff,* in which
the author laments the constant use of snuff among all
classes:—

> ———— "now, 'tis by every sort
> And sex adored, from Billingsgate to court.
> But ask a wench, ' how oysters sell ?'—if nice,
> She begs a pinch before she sets a price.
> Go thence to 'Change, inquire the price of Stocks ;
> Before they ope their lips they open first the box.
> Next pay a visit to the Temple, where
> The lawyers live, who gold to heaven prefer ;
> You'll find them stupify'd to that degree,
> They'll take a pinch before they'll take their fee.
> Then make a step and view the splendid court,
> Where all the gay, the great, the good resort;
> E'en they, whose pregnant skulls, though large and thick,
> Can scarce secure their native sense and wit,
> Are feeding of their hungry souls with pure
> Ambrosial snuff. * * * * * *
> But to conclude : the gaudy court resign,
> T' observe, for once, a place much more divine,
> Where the same folly's acted by the good,
> And is the sole devotion of the lewd ;
> The church, more sacred once, is what we mean,
> Where now they flock to see and to be seen ;

> The box is used, the book laid by, as dead,
> With snuff, not Scripture, there the soul is fed ;
> For where to heaven the hands by one of those
> Are lifted, twenty have them at the nose ;
> And while some pray, to be from sudden death
> Deliver'd, others snuff to stop their breath."

In his preface the author says : "The principal maladies produced by the misapplication of snuff take their rise, from the violent convulsive motion that nature makes use of in sneezing;" and he then continues, "I don't remember, nor do I believe, that sneezing has hitherto been reckoned by any author, ancient or modern, amongst the causes of consumption." He then adroitly turns aside to his own purpose the old custom of invoking a blessing on sneezers, a custom which dates from the most remote times, by asking: "I should be glad to be informed how the common salutation, 'God bless you!' when anybody sneezes, became so much in vogue ; if it were not from the dreadful convulsions, and sometimes sudden deaths, that have been the fatal consequences of those impetuous shocks." The following story, apropos of this, is in *Ménagiana* :—

> " Un petit-maître, après mauvais chance,
> Sortoit du jeu la tabatière en main.
> Un gueux passoit, qui vient à lui soudain
> Lui demandant l'aumône avec instance.
> Des deux côtez grande étoit l'indigence.
> Il ne me reste, ami, dit le joueur,
> Que le tabac. En veux tu ? Serviteur,
> Répond le gueux, qui n'étoit pas trop nice,
> Nul besoin n'ai d'éternuer, seigneur,
> Chacun me dit assez, 'Dieu vous bénisse.' "

In addition to the snuffs already described, we may note others introduced about the middle of the last century, and among them *Violet Strasburgh*, a snuff originally manufactured in the old German town whence it is named, and consisting of rappee and bitter almonds reduced to fine powder, to which amber-gris and attar-gul was added as a scent; it was snuff much in request with ladies at this period, and constantly patronised by the late Queen Charlotte, whose example made snuff-taking a fashionable thing among court ladies; the queen also used Spanish snuff, and was in the habit of adding a tea-spoonful of green tea to her box every morning.* *Macauba* was another highly scented snuff, brought from the island of Martinique, which was extensively patronised by dowagers. The list of prices and names given by Wimble, the snuff-seller, about 1740, is curious now; he adds to the end of it this note : " To small quantities under two ounces something will be added, on account of the extraordinary trouble and waste."

RETAIL PRICES OF WIMBLE'S SNUFFS.

	per lb., s. d.			per lb., s. d.
English Rappee	3 0		Best English Rappee	4 0
Do. do.	3 6		Common do.	2 0
Bolongaro's Hollanda	4 0		Good Plain do.	2 6
English Round Rappee	3 6		Best Scotch	2 6
Strasburgh	3 0		Common do.	2 0
Do. Violet	4 0		Ordinary English Rappee	2 6
Scented Rappee	2 6		High-flavoured do.	3 6
English Bran	3 0		Composite do. do.	2 6

---

* The author is acquainted with a gentleman who fills his pipe with *tea* for smoking.

per lb.,	s.	d.	per lb.,	s.	d.
Fine English Rappee	3	6	Rappee Bergamot	2	0
High-flavoured Coarse do.	3	0	Low Rappee	1	0
Ordinary English Bran	2	6	Plain Scotch	2	0
Carrot Rappee	4	0	Natural English Rappee	3	0
Romano's Hollande	4	0	High-flavoured do.	3	0
Best Dunkerque Rappee	3	6	Cephalic	5	0
Macabao	8	0	St. Domingo	6	0
Scotch	2	0	Brazil Imitated	5	0
Fine do.	3	0	Best Brazil	24	0
Scholten's Best Rappee	6	0	Second do.	20	0
Bolongaro's St. Vincent	4	0	Third do.	16	0
John's Lane	2	0	Best Spanish	10	0
Spanish Bran	6	0	Second do.	8	0
Common Scotch	1	0	Best Havannah	6	0
Fine Irish	2	0	Common do. *	4	0

The Cephalic snuff mentioned in the previous list was one of those compounds of herbs, &c., put forth like " Grimstone's Eye Snuff," and extensively bought toward the end of last century, from a belief in its efficacy in freeing the head of bad humour, and imparting clearness in vision, in which it was imagined to be "most sovereign." The inventor of this " cephalic and ophthalmic snuff" published in 1722 a pamphlet on its virtues, in which he assures us, that " the Virginia tobacco from which this tobacco is prepared, being here divested of its malignant *ill* qualities, and strengthened in its *good* ones, will, when taken in snuff, answer the desirable ends and intentions of

* Another trader of the period thus notes his wares : "John Bowden, at the Highlander and Black Boy in Threadneedle Street, London, makes and sells the best Scotch snuff, plain and scented St. Domingo, Dutch and Strasbourg, Hoxton and all other sorts of Rappee, Spanish, Seville, Havanna, Brazil, Portugal, and Bergamot; Aloe, Pigtail, and Mild Tobacco ; with all sorts of perfumer's goods, wholesale and retail."

snuff; as, for example, to make an evacuation of offending humours from the head, eyes, &c., without the usual ill consequences of it." Thus, tobacco being washed and deprived of its native virtues, was impregnated with foreign ingredients, and sold as a much-improved article! The author's directions for its use are as follow:—

"Take some of this tobacco, and dry it either in the sun or before the fire, till you can rub it into a gross powder, and put it into your snuff-box, either alone, or you may mix it about half one and half the other, just as you please, with your other snuff that you usually take. And so at times take it, and you will find it fragrant, odoriferous, delicious, and pleasant, recreating and refreshing the head and brain, and will answer at once what is to be wished for in the taking of snuff."

One of these quack snuff-vendors issued an advertisement of so grandiloquent a nature that it is here reprinted as a curiosity from the *General Advertiser* of June 21, 1749:—

"Once more I desire you to remember, I have published my *Imperial Snuff*, for all disorders in the head; and I think I might have gone farther, and said, for all disorders of body and mind.—It hath set a great many to rights that was never expected, but there is but few, or none, that careth to have it published they were a little out of their senses, although it be really an ailment that none can help; but here is present relief, if not a cure: but I hope both, as by

God's assistance it hath been performed already on many. And I think it my duty to let the world know it, that they may not bear so many miserable ailments that is capable of curing. I hear it is reported abroad, I am dead, and that the world is imposed on; but, thank God, I am alive, and put my dependence on him, and that he will give me leave to do some more service before I go hence. But suppose I was dead, my Snuff is alive, and I hope it will live after I am dead, as it is capable of keeping the world in sprightly life and health, which must be allowed to be the greatest blessing in the world. But what is riches without that? And what would some have given for some of these reliefs before it was advertised? But you are all heartily welcome at this price of sixpence, at present, but I should be glad of more from the rich. I do assure you it is sold at this price in regard to the poor only.

" I am yours, &c.,

" Samuel Major.

" In Swedland-Court, against the end of
Half-Moon-Alley, Bishopsgate-street."

" This Snuff is sold by George Horselyham, servant at Mr. Ashley's Punch-house on Ludgate-hill, and at Mr. Child's, Sam's Coffee-House, near the Custom-house; of whom you may have a true character of this Snuff, it having repaired his constitution. It is left at the bar of the said house for conveniency of merchants, masters of ships, and others, where you may have a book and a bill of directions."

Snuff-takers could boast at this time a large array of important persons in Church and State, who indulged in the practice, from royalty to curacy. Indeed, Churchmen of all denominations were great patrons of snuff—none more so than the Roman Catholic clergy, whose love for induging in a pinch had made St. Peter's echo, and excited the ire of Pope Innocent the Twelfth, who solemnly excommunicated all who should dare to do it after the " year of grace," 1690, when he denounced the pious snuff-takers. The priests modestly excused the custom, on the plea of its anti-aphrodisiac virtues ; and its social qualities might also be pleaded, for the offer of a pinch was a civility few could resist. Sterne has noted, in his *Sentimental Journey*, the effect of the offer when made by the poor Monk after an uncharitable tirade against " the cloth." It has been a *silent* mode of friendship in travel, frequently adopted between foreigners who know not each other's language ; and the heart opens to the open box of a true gentleman, of whatever country he be, or however humble be his station.

In Read's *Weekly Journal* for Feb. 21, 1761, is given the following—

SIX REASONS FOR TAKING A PINCH OF SNUFF.

When strong perfumes, and noisome scents,
   The suff'ring nose invade,
Snuff, best of Indian weeds, presents
   Its salutary aid.

When vapours swim before the eyes,
   And cloud the dizzy brain,
Snuff, to dispel the mist, applies
   Its quick-enliv'ning grain.

When pensively we sit or walk,
    Each social friend away,
Snuff best supplies the want of talk,
    And cheers the lonely day.

The hand, like alabaster fair,
    The diamond's sparkling pride,
Can ne'er so gracefully appear,
    If snuff should be denied.

E'en Commerce, name of sweetest sound
    To ev'ry British ear,
Must suff'ring droop, should snuff be found
    Unworthy of our care.

For ev'ry pinch of snuff we take
    Helps trade in some degree ;
As smallest drops of water make
    The vast unbounded sea.

Among men of large intellect, snuff-taking has been
rather common ; it may have been felt by them as a
counter-irritant to the over-worked brain. Pope and
Swift were snuff-takers ; the latter made his by mixing
pounded tobacco with ready-manufactured Spanish
snuff. Bolingbroke, Congreve, and Addison indulged
in it. Gibbon was a confirmed snuff-taker, and in one
of his letters he has left this account of his mode of
using it : " I drew my snuff-box, rapp'd it, took snuff
twice, and continued my discourse, in my usual attitude of my body bent forwards, and my fore-finger
stretched out." In the *silhouette* prefixed to his
miscellaneous works, he is represented indulging his
habit, and looking, as Colman expresses it,—

" Like an erect, black tadpole, taking snuff."

Frederick the Great loved it so entirely that he had

capacious pockets made to his waistcoat, that he might
have as little trouble as possible in getting for immediate use the largest quantity he could desire. It is
said that, unlike the fraternity of snuff-takers, he
disliked others to take a pinch from his box, and,
once detecting a page doing so from one lying in an
adjoining room, exclaimed, "Put that box in your
pocket; it is too small for both of us."* George II.
had the same selfish dislike, but expressed it more
rudely, when he threw away his box in great anger
at a masquerade, because a gentleman took a pinch.
Napoleon carried snuff in a similar way ; and many of
the sovereign pontiffs of the Romish Church have
been confirmed snuff-takers.

In the *Memoirs* of Barré Charles Roberts, he says,
"When my father was at Paris in 1774, he was told by
Count Clouard, then an old man, that he remembered
a time when persons were stationed on the Pont Neuf
at Paris, with boxes of snuff, which they offered to the
passengers. This was a scheme of the manufacturers
to introduce it into general use. At the time this was
told my father, there was no person in France, of
whatever age, rank, or sex, that did not take snuff."

With our brothers of Scotland snuff has found much
favour ; they are so far identified with its use, that a

---

* During the coronation of his mother, the first Queen of Prussia, she
anxiously awaited a chance to get a pinch during the long ceremony. She
at last took an opportunity, when the King's attention seemed engaged ;
but he saw the act, and sent one of his gentlemen to ask her, "whether she
remembered the place she was in, and the rank she held there." It was
at that time considered an act of levity or contempt to take snuff before
respectable persons, or during conversation.

figure of a Highlander helping himself to a pinch was generally sculptured in wood, and placed as a " sign " beside the snuff-shop doors, until within the last thirty years, when such distinction ceased. These figures were sometimes the size of life, painted in natural colours, and placed at the door-jamb. The Scots have well earned their distinction; for, in Scotland alone, according to the computation of the late Rev. Dr. Chalmers, the people lay out six thousand pounds per year on snuff; a reckoning probably within the mark.

The old Scottish snuff-mill was a much more rational invention for ensuring a pure snuff, retaining the full virtues of the tobacco, than the French and English rasp; and the washing and scenting the powder thus produced. Jamieson in his *Etymological Dictionary of the Scottish Language,* says : " When tobacco was first introduced into this country, those who wished to have snuff were wont to toast the leaves before the fire, and then bruise them with a bit of wood in the box, which was therefore called a *mill* from the snuff being *ground* in it."

We here engrave one of the earliest specimens of the genuine old snuff-mill we could obtain. The original is in the possession of  Mr. Paton of Dunfermline; and is traditionally said to have originally belonged to Maggie Lang, who was

burnt for witchcraft at the Cross of Paisley, in the close
of the seventeenth century. She was one of the "witches
of Bargarren, Renfrewshire," whose story is related in
Sinclair's volume *Satan's Invisible World discovered*.
Poor Maggie's box is a small wooden receptacle, upon
which fits a solid cover, with a strong handle above,
and a conical projection beneath; the tobacco is placed
in the box or mill, and pounded into dust by the cone,
the lower part of which is shod with rough metal to
assist the operation. The cut exhibits each portion of
the mill separate, as well as conjoined in the way it
would appear when the snuff was making.

This old form is therefore essentially different to
the more modern snuff-mull, which is used as a recep-

tacle for ground snuff. The engraving
exhibits one about a century old, which
still resembles the older form of the
pounding machine ; but is simply covered
with a wooden lid, and was carried like
the modern snuff-box about the person.
This sketch may assist in illustrating
the process by which snuff-boxes or
horns came to be called *mills* (pro-
nounced *mulls* by the Highlanders). Snuff was termed
*snush** and *sneeshing* in the North. Among Tannahill's *Songs* is *The Highlander's Invitation*, who urges
among other attractions to his *bothy*—

---

* In the *History of Scaramouch*, 1698 (quoted p. 254), snuff is always
called *snush*.

" There'll be plenty of pipe, and a glorious supply
Of the good *sneesh-te-bacht*, and the fine cut-and-dry ;
There we'll drink foggy Care to his gloomy abodes,
And we'll smoke, till we sit in the clouds, like the gods."

The Museum of the Society of Antiquaries of Scotland possesses a rappoir or snuff-grater of Ivory,
beautifully carved and probably of Italian workmanship, said to have belonged to Prince Charles Edward,
known to " disloyal Southrons " as " the Young Pretender." They also have a curious conical snuff-box
of horn (here engraved) which was given
to Mr. George Barclay, of Cavill, by
Pope Innocent XIII., when he was at
Rome, 22nd August, 1722. They have
also specimens of the Scottish *mulls* of
wood and horn ; ultimately they were
made of horn only, with a tight-fitting
cover of the same. Dr. Nott in a note
to his edition of Dekker's *Gull's Horn-*
book, says : " the Scotch mull, or sneeshing mull, with a spoon and hare's foot
appended by chains—the one for applying snuff to the nose, and the other for
wiping the upper lip, is of no very

distant date. I well remember to have seen Bad-
deley the actor come upon the stage with such an
apparatus, as *Gibby*, in *The Wonder*, when Garrick
was playing *Don Felix*." This mull of curved horn is
peculiar in its nationality ; and was furnished in olden
time, if belonging to a person of consequence, with a

variety of small articles attached to it by small silver
chains, to assist the snuff-taker in the most luxurious
style.   They consisted of a hammer to hit the side of

the mull, should the snuff adhere ; a
bodkin to pierce and separate it if it
stick together by damp ; a rake to
collect it into the little shovel ; and
a hare's foot to brush loose parti-
cles from the nose ! Plain people
were contented with plain horn ;
and our cut exhibits the box which
one of Scotland's greatest men, the

Poet Burns, used; and which is now properly valued
in the Museum of the Society of Antiquaries of Scotland.   Its surface is divided into squares, alternately
plain with silver studs in the centre, or ridged in
parallel lines. A small silver plate in the middle
might receive the initials or name of the owner.   It
was given by Burns to his friend Blackie, at one of
the convivial meetings which they held at the Haugh
of Urr, and was presented to this national collection
by his son.

James Boswell in his *Shrubs of Parnassus* has the
following little poem in praise of a pinch of snuff :—

"Oh Snuff! our fashionable end and aim!
Strasburgh, Rappee, Dutch, Scotch! whate'er thy name;
Powder celestial! quintessence divine!
New joys entrance my soul while thou art mine.
Who takes—who takes thee not! where'er I range
I smell thy sweets from Pall Mall to the 'Change.
By thee assisted, ladies kill the day,
And breathe their scandal freely o'er their tea;
Nor less they prize thy virtues when in bed,
One pinch of thee revives the vapour'd head,
Removes the spleen, removes the qualmish fit,
And gives a brisker turn to female wit,
Warms in the nose, refreshes like the breeze,
Glows in the head, and tickles in the sneeze.
Without it, Tinsel, what would be thy lot!
What, but to strut neglected, and forgot!
What boots it for thee to have dipt thy hand
In odours wafted from Arabian land?
Ah! what avails thy scented *solitaire*,
Thy careless swing and pertly tripping air,
The crimson wash that glows upon thy face,
Thy modish hat, and coat that flames with lace!
In vain thy dress, in vain thy trimmings shine,
If the Parisian snuff-box be not thine.
Come to my nose, then, Snuff, nor come alone,
Bring taste with thee, for taste is all thy own."

In a satiric spirit did a later rhymer thus write, under the false pretence of " Praise of Snuff-taking," in the *European Magazine* for 1807 :—

When Honour sinks into the silent grave,
When Valour bleeds his country's cause to save,
The Muse in gratitude prolongs his fame,
And hands to late posterity the name;
Tells how the hero lived, the victor's doom,
And sheds her passing tribute o'er his tomb.
  But say, can she your prowess praise enough,
At once o'erwhelm'd in poetry and snuff?
Tell how you loved the sweet Parnassian shade,
How on the brow of Helicon you stray'd;
Tell how in snuff you sought relief from pain;
Tell how you sniff'd and sneezed, and sniff'd again.

No more let arts and science bear the bell ;
Go, Cleanliness, I chant thy fun'ral knell.
Come, Caledonian custom, list my call ;
Hither French fashions, beastliness, and all.
Come, kindly goddess of the Indian shore !
Bring here your snuff, and grime our noses o'er.
　Snuff's my delight ! let other youths declare
Their minds to Celia or to Chloe fair ;
Let them in sportive glee lead down the dance,
And shyly steal the love-inspiring glance ;
Beauty and all its charms are foolish stuff,
If you compare it to a pinch of snuff.
　Science avaunt ! what are thy pow'rs to me,
Whose whole delight is Scotch and black rappee ?
Newton and Euclid now no more can please,
All knowledge shall be center'd in a sneeze :
Vain are the problems you may wish to draw,
None, none can please the sense like macabau.
　No more let music pour its soothing strain,
Or teach in echoes mountains to complain ;
Enrapt the soul with soft melodious thrill,
And make the senses act against the will ;
Say, can it equal with its pow'r divine,
The pleasing sound of "Take a pinch of mine !"
　No more let poets in their am'rous lays
The sweets of flowrets or of west wind praise,
Or citron groves that Egypt's coast adorn,
Or praise the rising blushes of the morn ;
For ev'ry day's experience only shows
That Strasburg is more grateful to the nose.
　Hither ye Graces ! listen to my call,
(Fish-wives from Billingsgate and Leadenhall,)
Here quickly haste, and all your boxes bring,
And let me dip my greedy fingers in.
This a treat is, this is my nose's heaven ;
This far exceeds old Hardham's 37.

The snuff mentioned in the last line of these rhymes,
took its name from the maker, who was a tobacconist
residing at No. 37, Fleet Street, he was also connected
with the theatres, acting as under treasurer to Garrick.
The late Mr. Minton of Oxford Street, was also an

actor, and cleverly impersonated old men, in the days
when the theatre was a school of acting, and not a
place for the display of *Spectacles*, as it too generally is
at present. Hardham's mixture was formed of Dutch
and rappee. *Masulipatam*, is a dark moist highly
scented snuff, brought from the coast of Coromandel.
Martinique takes its name from the Island in which it
is fabricated. *Princeza* is made at Lisbon. *Bolongaro*,
takes its name from the maker, an Italian who resided
near Frankfort, but retired to Italy with a large fortune. *Penalvar* is a mixture of tobacco and red earth,
brought from Havanna, and of great pungency. As a
dentrifice, this so-called snuff is much and successfully
used.* *Prince's mixture*, a compound of rappee,
scented with attar of roses, was named after George IV.
when Prince Regent. *Gillespie* takes its name from
that of the original manufacturer at Edinburgh, who
made a large fortune thereby.† *Cuba* takes its name
from the place of its birth. *Latakia* is made from the
light tobacco of Persia. Many snuffs have taken their
names from the noblemen who have patronised, or
invented, a particular mixture; of all the number, none
were more remarkable than the late Earl of Harrington,
who spared no expense in procuring snuffs of all kinds,
and devoted one room of his mansion in Whitehall

---

* I am indebted to a clever little book published by Tyas of Cheapside
in 1840, and termed *A Pinch of Snuff*, for these particulars.

† Henry Erskine proposed the motto for the arms on his carriage :—

" Who could have thought it
That noses had bought it ? "

Gardens to properly storing them all. That room was
a curiosity in its way, with its rows of well-made
jars, and proper materials of all kinds for the due
admixture and management of the snuffs they contained, under the able superintendance of a well-
informed man, who was the guardian angel thereof.
After the Earl's death, the collection was sold; and
prices that seem fabulous to the uninitiated, were realised for the finest sorts.

It may almost be doubted whether smokers feel so
large an amount of gratification in their mode of
consuming tobacco, as the snuff-taker does. There
seems an extra amount of excitement and exhilaration
from its use. Smoking may, like angling, be "the contemplative man's recreation;" but snuffing seems to be
the joy of the more mercurial, hence its great popularity in France, and with men of quick intellectual
capacity. The following clever lines *To my Nose*
convey a due sense of this pleasure :—

> Knows he that never took a pinch,
> Nosey, the pleasure thence which flows ?
> Knows he the titillating joys
>   Which my nose knows ?
> O nose ! I am as proud of thee
> As any mountain of its snows ;
> I gaze on thee, and feel that pride
>   A Roman knows ! *

The high-dried snuffs are favourites in Wales and
Scotland. There is a powerfull snuff of this kind
which is said to have originated by accident in Ireland.

* These stanzas first appeared in Miss Sheridan's annual *Comic Offering*
for 1834, and were written by the talented artist-author, Alfred Crow-
quill.

It is known as *Lundyfoot*, or *Irish Blackguard*. The first name is from that of the maker Lundy Foot, who resided at the entrance of Essex Bridge, Dublin; the second, from its being highly approved of by the lower classes of Irish to whom it was given as spoiled material, or from the blackguard who had spoiled it. Tradition is not clear on this point.* The popular story of its origin is, that it was the neglect of a man who had gone to sleep while the snuff was drying in the kiln, that burnt the snuff, and induced the proprietor to put it in a tub at the door for all poor passers by to help themselves, and so rid him of his waste. Another version of the story is, that Foot bought a large quantity of tobacco, from the ruins of a tobacco warehouse in Dublin, and ground the charred material into snuff, which was sold very cheaply to the poorer classes of Irish; until its pungency and flavour became gradually known to the middle and upper classes, and similar snuff demanded.† Foot never forgot the poor, who helped to make his fortune; and a keg of *blackguard* was always placed at his door for all comers; a custom continued by his descendants.

An Irish clergyman celebrated the pleasures of a pinch in a poem, which a few private friends knew, but

* One version of the story is, that the snuff was so called because it was made for the poor of Dublin of the stalks and refuse part of the tobacco.

† This part of the story is also differently told. A messenger had been sent from the Castle to Foot's shop for snuff, and he tried a pinch of the over-dried article, which Foot had on his counter to get rid of to the poor in "ha'porths," and was lamenting his loss; when the "correct nose" of the messenger appreciated the flavour, took some to the Castle, and made it famous.

which has never been printed. It was written about
1788 by the Rev. William King of Mallow, and my
extracts were made from a copy in the possession of
Crofton Croker. The author notes his own habits
freely; and in so doing, gives us a true insight of the
philosophy of snuff-taking. He says:—

> "——— before I budge an inch
> I hail Aurora with a pinch;
> After three cups of morning tea
> A pinch most grateful is to me;
> If then by chance the post arrive,
> My fingers still the deeper dive.
> When gallant Nelson gains his point,
> I sink in deep to middle joint;
> And soon as e'er the work he clinches,
> Oh, then I take the pinch of pinches!
> But if our heroes chance to fail,
> I seldom go beyond the nail.
> If I on ancient classics pore,
> Or turn their learned pages o'er,
> I take a pinch at every pause,
> A tribute of my just applause.
> Whenever I dip in page historic,
> Or pass an hour in wit with Yorick,
> I relish more each paragraph
> If season'd with a pinch and laugh.
> Or if discussing subjects curious,
> I revel in a pinch luxurious;
> E'en joyous friends and claret rosy
> Insipid are *sans* pinches cosy.
> Whate'er I do, where'er I be,
> My social box attends on me;
> It warms my nose in winter's snow,
> Refreshes midst midsummer's glow;
> Of hunger sharp it blunts the edge,
> And softens grief as some alledge.
> Thus, eased of care or any stir,
> I broach my freshest canister;
> And freed from trouble, grief, or panic,
> I pinch away in snuff balsamic.
> For rich or poor, in peace or strife,
> It smooths the rugged path of life."

Lord Stanhope once made an estimate of the time wasted by a snuff-taker :—" if we suppose this practice to be persisted in for forty years, two entire years of the snuff-taker's life will be dedicated to tickling his nose, and two more to blowing it." He ends by declaring, that " a proper application of the time and money thus lost to the public, might constitute a fund for the discharge of the national debt."

The following outrageous attempt at satirising the habits of snuff-taking to excess, appeared in the *London Journal* about thirty years ago : " A provincial paper says, that a gentleman in Devonshire has invented what he calls a snuff-pistol ; it has two barrels, and being applied to the nose, upon touching a spring under them with the fore-finger, both nostrils are instantly filled, and a sufficient quantity driven up the head to last the whole day !"

We will conclude with a few remarks on snuff-boxes, native and foreign, to complete those scattered through this chapter. And first of the primitive snuff-mills. Of these a writer in the *New York Literary World*, for 1834 gives the following account. He says :—

" Old Brazilian Indians were the fathers of snuff, and its best fabricators. Though counted the least refined, or in other words, the most savage of Americans, in one respect their taste was as pure as that of the fashionable world of the West. Their snuff has never been equalled, nor in simplicity and originality their implements for making and taking it."

The following is a description of their milling and
sniffing machinery—machinery, we believe, never
figured and published before :—

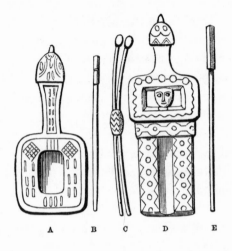

The figure A at the right of the engraving is a slab
of jacaranda (rose-wood) resembling a spatula ; the
length ten inches, of which five are taken up by the
handle.   The blade four inches wide, and nearly half
an inch thick in the middle, but reduced to a quarter
at the edges.   Except the cavity in the centre the
entire face of the instrument is covered with carvings,
as shown in the cut.   The back is plain, and void of
ornament; the extremity of the handle represents the
head of a serpent, with the tongue protruded ; the eyes
are imitated by two pieces of bone or white shell, which
strongly contrast with the dark hue of the wood.   The
effect of colour is further attempted, by filling the

grooves of which the carving consists, with white and yellow pigment.

B, a pestle or rubber—a smoothly polished cylindrical stick of rose-wood, nine inches long, and three-fourths of an inch in diameter ; the upper part is squared, the lower end bevelled and considerably worn.

Now, let us see how the owner put this apparatus in play. In the first place he took a seat on a log on the ground, drew from a *chuspa*, commonly suspended over the right shoulder, a few pieces of dried leaves of tobacco and placed them in the cavity of A. Then grasping the handle of the mill in one hand he began to grind them with the pestle or rubber B in the other, the blade of A resting on the knee or lap. In a few moments the leaves were reduced to a powder much finer than the mortar could make—in a word, to a rich and *fragrant* snuff. Not a fragrance due to the substance ground, but to the material of the mill! The heat developed by the friction of . two pieces of jacaranda evolves a delicious aroma, which impregnates whatever is ground between them. This was the secret of the superiority of primitive snuff—a knowledge of it may be worth something to modern manufacturers.

The article being thus prepared, the next thing was to transmit it to its destination, ere it grew cold or its odour became weakened by evaporation. The apparatus for this part of the business is figured at C, a double tube, consisting of two thin, light, cylindrical, and parallel bones, fourteen inches long, three-eighths of an

inch bore, and slightly curved ; probably the leg bones
of a species of crane.   They are united by a neat and
ornamental piece of needle- or platted-work. The upper
ends are finished off with little round ferules of wood,
the opposite ends have no additions.   The reader has
doubtless anticipated the rest : No sooner was the tritu-
rating operation ended, than the pestle was dropped,
and this double tube taken up, the plain ends plunged
into the smoking powder and the ferruled ones applied
to the nostrils—the mouth had meanwhile been closed
—a smart inhalation instantly followed, and the warm
scented powder in a trice was diffused over the olfac-
tory palate ! The apparatus was then hung round the
neck, and the proprietor, if alone, arose, we may suppose, and went on his way rejoicing.

The figure D represents another mill. It is larger
than the preceding one, being fifteen inches long and
of a different form, showing how fancy exerted her influence over South American artists in bygone days. The
grinding receptacle is in the shape of a gutter running
out to the end of the blade.   The ornamental work is
more elaborate, part being pierced entirely through.
The handle represents a serpent with its tongue thrust
out and the head inclined upwards.   The eyes are
pieces of shell secured by wax. A human face is
tolerably worked out, the mouth being represented by
a piece of shell with an edge finely serrated to imitate
teeth.   The rubber is shown at E ; its form is more
distinct in this, than in our other example. Both mills
seem to have done considerable service.   There was

another pair of sniffing-pipes, but they varied so slightly from those we have figured as to render a sketch of them unnecessary. The bones of both were very thin, round, of uniform bore, white, and relieved by the black bulbs of rose-wood.

Such was the snuff-making devices of old copper-coloured artists, and such the fashionable mode of imbibing the sweet-scented dust by red warriors and ladies. Has either been improved by white inventors? The mill is so simple, portable, cheap, and durable, that in these respects it cannot be beaten. As regards the singular attribute—so foreign to its chief design—of communicating an agreeable perfume, what modern engine can stand before it? Of the sniffing-tubes it may safely be said, that while for cleanliness and economy they are far superior to fingers and thumbs, in a philosophical point of view they are the oldest illustrations extant of elevating dry substances through pipes by atmospheric pressure. The custom of embellishing and carrying the whole apparatus as personal ornaments may be excepted to, but in this matter fancy rules, and more costly pendants are not always more useful. On the back of the handle of A is an angular recess worked out, probably for kindling fire by friction; thus uniting in these rose-wood jewels the tinder-box, snuff-box, and snuff-mill. Lastly, for the snuff itself: if we may trust a first-rate judge, there is no comparison between its warm, odoriferous, and grateful flavour when made and taken as just described, and the fetid poisonous stuff manufactured even in the royal factory of Spain—said

U

to be the best extant; nay, we are assured if but half
the process of fabrication followed there were made
known, amateurs of the article would eschew it for ever.

Modern Indians are as warm admirers of snuff as
their ancestors.   Their apparatus for making and
taking it is also similar to those described.   I have
seen neat circular mills, varying from two to five inches
over; with conical and pyramidal pestles or mullers,
one and a half and two and a half inches long.   The
sniffing-pipes are more portable and compact than
those figured above.   They seldom exceed eight inches
in length, and sometimes are not over four.   They are
often composed of three bones—the lower extremities
of the pair applied to the nostrils being united (by wax)
to a shorter and rather larger one; precisely like one
suction-pipe serving two pumps.

The Eastern nations make use of a box of hard
wood or ebony of an oblong spherical form about the

size of a pear; it has a narrow opening at the top, through which the
snuff is shook upon the hand; as it
is moist, and may adhere to its sides,
an ivory *stylus* is used to stir it; and
when the box is closed, it is done by
thrusting this down the centre of the
box, and screwing its head over the
aperture, as shown by the dotted lines
in the cut.

The Chinese use a similar kind of snuff-box, looking
like a smelling bottle, and to their stoppers is appended

a little spoon or shovel; after the fashion of those adopted among ourselves for cayenne-pepper bottles. With this they take out the pungent dust, and place it upon the back of the left hand, which is closed; and a receptacle formed at the root of the forefinger and thumb, from which it is drawn up the nose. This plan is sometimes adopted by the Scotch.

A Moorish snuff-box from Mogador is here engraved; it is formed from a hollow bamboo, each end being secured by a plug of cork, capable of removal at the pleasure of the snuff-taker. The surface of the reed is decorated with incised lines cut with a sharp tool; and filled with red and blue colour. It is a cheap, convenient, and portable thing.

European boxes present an enormous variety of design; it is not possible here to name a tythe of them. The luxurious boxes of gold and silver, patronised by the rich, or the diamond-studded boxes which Royalty presents as "memorials" to favoured statesmen, are examples of what art and taste, united to wealth, may do for so apparently simple a thing as a receptacle for snuff. The plain wooden box of slight value, which only accommodates the necessary wants of the snuff-taker, may thus by a series of substitutes and additions, the invention of goldsmith, jeweller, and painter, become the most costly article a nobleman can carry.

There has been a very pretty "social-box" manufactured, to roll round the table after dinner is concluded
at clubs, and social gatherings of a public nature. It
represents a Cupid guiding a closed barrow, whose lid

when opened displays a fair supply of snuff. Large
boxes of favourite snuffs are generally kept for such
gatherings, at the cost of the landlord of the house.
Boxes decorated with paintings were great favourites in
the days of Anne and George I.; having pastoral scenes
as described in Arbuckle's *Poem on Snuff*, 1719 :—

> " Here bends the milkmaid to the laden cows,
>   And there fat sheep in lusty pastures browse,
>   Fond cooing turtles through the meadows stray,
>   And nymphs and shepherds not less fond than they."

Very large sums have been expended in painting
such boxes; and artists of much eminence have
devoted their talent to the work. Many that emanate

from the *ateliers* of France and Holland, show more ability than delicacy. Sometimes the French boxes have been used politically; thus the Bonapartists during the banishment of their chief to Elba, and while plotting his return, filled their boxes with *violet*-scented snuff, the violet being Napoleon's distinctive flower, and when offering a pinch, would significantly inquire "Do *you* love this perfume?" Talleyrand argued that snuff-taking was *essential* to all great politicians, as it gave them time for thought in answering awkward questions while pretending only to indulge in a pinch; or a proper management of the box, enabled them to adapt themselves to many temporary necessities of diplomacy.*

Boxes are often constructed of "relics," or woods which are associated with some great name, such as Shakespeare's mulberry-tree,† Nelson's ship, or Wellington's table. Of the first named so many were constructed, particularly after Garrick's jubilee, that it rivalled the wood of the "true cross" in quantity, which has been calculated to be sufficient for the construc-

---

* The author of the *Pinch of Snuff*, 1840, says : "Of the importance of snuff-boxes as a means of keeping up friendly relations with foreign powers, we need only quote, from the account of sums expended at the coronation of George IV., the following entry :—

	£	s.	d.
"Messrs. Rundell and Bridge, for snuff-boxes to foreign ministers	8205	15	5."

† The tree was cut down by the (Ir-)Reverend Francis Gastrell, to save himself the trouble of showing it to strangers. He rented Shakespeare's house (New Place) and grounds, and he ended by pulling the house down in revenge for the taxation he paid during his absence from it.

tion of a Ship of War. We engrave one of these boxes,
constructed from the famous mulberry wood, soon after

the tree was cut down, and
before it was so greatly
prized. It was made by
William Sharpe of Stratford
on Avon, who bought the
wood, and by oath testified
to the genuine character of
the works he made; an oath he again registered on
his death-bed. His work is well known by its rude
and peculiar character, and the introduction of the
mulberry as a decoration, as we see it on the lid of this
box, which has been constructed from a portion of the
root of the tree, one of its bosses being cut into a
medallion of Shakespeare.

Boxes of China, tortoise-shell, and horn are not
considered good for snuff by connoisseurs, as they allow
it to become dry too quickly. Horn is the material for
the Scottish mull; but that is an entire horn, well
stopped by a cover, almost "plugged" in the opening,
and the climate of Scotland is colder and damper than
our own. Very neat wooden boxes covered externally
with a pattern of various-coloured Tartans and known
as "Lawrence-Kirk boxes" were in much favour some
few years since. They were remarkable for neatness,
cheapness, and the excellence of their joints, which
were also of wood. They were invented by one
James Sandy, a poor mechanic of Perthshire, who
had lost the use of his legs; but whose long life

passed happily in the ingenious fabrication of these boxes.*

Quaint forms are as common to snuff-boxes as to tobacco-pipes. One favourite in the last century was *A Ladies Shoe* (Fig. 1.), carved in wood and inlaid with threads of silver to imitate ornamental stitches.

1 2 3

Coffins were also hideously adapted to hold the fragrant " dust." *A coiled snake* whose central folds form the lid, was a box for a naturalist (Fig 2.); *a book* might serve for a student, and a *boat* (Fig. 3.) for a sailor. All persons, and all states, may be " fitted " with a proper receptacle for the pungent dust they love so well; and of which the rhymester last quoted sings :—

> " What strange and wondrous virtue must there be
> And secret charm, O Snuff, concealed in thee !
> That bounteous Nature and inventive Art,
> Bedecking thee, thus all their powers exert ;
> Their treasures and united skill bestow,
> To set thine honours in majestic show !
> But oh, what witchcraft of a stronger kind,
> Or cause too deep for human search to find,
> Makes earth-born weeds imperial man enslave,—
> Not little souls, but e'en the wise and brave !

---

* A very interesting notice of this man's habits of life is given in *Hone's Table Book*, vol. ii.

CHAPTER VI.

THE CULTURE, MANUFACTURE, AND CONSUMPTION OF TOBACCO.

TOBACCO requires a large amount of care throughout its growth, and an equal solicitude to ensure its safety from damage, when sent to a distance for the use of the consumer. In the outset it is necessary to secure the best land for its cultivation, and that land is soon impoverished by the plant, if it has not the adjunct of good manure. The seed is usually set in beds of made soil, comprising the most unctuous native earth, enriched with wood-ashes, and other manures. March or early in April is the period chosen for placing the seed in the beds, where the young plants remain till May or June, carefully protected against frosts; when the leaves have grown to the size of a dollar and four or five appear, they are then transplanted into the tobacco-field, a day of warm rain being chosen for the purpose. The field is hoed into rectangular hollows, with small raised hillocks between each. The young plants are then drawn from their native bed, and brought in baskets to the field, one being laid on the top of each mound of earth. The planter then makes a hole in the centre of each hillock with his fingers, and having adjusted the tobacco-plant in its natural position, presses the earth gently round the roots with the hand. The field requires constant care to prevent growth of weeds; and the plant in its early stages is liable to injury from the attacks of the horn-worm, or tobacco-worm; a caterpillar which, if left to grow, will increase to the size of a man's finger, and commit great devastation in the crops. It is furnished with a thorn-like protuberance at its extremity, from which it obtains the name of horn-worm,* and by which it is seized and pulled from the plant; the act of destroying these worms is termed *worming* the tobacco. The next operation is that of " topping " the plant, which hinders the leading stem from running up too quickly to flower and seed, and so starving the leaves; to prevent this, the top is nipped off with the thumb nail, which is considered to be better than any instrument that could be adopted, because it partially closes the wound and does not allow the plant to bleed.† The custom is to " top " the plant to nine, seven, or five leaves, according to the quality of the soil, and the strength

---

* It is ultimately transformed into a large brown moth, with variegated wings, measuring about 4½ inches from the extreme of each tip ; the body having patches of dull red upon it. It is popularly termed the Tobacco-hawk. It is the only insect that feeds upon the plant. No animal will touch it.

† Tatham, in his *Essay on the Culture of Tobacco*, 1800, says, " many of the Virginians let the thumb nail grow long and *harden it in the candle* for this purpose ; not for the use of gouging out people's eyes, as some have thought fit to insinuate."

of the herb, the result ensuring large well-grown
leaves ; upon the same principle adopted by the
growers of fine wines, who are usually careful to
restrain the fruit to a few bunches, and the vine to a
small plant. The next operation performed on the
tobacco-plant is equally important, and is done in a
few weeks after the preceding one. It is termed
"suckering;" and consists of removing the suckers
or shoots which now make their appearance at the junction of the leaves and about the roots of the plants,
the result of that vigorous growth retarded by the topping process, and which if allowed to continue, would
injure the proper development of the tobacco-leaves,
the great end the planter has in view; he therefore
removes all these off-shoots with the thumb-nail as in
the previous process. The older planters of Virginia
were so particular in attending to all these duties, and
so anxious that the character widely established of
the quality of their tobacco should be preserved, that
they were enforced by law; and as it was sometimes
the custom with planters to reset the suckers, and thus
grow a double crop on one field, such conduct was
disallowed; for the reason that the crop was inferior,
and the more honest grower, who conscientiously
cleared his plants, and gave them abundance of room
to grow, was dishonestly competed with ; and the first-
rate character of the Virginian crop prejudiced by the
action. The constables were therefore strictly en-
joined *ex officio,* to make diligent search for such
crops, and to employ the *posse commitatûs* in destroy-

ing them. A law rigidly enforced, but seldom found necessary. Consequently dealers were "safe" in trusting to the quality of genuine Virginian leaf.*

During very rainy seasons, and in some kinds of unfavourable soil, the plant is subject to a malady called "firing." It is a kind of blight produced by the moist state of the atmosphere, or of the ground in which the plant grows; it is also liable to the opposite extreme of heat or drought. The injury is much dreaded by the planter, as it spots the leaf with a hard brown spot, which perishes, and produces holes fatal to the value of the crop. The leaves as they ripen, become rougher and thicker, assume a tint of yellowish green, and are sometimes mottled with yellowish spots. The crop being ready for gathering, the planter is careful to secure it before any autumnal frosts occur; for the plant is among the first to feel its injurious influence. Judgment is also required in cutting the plants, and this operation is consigned to the best and most judicious hands employed in the culture. Each person so employed, being provided with a strong sharp knife, proceeds along the respective rows of plants, and selects only such plants as appear fully ripe, leaving the rest a short time longer.

* " The valuations of an ordinary price current afford a good criterion by which to judge of the quality of the different sorts of tobacco, as far, at least, as they are presented in our markets. I quote the highest quality of each sort : Canada, 4d. per pound ; Kentucky, 6d. ; Virginia, 7d.; Maryland, 9d. ; St. Domingo, 8d. ; Turkey, 9d. ; Columbian, 10d. ; Cuba, 1s. 6d. ; Havannah, 3s. 6d."—Mr. Johnston, in *The Journal of the Statistical Society*, vol. 16.

The stem of each plant is severed as near as possible to the ground, and such plants as have thick stems are divided longitudinally, to admit the air and dry them quicker. The plant is then laid gently on the ground, so that the leaves be not damaged, and is allowed to remain exposed to the rays of the sun throughout the day, or until the leaves are entirely "wilted," as it is termed; that is, till they are flaccid, and will bend any way without breaking.

The drying of the leaves is effected in houses where free ventilation is secured. They are often simply constructed of logs of timber, the edges of each one resting at right angles on its neighbour, by which means thorough draught is secured; the spaces allowing the insertion of smaller poles, upon which the plants are hung to dry. In about a month the leaves will be thoroughly dried. Should the weather be wet, as the plant is so easily affected by the humidity of the atmosphere, artificial aid must be ensured by smouldering fires of bark and rotten wood, made on the floor of the drying-house. Sometimes another process precedes this, termed "sweating the tobacco," when the leaves are laid in a heap on the barn-floor, and allowed to partially ferment; being turned every twenty-four hours, so that they all fare alike. The longer they thus lie, the darker the tobacco becomes. They are then hung on the poles to be entirely "cured."

The plant is said to be "in case," or proper condition for packing and removal, when the leaves are dry enough to bear handling, and have a certain elasticity, which is tested by stretching them gently over the ends of the fingers and knuckles, and they pull like kid leather, glowing with a kind of moist gloss, not dry enough to break, or damp enough to ferment. They are now unhung from the poles, and the leaves stripped from the main stem, are gathered in small bunches termed " hands," each of these are tied round at the base of the stalks with another leaf, making a kind of bandage. They are now packed upon each other in regular rows, to dry sufficiently to be placed in the cask. It will thus be seen, that from the first planting of the seed to the ultimate packing of the dry plant for exportation, it is a constant solicitude to the planter.

The hogshead to hold the tobacco is regulated by standard to four feet six inches in height; and will hold a 1000 pounds of tobacco,* which is compressed into a very solid mass. The small bunches being dipsosed in layers, close to each other across the hogshead, with the points of the leaves one way; the next course or layer is reversed, with the points in an alternate direction; and the interstices are filled up with smaller plants, so that a general even surface be ensured.† The hogshead being about one-fourth part filled, the whole is subjected to a strong pressure

---

* This is by custom understood as the usual average. The legal requirement is 950 lbs.

† The leaves are sometimes flavoured by sprinkling them with diluted rum and molasses; this is the custom in Virginia; in Brazil a decoction is used of an infusion of tobacco leaves and gum copal.

until it is reduced to one half its bulk; then another similar layer is placed upon it, again squeezed, and succeeded by as many as are required to fill the cask.

The cask has now to be transmitted to the shipping warehouse, and a rude mode of doing this fifty years ago is described and pictured in Tatham's book on *Tobacco Culture;* and consisted in affixing a couple of shafts of hickory-wood by a pin into each end of the cask, so that the whole looked something like a garden-roller. The cask was dragged along the country thus, and was protected with an extra hooping of hickory-wood, to prevent undue wear; or by a series of blocks like segments of a circle, fixed round the circumference of the tobacco-hogshead by means of augur holes, and wooden pins driven into the bulk of tobacco, through the staves of the cask.

The export warehouses receive the planter's stock, which is inspected by proper officers. The cask is broken open, and the closely packed leaf is cleaved by a wedge driven into its bulk by a huge hand-mall, from this a few bundles are taken for examination; and should necessity arise, the operation is repeated in other parts of the mass. If the leaf appears to be well cured, and not of bad quality or grown from "suckers," they generally "pass" the tobacco on the spot, and it may be sold; but should the contrary be the case, the whole hogshead is condemned and burnt. If "passed" as good and marketable, it is replaced in the cask, subjected to another pressure, and made more secure by an extra amount of cooperage, for rough usage in a sea-voyage, consisting of tray-shaped heads to the barrels, and extra hoops and clamps.*

Only certain ports have the privilege of receiving vessels laden with tobacco. The moorings of such vessels are regulated by the officers of the customs, who may come on board the vessel when within four leagues of the coast, and demand the official record of freightage. They then batten down the hatches; in which operation the crew must aid if required; and should they be improperly opened by any but the government officers, a fine of £200 may be inflicted, or the vessel and cargo forfeited, as well as the master fined, if the tobacco be unladen before the custom-house officer authorises it.

We may now imagine the barrels or hogsheads unshipped and ranged in the English dock-yard. The tobacco-warehouse at the London Docks is one of those metropolitan sights which could only be seen in a city of great commercial power. Sometimes 40,000 hogsheads may be seen ranged in long alleys under the vast roof of this emporium, with passages between each, only wide enough for necessary removal. In the interview the tobacco-traders had with the Chancellor of the Exchequer in November 1857; the usual London stock was stated to be 40,000 hogsheads; but owing to bad crops, it had decreased to

---

* The pressure is so great, and the mass of leaf so impervious, that instances are on record of tobacco washed from wrecked ships, the exterior of the mass completely rotted, but the interior dry and sound.

26,000 during the three previous years. The tobacco
pays no duty while in these warehouses. It is "in
bond" as it is technically termed; the officers giving
a receipt for it, cancelled when the duty is paid and
the salesman removes it. This bonded tobacco used
to cost the country 40,000*l.* per annum in warehouse-
room, for which a nominal rent only was charged; but
in 1857 this was altered, by which a sum of about
27,000*l.* was saved to the revenue. Should any portion
of the tobacco be injured by bad packing or sea-water
getting to it, the mass is turned out of the hogshead,
and the damaged parts chopped away with huge blades
like scythes, but straight, affixed to strong handles.
They are wielded by both hands, and require a vigorous arm to use, such is the density of the mass.
The damaged part is burnt, and remainder weighed,
the proper amount of duty charged only on it. A
large kiln is prepared at the docks for the burning of
this tobacco; its external appearance is that of a tall
cylindrical shaft, which is jocularly termed "Her
Majesty's tobacco-pipe."

Arrived at the manufacturer's, the tobacco-hogshead
is broken open, and by wedge and lever the solid mass
is split into a series of flat circular cakes, over which
water is sprinkled, to induce them to swell or separate,
that the bunches or "hands" may again assume something of their original form. These masses were formerly weighed in the presence of a government officer
of the excise, and the amount required for present use
left in the manufactory; the rest was locked in a

warehouse by the officer, and although the property of
the manufacturer, could not be touched by him till the
custom-house officer again weighed out another supply.
Now a return is made of the manufactured quantity kept on sale, so that it may be seen how that
tallies with the quantity of leaf delivered from the
docks ; the old restrictive policy was occasionally injurious to the manufacturer, whose work sometimes
stood still for want of access to the leaf-tobacco in his
own warehouse.

The tobacco "hands" are now "weighed out" in
certain quantities to women employed in the warehouse, termed "strippers;" it is their business to
"strip" from the centre of each life, the main stalk,
which is never retained in the tobacco used by the
smoker, except in one instance—the manufacture of
"bird's eye;"—when the stalk is cut up in the leaf,
which is carefully laid at right angles with the knife, the
section made through it produces the thin circular
slices appended to the long fibres of the leaf ; this
name has been given to the tobacco from a fancied
resemblance to the eye of a bird ; for the same reason
it has been also appropriated to spotted woods, pocket-
handkerchiefs, and cotton gowns !

The "stripper" performs her duties by folding the
tobacco-leaf, and with a thick-backed knife (an old
razor being usually preferred) cutting under both sides
of the thick end of the stalk ; retaining the hold thus
given, securing the two sides of the leaf in the left
hand, and so rapidly drawing out the large central

x

stalk, without disturbing the minor branches which cross the leaf, or tearing the leaf in any degree; a facility of hand only to be obtained by practice, for a leaf would be torn to shreds by a person unused to the trade, while practised strippers can take the stalk out of a hundred weight of tobacco, in a wondrously short time, with a certainty and absence of all risk to the leaf. Some leaf is packed in the plantation with the stalk already extracted, and is termed "strip-leaf" by the English manufacturer. It is so packed when the grower has any reason to fear that the juices in the stalk might endanger the safety of the cargo, by producing mildew or spots, just as mischievous as the "firing" already alluded to in the growing crop. The technical name given to tobacco with the stalk in it is "hand-work."

The tobacco-leaf is now ready to be manufactured for the smoker, and cut into shreds for his pipe. The first thing done toward this is the placing of the leaf in a trough, and wetting it thoroughly with water; to which sometimes a little salt is added, and sometimes treacle; neither being strictly considered necessary or allowable in first-rate manufactories, and are usually adopted to disguise the bad flavour of common or damaged leaves. The tobacco is generally subjected to this process, or "liquoring" as it is termed by the workman, over night as he leaves his work; and is allowed to remain soaking all night, because as the water is only sprinkled over each layer of dry leaf, it takes a considerable time to spread and soak, giving

the leaf again the elasticity it had, when declared to be
" in case " by the grower.

The lighter kinds of tobacco such as *Returns,*
Orinoco, &c., are very sparingly wetted; only just
sprinkled, and not allowed to soak. They are just
sufficiently damp to squeeze into form in the box;
and owing to their dryness, are less easily cut than
damper tobaccos, which owe their dark colour principally to "liquoring ; " and to increase this, the manufacturer saves the stained water which drains from the
leaves, to wet the tobacco with, over and over again;
nothing is " wasted " in a tobacco manufactory, as our
snuff-making notes will show.

These leaves, or rather the half-leaves, having soaked
sufficiently, are now lifted in masses by both arms
toward the breast of the workman, and so thrown
dexterously forward, that they fall on the floor in
regular layers ; a process, like many others used by
manufacturers, most difficult to teach, or to be done by
the uninitiated, but effected with ease and rapidity
by the practised hand. The layers are then placed in
shallow wooden boxes, measuring about fourteen inches
each way and two inches deep, and are piled in them
to the height of six inches; each tray is then placed in
a press, and others similarly filled are placed over them,
until the press is filled; the whole are then squeezed
till they are reduced to one third their bulk, or till the
boxes touch each other; and the six inch depth of the
tobacco leaf, has been compressed into a solid cake of
two inches in thickness. Here it remains several

hours, and is ultimately taken out and placed in the
cutting-machine.

The cutting-machine is a comparatively modern
invention, looked upon as a degeneracy by the men
of the last century, who cut up their tobacco roughly
for their own use, from cakes or carottes as the taste
might lead. The oldest form of cutting instrument
used by manufacturers, was like the chopping-machine
of the sausage-maker; and was called a "jigger" by
the workman, probably from the jerking motion they
were obliged to use, in bringing the knife and handle
upon, and through, the tobacco-cake. It was very hard
work for the men, and demanded all that waste of
muscular energy, so lavishly bestowed without reason
in the old workshops, on processes now receiving very
little. At the commencement of the present century,
a "hand-engine" was used, with a fly-wheel and winch
handle, which by comparatively easy turning lifted a
knife to cut the tobacco-cake, which was pushed
forward at the same time, for another cut as the wheel
revolved. It will be best understood by our cut. The
cutting-knife a is lifted at one side by the action of a
crank connected with the wheel turned by the workman;
a circular bar affixed to the other end of the knife
passes to the back of the machine, and by its motion
lifts with every cut, by a pinion at b, the wheel c,
prevented by another pinion at d, from a retrograde
movement; this wheel acts on a screw, and propels the
cake of tobacco sufficiently forward to cut a fresh
slice through the mass; the cake having been placed

in a frame, held fast between grooves at *e e,* and which
when the screws upon it are removed, allows the mass
of cut tobacco to be drawn out in the trough *f.* The

width of the fibres thus made occasionally differs:
" shag " tobacco is cut the finest; " broad-cut, " as its
name implies, is nearly an eighth of an inch in width.
The cutting is regulated by changing the cog-wheel,
and the two sorts are technically known as " short cut "
and " long cut," the first being originally adopted for
smokers, the second for chewers.

Sometimes horses are employed in turning the
cutting wheels; and in large warehouses tobacco is now
cut by steam power.

The mass of cut tobacco when removed from the
machine, is next placed in a brass drying-pan over a
slow fire, and so kept till the damp evaporates in thick
white steam. This is a final process which has to be
conducted with much judgment; for a sufficient amount
of damp must be retained to preserve its moisture in
the salesman's cask. When the tobacco is dried to
this point, which is decided by " the feel " of the heated
mass to the workman's fingers, it is taken from the

pan, spread out to cool, and ultimately sent in casks to the shop-keeper.

We have noted some of the older processes of the tobacco warehouse, in the incidental mention of the carotte and spun tobaccos. Carotte was formed by enswathing a number of leaves, when cured, on each other, after the ribs had been taken out, and rolling them round with packthread, till they became cemented together. These rolls commonly measured about eighteen or twenty inches in length, and nine round the middle part. Two modes of tying the tobacco was in use in the middle of the last century, and are represented in our engraving; one termed in the French market " filer à la Françoise," and the other " filer à la Hollandoise," the latter being the one most generally adopted ; it consisted in enclosing the roll of leaf in a thread which was twisted and knotted at each turn ; the former mode only wound the thread round the mass. A holder with a quantity of thread upon it was used by the workman, it had a pointed head to pass under the thread, and assist him in knotting it. When the mass was thus secured, some large leaves were used to cover the whole. The operation required great nicety and exactitude, and could only be successfully done after long practice.

Our engraving exhibits the mode of tying the carotte in the French style at A. The Dutch style is shown at B, with the workman's implement at C, and the mode by which the knot was secured. It is copied from an engraving dated 1768. These carottes were sometimes steeped in new rum or sugar, to give richness to the flavour of the leaf, and were in much favour with sailors for chewing.

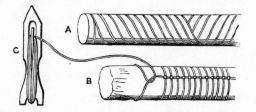

The process of forming roll tobacco is exhibited in our cut on p. 129. Tobacco is thus made up into rolls, as well by the inhabitants of the interior parts of America as ourselves, by means of a machine called a tobacco-wheel. With this machine they spin the leaves after they are cured, into a twist of any size they think fit, and having folded it into rolls of about twenty pounds each, it is put into a press for some days, and then laid by for use. In this state it will keep for several years, and be continually improving, as it always grows milder. Smaller rolls of this tobacco called "negro head," weighing six or eight pounds each, are also manufactured for the market; and a still smaller package of thinner twist, termed "pig-tail," is frequently imported.

Kanaster is a favourite tobacco in Holland. It takes its name from the rush baskets in which it was originally packed; it then consisted of selected leaves from the finest plants, in accordance with old Indian custom (see p. 23); it is now a coarsely cut tobacco of a dry kind, made from the best Havannah leaf, and packed in cases. The uncut tobacco known as Cavendish, is entirely formed of fine leaf, pressed closely in small cakes; and cut up as wanted for the pipe, a small hand-knife fastened to a lever being used by the smoker; or a strong knife and wooden trencher according to the old form (see cut p. 57). This kind of tobacco is much valued by connoisseurs, who find in it the purest flavour and full sweetness of the leaf, which is apt to be injured by the wettings and pressings it undergoes in the European warehouses before it is subjected to the cutting-machine. The process of drying and the thinness of the shreds into which it is cut, gives still further chance of continuous loss of flavour. Old tobacco-takers used always to "lament the weakness of these latter times," which insisted on fine cutting; they delighted in the coarser-cut fuller-flavoured tobaccos of their youthful days.

Cigar-making is practised by workmen who are quite distinct from the tobacco manufacturer. The two trades are never combined in the same individual. Thirty years ago, when cigars were looked on as luxuries, and only sparingly smoked, it was the custom in the tobacco trade, to engage the cigar maker for a few days' work now and then, according as the stock was sold. The chief workman would arrange with the tobacco manufacturer, and bring with him his staff of workmen, who were under his ˙sole control; he contracting for the value of the conjoined labour of all, and carrying them about from warehouse to warehouse.

They all earned more than the tobacco-cutters, and were looked upon as *the artists* of the trade. They had the privilege of picking the finest leaf from the hogshead for their use; and the first process with them was to strip the central stalk away; a process usually effected by boys. The cigar maker received the leaf on his bench in small quantities, and spread each half leaf on a square block of wood before him, cutting it into gore-shaped pieces, which were used to roll round the central tobacco, consisting of a gathering of the smaller pieces cut off, and the leaves which were torn, or with holes; and which though equally good, will not do for coverings. The proper size of each cigar is then tested in a gauge; trimmed to its proper length; and finally rolled in a strip of leaf, which spirally envelopes it, and is twisted at one end to secure it. This end is the first thing cut off by the smoker when the cigar is put between his lips.

In our previous chapter we have noted the great increase of the cigar trade, the large variety of cigars manufactured, and their names and qualities. The rate of duty on foreign cigars is very high, and amounts to a restriction of the article to the humbler classes. Nine shillings per pound duty thus imposed on tobacco leaf requiring so small a cost in manufacture, (much less than is bestowed on cut tobaccos, the leaf itself being worth about seven-pence a pound), has the effect of restraining choice foreign cigars to the morocco cases of the wealthy. But as this has little to do with the quality of the leaf, and imposes a completely

fictitious value on the cigar ; very good ones may be
manufactured of the same leaf, at home, for one half
the money.   The buyer of foreign cigars consoles
himself for his heavy tax, by a belief that the best
leaves of the crop have been selected at the planters',
before the shipment of any elsewhere.

In both these processes we have noted the rejection
of the leaf-stalk (except in the manufacture of bird's
eye); these stalks are laid in a chaff-cutting machine,
and cut into short pieces, which are then packed in bags
and sent to the snuff-mills, to be dried and ground to
powder.   Almost all the snuff ground for the London
traders is done at the mills at Mitcham in Surrey.
The Scotch snuff is the purest ; being made from the
powder of the stalk, its light colour is owing to its never
being sodden in water, or subject to "liquoring," or
scenting.   It is pure tobacco in its simplest form.
Next to this comes Irish high-dried, and Welsh snuff.
Other snuffs are darkened by mixtures and scents ; and
have a large variety of names, as already noted and
partially explained in our previous chapter.   "Prince's
mixture" is generally considered in the trade to allow
of most unfair mixing ; all portions of damaged tobacco,
the sweepings of the tobacco warehouse, &c., are incorporated in this.   It is impossible to hinder small fragments of tobacco from falling on the floor of the manufactory ; and the workmen's feet are always carefully
scraped into a box, which afterwards helps to fill the
more elegant box of the snuff-taker.   The "smalls," or
fragments which fall to the bottom of tubs or canisters

used in the tobacco shop, add their quota to the mass.* When the whole is placed in the " snuff bin," it is well wetted, and allowed partially to ferment ; as it heats it is turned with a shovel, and the mass ultimately assumes that dark colour valued in rappee ; the blacker kind of that snuff being subjected to a longer residence in the bin. Agreeable and delicate as scents may be, they are generally eschewed by all who admire tobacco for its own sake. Some of the old snuff-takers, who were sticklers for pure Scotch, did not object to place a Tonquin-bean in their snuff, which gave out a slight aroma like the scent of new hay ; a power the bean retained for years ; but even this was objected to by many snuff-takers, who held that this, as well as all other scenting, was injurious, and tended to produce headaches.

We have already reverted to the simple old process of rasping the tobacco rolls to form a rough snuff, and how these coarse " brans " were afterwards pounded in mortars with a pestle of peculiar form. Snuff thus made by hand-labour was not supplied equal to the demand, it was also too expensive, and snuff-mills

---

* Soyer, in his *Shilling Cookery for the People*, has an awful story about snuff adulterations. He says : "In many parts, and even in Ireland during the year of the famine, those who were starving would not partake of ox-liver. These are bought up in that country, put into casks with salt, sent over to a seaport in England ; they are then subjected to a cold pressure by which the liquid is extracted, which is used for adulterating an article in universal use ; the remains are then dried in ovens, pounded, and sent back to Ireland to be made into snuff." The wood of old coffins, broken up by dishonest sextons, was also popularly believed to have been ground down for snuff. But we believe all these tales " weak inventions of the enemy" to snuffing !

turned by horses were invented. One of the earliest of these mills is here represented ; it is copied from the shop-bill of Abraham Delvalle of St. Mary Axe, Lon-

don, from whence we have also copied the pounding process on p. 251. The horse in the foreground conti-nually encircles the mill, and it is usual to cover his eyes while doing so. His labour gives motion to two heavy grindstones, which passing over so small a sur-face, turn the snuff in every way and ultimately reduce it to a fine powder. It is stirred by a man from time to time, towards the centre. A crank is connected with another grinding-mill for finer snuffs, where a series of small pestles (precisely similar to those used by the hand labourer in the cut on p. 251) are in use ; by their peculiar form the snuff is stirred up from the bottom, and ground by the globular muller, over and over again, until it is properly triturated. The most modern form of the snuff-mill retains this old feature of the original manufacture, which will be best understood by our cut of a section of the receptacle for the snuff, with the muller or grinder ready for use.

The excise regulations were formerly as stringent on the snuff as on the tobacco manufacturer. He was obliged to place his snuffs in a storeroom which was locked up by the excise officer, nor could he dare to touch his snuff, until such time as the officer came to open the store, and give him out his own property.

Such are the modes by which tobacco is prepared for the luxurious use of the modern civilised world. Its medical uses are few, although as we have seen, they were originally its chief recommendation. Of its curative virtues we have already given vouchers from the older books of the faculty. At the commencement of the present century, the Perth *Encyclopædia* tells us, tobacco was sometimes used externally in unguents for destroying cutaneous insects, cleansing old ulcers, &c. Beaten into a mash with vinegar, it has sometimes proved serviceable for removing hard tumours of the hypochondres. Dr. Page in the 18th vol. of the *Edinburgh Medical Journal,* tells of the cure of an inflammation of the substance of the lungs, which had proved obstinate, in spite of the abstraction of ninety-five pounds of blood, and the application of vesicatories ; and which was effected by the injection into the rectum, of an infusion of a drachm of the leaf to twelve ounces of water.

According to Merat, the Swiss and Dutch, were in the habit of injecting the smoke, in this way, to persons asphyxiated by submersion. Clysters of tobacco water were frequently used in the last century in cases of obstinate constipation. For catarrh and bronchitis it was also recommended, and then mixed with brandy ; Neander applauds its use in this way as a most effective emetic, which we do not for an instant doubt. *Tobacco wine* was thus made :—Leaves of tobacco 1 oz ; Spanish white wine 1 lb. Macerate for seven days, and strain through paper. Under this form tobacco has been used as a diuretic in dropsy. Dose 30 drops, gradually increased to 60 or 80, twice a day. *The London Medical Gazette* vol. ii. records several cases of epidemic scarlatina, which was very prevalent in some parts of Germany a few years ago, being entirely cured by the doctors' administration of powdered tobacco; in doses of a quarter of a grain to two grains a day, according to the age of the patient ; and which saved fifty patients a week, when belladonna, prussic acid, and other remedies, had been tried in vain. Sir Astley Cooper has declared it to be the most powerful and successful agent we possess to reduce hernia; but it will not be necessary or agreeable in a non-medical book to recapitulate all its uses ; we will therefore conclude in the words of Dr. Cleland :" In the treatment of lapsus uvulæ, ranula, polypus nasi, carbuncle, ernio, sciatica, urinary calculus, hemicrania, mammary engorgment, worms, ileus, surditas, and a multitude of other diseases ; tobacco has, like every other remedy,

been repeatedly capricously employed; but space for-
bids any further enumeration, nor indeed, would any
profit result at all commensurate with the time which
must have been spent in the investigation."

Let us now consider the rise and growth of that vast
commerce in the plant, with which the world has
heavily, but willingly, taxed itself, from the days of
Elizabeth to those of Victoria. The revenue brought
to our present Sovereign Lady, from this source alone,
is greater than that Queen Elizabeth received from the
entire customs of the country. The narrow view of
commercial policy held by her successors, the Stuarts,
induced them to hamper the colonists of America
with restrictions; because they were alarmed lest the
ground should be entirely devoted to tobacco, and no
corn grown, as the latter was much less profitable
than the former. In p. 105 we have given Sir Edwin
Sandys' view of the dangerous state of the English revenue in 1620, in consequence of the dealing with Spain
for tobacco. Nineteen years after this, the Virginians
agreed to restrict the growth of their tobaccos, and limit
the produce of the district in 1639, to 1,500,000 lbs.,
and to 1,200,000 lbs. in the two years next ensuing.
This was agreed to at an assembly with the Governor,
Sir Francis Wiatt, and the principal men of the
country; and it was done that the market should not
be overstocked by an inferior article, grown anywhere,
and anyhow, to meet the demand; and which they
feared would affect the high character which Virginian leaf held. Imposts and taxes were imposed on

New England tobaccos by Charles II.; they were restricted in 1766 to two shillings per hogshead. Just before the American War, Virginia exported about 55,000 hogsheads of tobacco, each hogshead weighing 1000 lbs. In 1758, the number increased to 70,000 hogsheads, which was the greatest quantity of tobacco ever produced in that country in one year. Some accounts of the exports of Virginia and Maryland at this period give 80,000 hogsheads as their usual yearly gathering, the freight of this, at thirty shillings per hogshead, amounting to £120,000. From 58,000 to 60,000 hogsheads was the usual quantity of tobacco obtained from this source alone till 1790.

The consumption in England during the foregoing periods, is said to have advanced to 41,170 hogsheads. According to the account and balance of imports and exports, between Great Britain and the American colonies, laid before Parliament, for eleven years preceding 1774, the advantage annually advanced to about £1,500,000 sterling. The yearly amount of the payment into the Exchequer, according to the account of the duties upon tobacco from 1770 to 1774, was £219,117 sterling. One half of this tobacco was imported to Scotland, and four-fifths of that half was exported to France, Holland, Germany, and other countries.

In 1775 the duties on tobacco arose to £298,002 sterling. The duties were at this time so excessively high, that in the same year 131 hogsheads of tobacco, exported on account of a merchant in Charleston, for Bristol in England, produced to the proprietor but £1307 4s. 1½d. sterling. The excise, with the net proceeds, amounted to £4912 8s. 0¼d.*

The following table gives the entire amount of tobacco exported from the United States of America, from October 1, 1791, to September 30, 1792, showing the average of each State :—

	Manufactured lbs.		hogs-heads.
New Hampshire	—	—	3
Massachusetts	110,525	and	1,221
Rhode Island	—	—	1,429
Connecticut	—	—	105
New York	1,600	and	1,952
New Jersey	—	—	5
Pennsylvania	2,140	and	3,203
Delaware	—	—	8
Maryland	780	and	28,992
Virginia	2,025	and	61,203
North Carolina	—	—	3,546
South Carolina	624	and	5,290
Georgia	180	and	5,471
Total	117,874		112,428

A statement of a similar kind made out for the year ending September 30, 1798, shows the amount of manufactured pounds to have been 142,268, and of hogsheads 68,567.

On p. 132, we have stated the nature of "drawbacks" allowed to the tobacco-merchant; and its effect on the revenues of a country obtained by the custom-house. The following statement exhibiting the amount of drawbacks allowed on dutiable tobacco exported

---

* White's *Essay on the Culture and Commerce of Tobacco,* 1800.

from the United States in three years, will make it
clearer :—

	Duties. dols. cents.	Drawbacks. dols. cents.
1793	898 26	444 49
1794	1890 16	272 59
1795	4255 4	18 59

The increase of the tobacco-trade in France, has
been thus narrated by Mr. Steinmetz, in his agreeable
little volume on Tobacco : "No law was passed against
tobacco ; but a duty was imposed upon it, extremely
small at first, and this lasted to the year 1673 ; but in
1674 the habit of snuffing and smoking becoming more
and more popular, the government of Louis XIV.
increased the duty, and converted the cultivation into
a monopoly. This was conceded to a speculator for
six years, in consideration of the payment of 700,000
francs, in three instalments ; the enormous sum of
more than £29,000 sterling. In 1720 the consideration for the monopoly was more than doubled; in
1771 it was nearly quadrupled, amounting to about
£1,100,000 per annum. As the consumption of tobacco
continued to increase, the government took upon
itself the entire monopoly, under the name of *Régie ;*
and some idea may be formed of the enormous increase
in the consumption of tobacco, when it is stated that
in 1844 the revenue rose to the sum of 102,000,000
francs ; more than £4,000,000 sterling ; since which
date it has been constantly and steadily increasing, at
the average rate of from 2,000,000 to 5,000,000 francs
per annum. It is very probable that the revenue for

the year 1856 exceeded that of England, which is set down at £5,220,388."

A good idea of the number of cigars smoked in a cigar-smoking country, may be obtained from the returns published by the Austrian Government. They are there an Imperial monopoly; the consumption is about a thousand millions yearly; of this number Vienna alone consumes fifty-two millions. During the last ten years, the use of cigars has increased one hundred per cent., and that of tobacco for pipes, proportionably diminished. In Hamburgh, where the population is only one-third of that of Vienna, the yearly consumption of cigars is estimated at 14,600,000. Rome has the fewest tobacco-shops of any large capital.

In the *Journal of the Statistical Society* vol. xvi. is given the following table of the increased consumption of tobacco in England, in a series of ten years:—

	Consumption. lbs.	Duty. per lb.	Population.	Consumption per head. oz.
1821	15,598,152	4s. 0d.	21,282,960	11·71
1831	19,533,841	3 0	24,410,439	12·80
1841	22,309,360	3 0 *	27,019,672	13·21
1851	28,062,841	3 0 *	27,452,692	16·86

The advantage of a customs duty over government monopoly and home production under licence, is made plain enough by comparing our own tobacco revenue with that of France, with seven millions more inhabitants, and more general consumers. In 1849 the

---

* With an additional 5 per cent. on duty.

tobacco revenue of France was only £4,285,000; but if
equally productive with ours, it ought to have been
£5,572,300; so that France loses by its grasping, and
by its trimming with rustic proprietors, above a million
and a quarter a year! In England it amounted in
customs, in the same year, exclusive of excise, to
£4,425,040, or close on four and a half millions. This
exceeded the sugar duties by £575,350, and was larger
than the customs on any one article, tea excepted—as
great a fiscal, and indeed social curiosity as itself; for
this last amounted to £5,471,422, being £200,000 above
the excise on malt, long the prime prop of the British
Treasury.

But our British duty sins most wofully by excess, and
has perseveringly done so now for thirty long years. The
duties are, on leaf or unmanufactured tobacco, 3s. 1⅗d.,
on snuff 6s. 3⅗d., and on cigars, or any manufactured
article other than snuff 9s. 5⅗d. per lb. The average
price of leaf tobacco may be fairly taken at 5d. per lb.; so
that we have here a duty on the cost value of 758, which,
after deducting a handsome sum for a legitimate tax,
leaves a very broad margin for smuggling and adulteration, both of them so extensively practised that some
have estimated the amount to equal one-third part of
the legal consumption. Of course, on a mere luxury
the tax may fairly be made as high as is compatible
with security from smuggling and adulteration; but
anything beyond this point is a premium to the smug-
gler and adulterator, an injury to the fair trader, and a
loss to the Exchequer.—*Examiner*, Jan. 17. 1852.

What the result of these frauds are, may be gathered from the fact, that tobacco has been sent carriage free, from manufacturers in the north of England to the south, at prices, clear of duty, twenty per cent under those at which the genuine article could be sold by the London manufacturers, with all their advantages of capital, connection, and experience.

In 1853 the consumption of tobacco in Great Britain amounted to 24,940,555 lbs. or 19 ounces per head to the entire population. In Ireland it amounted to 4,624,141 lbs., giving the rate of 12 ounces per head to each inhabitant. The duty on tobacco and snuff amounted in the year 1858, to £5,272,471. Upwards of £8,000,000 are annually spent on both.

The writer in the Journal quoted p. 323, reckons that if the population of the Earth be taken at a thousand millions, and the consumption reckoned as equal to that of the kingdom of Denmark, or seventy ounces per head, the produce of the whole world will amount to near two millions of tons (1,953,125) a year. Seventy ounces a head, of course, far exceeds the average consumption of Europe, in most of the countries of which tobacco is heavily taxed. It is certain however, on the other hand, that it falls far short of the consumption of Asia, containing the majority of mankind, where women and children smoke as well as men, and where the article moreover is untaxed. Nearly half the British tonnage which " entered inward " or " cleared outward " last year, would be required to convey the quantity of this American weed; of which the

value, at two-pence per pound, will amount to nearly
thirty six and a half millions sterling (36,462,500).

From these different statements a tolerably approxi-
mate calculation may be obtained, of the progress
of the tobacco trade, from the earliest introduction of
the plant into Europe.   It is certainly one of the most
curious that commerce presents.   That a plant originally
smoked by a few savages, should succeed in spite of
the most stringent opposition in Church and state, to be
the cherished luxury of the whole civilised world : to
increase with the increase of time, and to end in
causing so vast a trade, and so large an outlay of money;
is a statistical fact, without an equal parallel.

In the course of this little volume, it has been
attempted to give such a general history of the custom
of tobacco-taking, in all its forms, as would interest
ordinary readers ; divesting it of the character of a
mere dry history; adding as much discursive infor-
mation as the subject would allow, and incidentally
displaying the opinions *pro* and *con* pronounced upon
a habit, second only in its universality to that of
taking salt.   Many from its first introduction have
condemned it, many have as strongly extolled it;
many still condemn, but more than many laud and
patronise it.   The historian and the chronicler have
to act impartially ; and to do this, as far as possible
they should be free from prejudice.   The author has
studied this subject without having acquired a taste for
the use of tobacco.   Had he been a smoker, he might
have written with greater enthusiasm, as a fisherman

would of fishing, or a huntsman of hunting. But he might also have felt, that his judgment, thus biassed, scarcely allowed him to speak as an impartial advocate ; anxious to allow to his fellow-man an innocent indulgence, in a proper spirit of fairness, and not permit prejudice to become persecution. He might thus, like Chapman's "Monsieur d'Olive" have become :—

> " Angry to hear this generous tobacco,
> The gentleman's saint and the soldier's idol,
> So ignorantly polluted."

Free from the prejudice that might be imputed to him had he held the pipe as well as the pen, he has been able from long observation which he has never ceased to make, to form a judgment upon certain facts which have accumulated over many years, and that judgment he thinks it right he should not withhold from the reader.

It has been, and is constantly alleged, that smoking leads to drinking. It certainly never induced our Saxon ancestors to drink; and they were notorious drunkards. The English, as a nation, were hard drinkers, long before the fumes of tobacco crossed their wine and beer cups. They are probably less given to drink at the present day, than at any period of their history : and while tobacco-smoking is on the increase. The Turks and the French smoke much, and both are essentially sober nations.*

* On the subject of this useful influence of tobacco-smoking in the East, see the testimony given by Lane, p. 158 of this volume.

But let us come to individuals of our own country, to those whom we have had opportunities of knowing, and give the result of our own practical observation. As a rule, we can pronounce that all great smokers are temperate men, and most of them extremely so, very many being water-drinkers, and particularly when smoking, as the use of wine and liquors destroys the palate for the appreciation of fine tobaccos. On the other hand, very many who do not smoke, and who are the most vociferous in condemning smoking, are habitual and daily drinkers of wine, beer, and spirits. Few drunkards smoke, at least, to any extent. If they smoke at all, it will be found that the love of drinking led to the use of tobacco; and not, as is often asserted, that they were induced to drink from smoking. Many may think these remarks too bold and trenchant; but let our readers look carefully around them, in their respective circles, and they will not fail to find their experience confirm our own. They may find some questionable exceptions to the rule; they may find, here and there, a sot who drinks and smokes; but take away from him his tobacco, he would be a sot still.

We remember on one occasion listening to the tirade of a tobacco-hater, who was denouncing in the usual unmeasured style all who indulged in the weed, and who imputed drunkenness and a whole train of vices to the practice. His eye was at last directed to a young lady present, down whose cheeks tears were falling; and a surprised inquiry, "What is the

matter ?" stopped the further display of his rhetoric.
" You insult my father and brothers, and then ask
what is the matter !" indignantly replied the lady.
Her relatives had distinguished themselves in the
army and navy, had risen by their own merit, and were
most exemplary in every act of their lives, men whose
honourable public career was most probably owing to
that moral discipline, in which they trained themselves by constant attention to their home-duties. The
loud and sweeping generalisations of reproach are, in
nearly every instance when individually tested, found
to be unjust.   Many great smokers we have found to
be men of particularly energetic minds,* and capable
of doing much mental and physical work ; and they
declare that smoking, with water and coffee, or without either, enables them to sustain an extra exertion
of mind and body, when the effect of wine, beer, and
spirits would weaken or wholly incapacitate them.   As
for longevity, whether it may be attributed to general
temperate habits, or to smoking, or to both, it is not
for us to say ; but we could enter into a long list of
smokers remarkable for retaining to extreme old age,
brightness of intellect and strength of limb.†   Some
member of the Statistical Society may probably be
induced to follow up this not unimportant branch of

---

* Instances may be found in pp. 146, 149.

† We may refer to p. 147 for the names of several.   In p. 10 is a more
familiar instance falling under the author's experience ; to which he may
here add the late Canon Bennett of Canterbury, a very great smoker, who,
when nearly 80, walked from thence to London as a joke, and when past
80, went into Wales fishing.

the subject; our chief aim has been to simply throw a
light on tobacco-smoking—

EX FUMO DARE LUCEM.

There can be little doubt that smoking, even more
than angling, deserves to be termed "the contemplative man's recreation." Most thoughtful men have
been smokers, nor have their excogitations over the
pipe been void of sound sense and morality.* In the
Pen and Pencil Sketches, recently published by the
son of Thomas Hood, the "bowl that cheers, but not
inebriates," is amusingly pointed at as the bowl of
the pipe :—

> Our shout for instance is alike,
>   I do not cry "Iacche."—
> But with a pleasure infinite,
>   I'll join in "Io Baccy."
>
> The god hath bowls of gems and gold
>   (Some plated though—a clear sham),
> And so have I !—but then they're made
>   Of china, clay, or meerschaum !
>
> He "fills the bowl" with Claret, Hock,
>   Champagne, or Mançanilla !
> And so do I ! but with Returns,
>   Bird's-eye, or Latakia !

Snuff has received a large share of clerical patronage, yet it may fairly be questioned whether it may
not have a more direct influence on the human system

* Witness the little poems in pp. 102 and 126.

than smoking has. The Continental clergy are much
addicted to the practice, and the elders of the Church
of Scotland, as well as many literary students, will be
ready to exclaim with Arbuckle in his Poem already
quoted, p. 292 :—

> " Blest be his shade, may laurels ever bloom,
> And breathing sweets exhale around his tomb,
> Whose penetrating nostril taught mankind
> First, how by snuff to rouse the sleeping mind."

We must not shut our eyes to the fact, that both
practices have been denounced by " the faculty" and
others, in no measured terms ; but we must also not
forget to observe, how tobacco has been blamed for the
production of ills impossible to be produced by its
means. If such imputations were not in print to be
referred to, the existence of such absurdities might
fairly be disbelieved.

A philosophic and charitable view of the minor
indulgences of life, would lead us to look with no
frowning eye on the simple pleasures of the poor ; and
tobacco has been called "the anodyne of poverty." He
would be harsh indeed who would deprive the poor
man of the hard-earned solace his pipe presents ; the
small recompense awarded a long life of toil. There
must be some charm which he in his narrow philosophy cannot comprehend ; which can recompense in
the pipe the toil and privation endured by the labourer,
the discomfort of the sailor on a stormy deck, or the
soldier in the trenches. As a comfort to the poor, as
a luxury to the rich, tobacco unites all classes in a

common pleasure; and there is much deep philosophy as well as sound sense, in the emblematic design by the German artist Rethel, with which we close our page; and in which the hand of Death holds up the balance, and enforces the lesson that the pleasures of the king's crown, and the poor man's pipe, are equal.

THE END.